# MONETARY AND FISCAL POLICIES IN THE EURO-AREA
## Macro Modelling, Learning and Empirics

# MONETARY AND FISCAL POLICIES
# IN THE EURO-AREA
## Macro Modelling, Learning and Empirics

WILLI SEMMLER[*],[**]
ALFRED GREINER[*]
WENLANG ZHANG[*]
[*]*Center for Empirical Macroeconomics
Bielefeld University, Germany*
[**]*New School University, New York*

2005

## ELSEVIER

Amsterdam – Boston – Heidelberg – London – New York – Oxford
Paris – San Diego – San Francisco – Singapore – Sydney – Tokyo

ELSEVIER B.V.
Radarweg 29
P.O. Box 211, 1000 AE
Amsterdam, The Netherlands

ELSEVIER Inc.
525 B Street
Suite 1900, San Diego
CA 92101-4495, USA

ELSEVIER Ltd.
The Boulevard
Langford Lane, Kidlington
Oxford OX5 1GB, UK

ELSEVIER Ltd
84 Theobalds Road
London WC1X 8RR
UK

First edition 2005

Library of Congress Cataloging in Publication Data
A catalog record is available from the Library of Congress.

British Library Cataloguing in Publication Data
A catalogue record is available from the British Library.

ISBN: 0-444-51890-8

♾ The paper used in this publication meets the requirements of ANSI/NISO Z39.48-1992 (Permanence of Paper). Printed in The United Kingdom.

Working together to grow
libraries in developing countries

www.elsevier.com | www.bookaid.org | www.sabre.org

ELSEVIER    BOOK AID International    Sabre Foundation

# Contents

# Part II    Fiscal Policy

viii

# Part III    Monetary and Fiscal Policy Interactions

# CHAPTER 1

# *Introduction*

## 1.1. GENERAL REMARKS

This is a book on the macroeconomy and monetary and fiscal policies in the Euro-area. The Euro-area is a unified currency union since 1999, yet attempts to coordinate monetary and fiscal policies have been pursued before the monetary unification of the Euro-area countries. Before and after the introduction of the Euro in 1999, policies were characterized by the challenges arising from the emergence of a new macroeconomy—the macroeconomy of the Euro-area countries. In this book the study of the learning of the new macroeconomic environment and the learning of appropriate policy responses are based on dynamic macroeconomic and macroeconometric models. We elaborate on many macroeconomic issues of the Euro-area, such as output stabilization, the Phillips curve, inflation rates, economic growth, employment, time-varying NAIRU, asset price bubbles, growth and fiscal policy, sustainability of public debt, the macroeconomic effects of fiscal consolidation, the empirics of monetary and fiscal policy interaction and so on. Yet, we want to stress that the response of policies can best be discussed in the context of dynamic macroeconomic and macroeconometric models. On the other hand, we are aware that such quantitative studies on the emergence of a new macroeconomy and the learning of the new macroeconomic environment and appropriate policy responses also face great challenges.

## 1.2. MONETARY POLICY

Concerning monetary policy, in general it is increasingly recognized that quantitative modeling faces great challenges because of (1) uncertainty on what the model should look like that the monetary authorities presume private agents are following (model uncertainty), (2) uncertainty about the actual situation of the economy (data uncertainty), (3) uncertainty about the size of shocks and (4) uncertainty concerning the effects of policy actions (uncertainty about short- and long-run real effects). It is of no surprise that in most countries neither private agents' reactions to monetary policy actions nor monetary policy behavior has been stable over time. Assumed models, underlying private behavior reaction coefficients of basic economic relations and monetary policy behavior change over time. Moreover, what has been called the NAIRU has changed over time too. Researchers have also characterized monetary regimes where, over some period of time, economic and monetary relationships as well as monetary policy appear to be relatively stable, subsequently followed by strong shifts and regime changes. This seems to be characteristic for many advanced countries, but more so for Euro-area countries. This leads to the question whether the monetary policy in Europe was too restrictive and what the appropriate policy should have been. Maybe there have been too strong policy reactions to past inflation pressures and the new macroeconomic environment has not been learned properly.

Numerous researchers have maintained that an important shift in monetary regimes, as far as the US is concerned, has taken place at the beginning of the 1980s after Paul Volcker was appointed the chairman of the Fed. Moreover, another important shift in monetary policy that can be considered is the central bank's shift from indirectly targeting inflation, through controlling monetary aggregates (money growth), to targeting inflation rates, through controlling short-term interest rates. Many observers maintain that this has also happened since the beginning of the 1980s. This shift was accompanied by a shift from passive monetary policy with strong reaction to employment but passive reaction to inflation, to an active anti-inflationary policy, namely monetary policy strongly reacting to inflation but less to unemployment. This seems to hold not only for the US but also for Euro-area countries.

## 1.3. FISCAL POLICY

There seems to have also been some regime changes of fiscal policy over time too. In the earlier time period before the 1980s fiscal policy does not seem to have been concerned with the problem of sustainability. It appears to have been the view of policy makers that there is a permissible time path of tax and expenditure that makes it feasible that the government's intertemporal budget constraint holds and fiscal policy is sustainable. In a later period, in the 1980s and 1990s, it was perceived that there do not necessarily exist tax rates (or expenditure paths) that make fiscal policy sustainable. As recent research has shown, for example, starting with Woodford (1996), fiscal regimes may also have implications for inflation rates. This has been an essential issue in the academic discussion on the creation of a single currency in Europe, the Euro.

Concerning short-run fiscal policy, Keynesian stabilization policy, economists have become skeptical regarding the immediate stabilization effects of such policies. The traditional macroeconomic policy of Keynesian type was that, when recessions occur tax reduction and spending increases to cushion the recession should be undertaken. Fiscal policy to cushion recessions through the automatic stabilizer as well as fiscal spending to increase employment is still favored by most macroeconomists. Yet, because of the uncertainty concerning the immediate effects of short-run fiscal policy, economists have become hesitant to favor fiscal policy— beyond its function as automatic stabilizer. Moreover, most countries show high fiscal deficit and debt and the space for fiscal policy has become very narrow. Because of this and the long delays in the effect of fiscal policy, monetary policy is frequently preferred to fiscal policy as discretionary policy. Monetary policy, so it is often argued, is likely to have a more direct effect on economic activity. Fiscal policy is nowadays seen as a less effective stabilization tool in particular for countries where high public deficit and debt prevail.

Today, fiscal policy is thus often relegated to set the right incentives for private agents and to provide the right infrastructure for the long run—for economic growth. We will discuss fiscal policy for the long run, namely how certain categories of public spending may enhance or retard growth. We will also consider the impact of budget deficits and public sector borrowing on economic growth and introduce formal tests of sustainability of fiscal policy. We also present a quantitative study of the impact of public debt stabilization programs on macroeconomic performance. We in particular will explore under what conditions short-run stabilization policy is still likely to be effective.

There has also been a new view arising on the interaction of fiscal and monetary policies. As far as inflation is concerned, an important issue concerning the interaction of monetary and fiscal policies is that, if the government budget is financed through the issue of money as well as treasury bonds, the difference of money and bonds becomes blurred in the long run, see Sargent (1986), Woodford (1996) and Sims (1997). As has been argued, fiscal policy can, even if there is a strict monetary policy, through independent central banks affect the price level. This has been called the fiscal theory of the price level, see Woodford (1996) and Sims (1997).

Since the intertemporal budget constraint has to hold jointly for both money and bonds, the recent literature has, therefore, classified two fiscal regimes—the Ricardian regime, when the intertemporal budget constraint can be enforced by a variable tax and expenditure for any given price level and the non-Ricardian regime when tax rates are not feasible to enforce the intertemporal budget constraint and the price level is the adjusting variable, see Woodford (1996).

Although in both cases the monetary authority may be able to steer the inflation rate toward the target inflation rate the price level is determined differently in the two regimes. Historically in the Euro-area countries, before the end of the 1970s a Ricardian fiscal regime seems to have been dominant, but since the beginning of the 1980s the non-Ricardian fiscal regime seems to have prevailed in countries of the Euro-area, since tax rates were less and less feasible instruments to enforce an intertemporal budget constraint.

## 1.4. MONETARY AND FISCAL POLICY INTERACTIONS

Recently, the interactions of monetary and fiscal policies and the issues concerning the uncertainties surrounding those two policies have come to the forefront in the discussion on policies in the Euro-area countries in particular since the introduction of a single currency, the Euro. The problem of the interdependence of monetary and fiscal policy is a particular issue for the Euro-area countries, since there is only one monetary policy, but decentralized fiscal policies of the different member states of the Euro-area. Economists, for example, have argued that the efficiency of monetary policy might be affected by fiscal policy through its effects on demand and by modifying the long-term conditions for economic growth. On the other hand, monetary policy may be accommodative to fiscal policy or counteractive. Therefore, in the last part of this book we will explore monetary and fiscal policy interactions in the Euro-area— not only policy interactions in member states, but also interactions between individual fiscal policy and the common monetary policy. Because of regime changes and uncertainty in macroeconomic models, monetary and fiscal policy interactions may have experienced important changes. Therefore, the time-varying interaction of monetary and fiscal policies will also be a crucial topic of the last part of this book. That is, the two policies may have been accommodative to each other in some periods and counteractive in other periods.

## 1.5. DYNAMIC AND ECONOMETRIC METHODOLOGY

In our quantitative study of the emergence of the new macro-economy of the Euro-area and the learning of the appropriate policies we apply certain methodological tools. These are tools from dynamic systems, dynamic optimization and non-linear econometrics. Both discrete-time and continuous-time models will be employed in this book to explore macroeconomic dynamics of the Euro-area.

In order to study those dynamics in the context of intertemporal models, we will employ different approaches of dynamic optimization. Optimal control theory, to be precise, the Maximum Principle (Hamiltonian), and dynamic programming (the Principle of Optimality), for example, will be employed. Optimal control theory and dynamic programming are used to solve dynamic optimization problems with control variables, which take the form of monetary or fiscal policy instruments in our models. In the case of need, a dynamic programming algorithm with adaptive rather than uniform grids will be employed for our numerical studies. With this algorithm, which has been developed by Grüne (1997) and extensively applied in Grüne and Semmler (2004a), we can deal with non-linear as well as linear state equations in dynamic optimization problems.

In order to explore time-varying behavior and regime changes, we will employ the Chow break-point tests and the Kalman filter. While the former can only explore structural changes at certain predetermined points, the latter can be used to estimate time-varying paths of unknown parameters. In the part of monetary policy the traditional state-space model will be employed to study regime changes, in the part of monetary and fiscal policy interactions, however, we will use the state-space model with Markov-switching, which can explore regime changes in shocks as well as changes in coefficients. As regards estimation of forward-looking models, we will employ the generalized method of moments (GMM).

In order to explore model uncertainty and learning in macro-economic models, we will employ both the recursive least squares (RLS) learning algorithm and the robust control theory. The classical optimal control theory can only deal with dynamic optimization problems without model misspecification; the robust control theory can, however, be used to study models with uncertainty. As will be seen, robust control helps one to seek the "best" policy reaction from the "worst" case. We will also use recent quantitative tools to discuss the issue of stability of the dynamic relationships under learning, a topic addressed in recent literature on macroeconomic learning. Finally we want to note that although the overall theme of the book is on the macroeconomy and monetary and fiscal policies and learning, more rigorous modeling of learning using adaptive and least squares algorithms is restricted to a few chapters.

## 1.6. OUTLOOK

The book is organized as follows. In Part I we will focus on the dynamics of the macroeconomy and monetary policy in the Euro-area. We will commence our study with some empirical evidence of the IS and Phillips curves and study backward- and forward-looking behavior, since these have recently been considered as core parts of macroeconomic analysis and thus have been used as a baseline model of monetary policy. We will then explore optimal monetary policy rules, at both theoretical and empirical levels, time-varying behavior and the stability of economic relationships under learning.

Part II explores fiscal policy in the context of dynamic macroeconometric models. We will consider fiscal policy and its change over time, both from the short-run as well as long-run perspective. We will explore not only the relation between fiscal policy and economic growth, but also sustainability of fiscal policy and the effects of fiscal consolidation on macroeconomic performance.

While Part I and Part II explore monetary and fiscal policies separately, Part III explores the interactions between monetary and fiscal policies in the Euro-area. We will explore not only policy interactions in member states, but also the interactions between individual fiscal policy and the common monetary policy.

PART I

# *Monetary Policy*

In this part we focus on uncertainty and shifts concerning monetary policy. An important econometric tool to study learning and shifts in policies will be the Kalman filter which is very useful to estimate time-varying private as well as monetary policy behavior. After estimating macroeconometric relationships such as the IS equation and Phillips curve for some European countries and the US, employing forward- and backward-looking expectations, time-varying economic and monetary relationships are estimated. Subsequently, optimal monetary control models with learning, robust control and time-varying (and state contingent) monetary policy reactions are studied. We also explore the question of what would have happened to output, inflation and employment if European monetary policy had followed American monetary policy rules. The last chapter in this part deals with the relationship of financial market volatility and monetary policy.

# CHAPTER 2

# Empirical Evidence of the IS and Phillips Curves

## 2.1. INTRODUCTION

The study of monetary policy is usually concerned with two important equations: the "IS" curve, which describes the relation between output gap and real interest rate, and the Phillips curve named after A.W. Phillips, which describes the relation between inflation and unemployment.[1] While the IS curve originally described the equilibrium in the goods market, the Phillips curve was originally developed by Phillips (1958) to describe the relation between the unemployment and the rate of change of money wage rates in the UK from 1861 to 1957.

While some researchers have presumed that the Phillips curve is dead, numerous researchers, Eller and Gordon (2003), Karanassou et al. (2005) and Mankiw (2001), for example, insist on the traditional view that there exists a tradeoff between inflation and unemployment. Mankiw (2001), however, defines the tradeoff between inflation and unemployment somewhat different from the traditional view. What he emphasizes is the effect of monetary policy, which may drive inflation and unemployment in opposite directions.

---

[1] Recently, the Phillips curve has been restated as a positive relation between inflation and output gap.

Karanassou et al. (2005) argue that there exists a tradeoff between inflation and output, even if there is no money illusion, because of "frictional growth". They further claim that there exits a *long-run* tradeoff between inflation and output.

On the other hand, following Phillips (1958), some researchers, Flaschel and Krolzig (2002), Chen and Flaschel (2004), Flaschel et al. (2004) and Fair (2000), for example, argue that two Phillips curves, rather than a single one, should be considered. Other researchers on macroeconomics and monetary policy, Rudebusch and Svensson (1999), Woodford (2001b, 2003b), Clarida et al. (2000), Svensson (1997, 1999a,b) and Ball (1997), for example, have, however, employed a single Phillips curve. This simplification is usually based on the assumption that there is a significant correlation between output and wage, which translates into the relationship of output and prices. Recently, there have been numerous attempts to provide some micro-foundation to the single Phillips curve. This line of research has put forward what is called the New Keynesian Phillips curve. In the research below we will, by and large, employ a single Phillips curve for simplicity, following the above mentioned recent work.

While the traditional Phillips curve considers mainly backward-looking behavior, the New Keynesian Phillips curve takes into account forward-looking behavior. Because of some drawbacks of the New Keynesian Phillips curve, which will be discussed below, a so-called "hybrid New Keynesian Phillips curve" has been proposed. The hybrid Phillips curve considers backward- as well as forward-looking behavior.

Another recent topic concerning the Phillips curve is its shape. While most papers in the literature have assumed a linear Phillips curve, some researchers have recently argued that the Phillips curve can be non-linear. These papers include Dupasquier and Ricketts (1998), Schaling (2004), Laxton et al. (1999), Aguiar and Martins (2002) and others. Semmler and Zhang (2004), for example, explore monetary policy with different shapes of the Phillips curve.

Flaschel et al. (2004) also claim to have detected non-linearity in the Phillips curve.

In most parts of this book we will focus on the linear Phillips curve, because there is no consensus on the form of non-linearity in the Phillips curve yet. Some researchers, Schaling (2004) and Laxton et al. (1999), for example, argue that it is convex, while other researchers, Stiglitz (1997), for instance, argue that it is concave. Filardo (1998), however, argues that the Phillips curve is convex in the case of positive output gaps and concave in the case of negative output gaps.

Next, we will present some empirical evidence of the IS and Phillips curves, since they are very often employed in the following chapters. While in section 2.2 only backward-looking behavior is considered, in section 2.3 we will estimate the two curves with both backward- and forward-looking behavior. This chapter estimates the IS and Phillips curves under the assumption that the coefficients in the equations are invariant, in the next chapter, however, we will estimate the Phillips curve with time-varying coefficients, since there might exist regime changes in the economy.

## 2.2. THE IS AND PHILLIPS CURVES WITH BACKWARD-LOOKING BEHAVIOR

In this section, we will work with the output gap in the estimation of the IS and Phillips curves. We here consider only backward-looking behavior, as used in Rudebusch and Svensson (1999):

$$\pi_t = \alpha_0 + \sum_{i=1}^{m} \alpha_i \pi_{t-i} + \alpha_{m+1} y_{t-1} + \varepsilon_t, \qquad (2.1)$$

$$y_t = \beta_0 + \sum_{i=1}^{n} \beta_i y_{t-i} + \beta_{n+1}(\bar{\imath}_{t-1} - \bar{\pi}_{t-1}) + \xi_t, \qquad (2.2)$$

where $\pi_t$ denotes inflation rate, $y_t$ output gap and $i_t$ the short-term interest rate. $\varepsilon_t$ and $\xi_t$ are shocks subject to normal distributions with zero mean and constant variances. The symbol "$-$" above $i_t$ and $\pi_t$ denotes the four-quarter average values of the corresponding variables. Quarterly data are used and the data sources are OECD and IMF. The inflation rate is measured by changes in the consumer price index (CPI, base year: 1995). The output gap is defined as the percentage deviation of the log of the industrial production index (IPI, base year: 1995) from its polynomial trend, the same as in Clarida et al. (1998).

The polynomial trend reads as

$$y^* = \sum_{i=0}^{n} c_i t^i,$$

with $n = 3$.[2] Because the IPI of Italy is not available, we use the GDP at a constant price (base year: 1995) instead. The Akaike information criterion (AIC) is used to determine how many and which lags of the dependent variables should be used in the estimation. The estimation results are presented below with $T$-statistics in parentheses. The equations are estimated separately with the ordinary least squares (OLS). We have also tried the estimation with the seemingly unrelated regression (SUR) and find that the results are very similar to those of the separate OLS regressions, since the covariances of the errors are almost zero. The countries we will look at include Germany, France, the UK, Italy and the European Union (EU) as an aggregate economy.

*Germany*: The short-term interest rate of Germany is measured by the 3-month treasury bill rate. The data from 1963.1 to 1998.2

---

[2] As surveyed by Orphanides and van Norden (2002), there are different approaches to measure the potential output. In the following chapters we will also use some other methods. While Clarida et al. (1998) use the quadratic trend to measure the potential output, we use the third-order trend because the data used here cover a much longer period and the third-order trend fits the data better.

generate the following estimates:

$$\pi_t = \underset{(3.314)}{0.004} + \underset{(13.049)}{1.082}\,\pi_{t-1} - \underset{(2.215)}{0.179}\,\pi_{t-2} + \underset{(3.796)}{0.184}\,y_{t-1}, \quad R^2 = 0.907,$$

$$y_t = \underset{(1.727)}{0.001} + \underset{(29.896)}{0.946}\,y_{t-1} - \underset{(2.330)}{0.046}\,(\bar{\imath}_{t-1} - \bar{\pi}_{t-1}), \quad R^2 = 0.868.$$

*France*: The short-term interest rate of France is measured by two different rates. From 1962 to 1968 we take the call money rate and from 1969 to 1999 we use the 3-month treasury bill rate, because the 3-month treasury bill rate before 1968 is not available. With the data from 1962.1 to 1999.4 we obtain the following estimates:

$$\pi_t = \underset{(3.158)}{0.003} + \underset{(19.120)}{1.402}\,\pi_{t-1} - \underset{(6.108)}{0.440}\,\pi_{t-2} + \underset{(3.167)}{0.165}\,y_{t-1}, \quad R^2 = 0.979,$$

$$y_t = -\underset{(0.980)}{0.001} + \underset{(7.521)}{0.603}\,y_{t-1} - \underset{(2.351)}{0.185}\,y_{t-2} - \underset{(2.227)}{0.041}\,(\bar{\imath}_{t-1} - \bar{\pi}_{t-1}),$$

$$R^2 = 0.683.$$

*Italy*: The short-term interest rate of Italy is measured by the official discount rate, because other interest rates are not available. The quarterly data from 1970.1 to 1999.3 generate the following estimates:

$$\pi_t = \underset{(1.094)}{0.002} + \underset{(16.761)}{1.412}\,\pi_{t-1} - \underset{(5.243)}{0.446}\,\pi_{t-2} + \underset{(2.250)}{0.236}\,y_{t-1}, \quad R^2 = 0.964,$$

$$y_t = \underset{(2.689)}{0.002} + \underset{(9.964)}{0.712}\,y_{t-1} - \underset{(1.596)}{0.107}\,y_{t-3} - \underset{(1.912)}{0.030}\,(\bar{\imath}_{t-1} - \bar{\pi}_{t-1}),$$

$$R^2 = 0.572.$$

*The UK*: The short-term interest rate of the UK is measured by the 3-month treasury bill rate. The data from 1963.2 to 1999.1

generate the following estimates:

$$\pi_t = \underset{(2.034)}{0.004} + \underset{(17.004)}{1.397}\,\pi_{t-1} - \underset{(2.909)}{0.413}\,\pi_{t-2} - \underset{(1.517)}{0.216}\,\pi_{t-3}$$

$$+ \underset{(2.408)}{0.192}\,\pi_{t-4} + \underset{(3.708)}{0.494}\,y_{t-1}, \quad R^2 = 0.954.$$

$$y_t = \underset{(0.076)}{0.00003} + \underset{(19.706)}{0.849}\,y_{t-1} - \underset{(1.810)}{0.015}\,(\bar{\imath}_{t-1} - \bar{\pi}_{t-1}), \quad R^2 = 0.735.$$

From the estimation of the IS and Phillips curves of the four main European countries above one observes that the $T$-statistics of the coefficients of $y_t$ in the Phillips curve and the real interest rate in the IS curve are significant enough. This indicates that there exists a significant relation between output and inflation, and between inflation and the real interest rate, supporting the above cited view by Mankiw.

Next, we undertake an aggregation of the EU-area economy. We undertake the estimation with the aggregate data of the four main countries of Germany, France, Italy and the UK (EU4) and then the three countries of Germany, France and Italy (EU3). The aggregate inflation rate and output gap are measured by the GDP-weighted sums of the inflation rates and output gaps of the individual countries. We use the German call money rate as the short-term interest rate of EU4 and EU3. Such aggregation of data can be found in Peersman and Smets (1999). There they have also justified using the German rate to measure the monetary policy in the aggregate economy of the Euro-area.[3]

---

[3] The justification of Peersman and Smets (1999, p. 7) reads

"The countries included have had a history of fixed bilateral exchange rates, with the German Bundesbank de facto playing the anchor role. As a result, the transmission of the German interest rate on aggregate output and inflation under a fixed exchange rate regime may be as close as one can get to a historical description of the effects of a common monetary policy in EMU".

The aggregate data of EU4 and EU3 from 1978.4 to 1998.3 generate the following estimates:

EU4

$$\pi_t = \underset{(1.979)}{0.003} + \underset{(15.860)}{1.175}\,\pi_{t-1} - \underset{(3.262)}{0.469}\,\pi_{t-3} + \underset{(2.424)}{0.265}\,\pi_{t-4} + \underset{(3.126)}{0.396}\,y_{t-1},$$

$$R^2 = 0.974.$$

$$y_t = \underset{(1.280)}{0.001} + \underset{(26.242)}{0.947}\,y_{t-1} - \underset{(2.055)}{0.033}\,(\bar{\imath}_{t-1} - \bar{\pi}_{t-1}), \quad R^2 = 0.900.$$

EU3

$$\pi_t = \underset{(1.652)}{0.003} + \underset{(17.182)}{1.235}\,\pi_{t-1} - \underset{(3.438)}{0.510}\,\pi_{t-3} + \underset{(2.121)}{0.240}\,\pi_{t-4} + \underset{(2.025)}{0.236}\,y_{t-1},$$

$$R^2 = 0.972.$$

$$y_t = \underset{(1.480)}{0.001} + \underset{(25.524)}{0.969}\,y_{t-1} - \underset{(2.141)}{0.039}\,(\bar{\imath}_{t-1} - \bar{\pi}_{t-1}), \quad R^2 = 0.901.$$

From these results one arrives at the same conclusions as for the individual countries, that is, there exists a significant relation between $\pi$ and $y$, and between $y$ and the real interest rate. Yet, one might argue here that the assumed backward-looking behavior is not suitable to explain price and output dynamics.

## 2.3. THE IS AND PHILLIPS CURVES WITH FORWARD-LOOKING BEHAVIOR

As mentioned by Clarida et al. (1999), the New Keynesian IS and Phillips curves can be derived from a dynamic general equilibrium model in which money and temporary nominal price rigidities are assumed. Clarida et al. (1999, p. 1665) write the IS and Phillips curves with forward-looking behavior as

$$y_t = E_t y_{t+1} - \varphi(i_t - E_t \pi_{t+1}) + g_t, \qquad (2.3)$$

$$\pi_t = \lambda y_t + \beta E_t \pi_{t+1} + u_t, \qquad (2.4)$$

where $g_t$ and $u_t$ are disturbances terms. $i_t$ is the short-term interest rate and $E$ denotes the expectation operator.[4]

Numerous researchers, Galí and Gertler (1999), Galí et al. (2001a), Woodford (1996), and Chadha and Nolan (2004) for example, have derived the New Keynesian Phillips curve 2.4. While Galí and Gertler (1999) derive the New Keynesian Phillips curve under the assumption that firms face identical constant marginal costs, Galí et al. (2001a) derive the New Keynesian Phillips curve under the assumption of increasing real marginal costs. Although there exist some differences between their frameworks, their models do have something in common, that is, the Calvo (1983) pricing model and Dixit–Stiglitz consumption and production models are usually employed. In the appendix of this chapter we will present a brief sketch of Woodford's (1996) derivation of the New Keynesian IS and Phillips curves.

Clarida et al. (1999) describe some differences of the above two equations from the traditional ones. In Equation 2.3 the current output can be affected by its expected value, and in Equation 2.4 one finds that $E_t \pi_{t+1}$, instead of $E_{t-1} \pi_t$ enters the Phillips curve.

The virtues of the New Keynesian Phillips curve have been described by Mankiw. Mankiw (2001), however, also mentions three problems of the New Keynesian Phillips curves: (a) It leads to "disinflationary booms", (b) it cannot explain "inflation persistence", and (c) it does not describe appropriate "impulse

---

[4] Some economists, Woodford (2001b), for example, argue that marginal cost rather than output gap should be used in the Phillips curve. Other economists, however, argue that there may exist a proportionate relation between marginal cost and output gap. See Clarida et al. (1999, footnote 15). The reader is referred to Clarida et al. (1999, pp. 1665–1667) for the interpretation of $g_t$ and $u_t$.

response functions to monetary policy shocks". Further criticisms on the New Keynesian Phillips curve can be found in Eller and Gordon (2003).

Because of the problems of the traditional and New Keynesian Phillips curves, a third type of Phillips curve, the so-called hybrid New Keynesian Phillips curve, has been derived and employed in macroeconomics. In the hybrid New Keynesian Phillips curve both backward- and forward-looking behavior is considered. The IS curve (with backward- and forward-looking behavior) and the hybrid Phillips curve have been written by Clarida et al. (1999, p. 1691) as follows:

$$y_t = \alpha_1 y_{t-1} + (1 - \alpha_1)E_t y_{t+1} - \alpha_2(i_t - E_t \pi_{t+1}) + \varepsilon_t, \quad \alpha_i > 0, \tag{2.5}$$

$$\pi_t = \beta_1 \pi_{t-1} + (1 - \beta_1)\beta_2 E_t \pi_{t+1} + \beta_3 y_t + \xi_t, \quad \beta_i > 0, \tag{2.6}$$

where $i_t$ is the short-term interest rate and $\beta_2$ the discount factor between 0 and 1.[5] $\varepsilon_t$ and $\xi_t$ are disturbance terms. The difference between the derivations of the New Keynesian Phillips curve and the hybrid New Keynesian Phillips curve consists in a fundamental assumption of the models. The former assumes that each firm adjusts its price with probability $(1 - \theta)$ each period and does not adjust its price with probability $\theta$. The latter, however, further assumes that there are two types of firms, that is, some firms are forward looking and the others are backward looking. Some estimations of the hybrid New Keynesian Phillips curves have been undertaken. Using the real marginal costs rather than output gap in the estimation, Galí and Gertler (1999), for example, conclude that backward-looking behavior is not so important as forward-looking behavior.

---

[5] Note that in case $\beta_2$ does not equal 1, $\pi_t$ and $y_t$ do not necessarily equal zero in steady states. In this case we have a non-vertical long-run Phillips curve. The topic of the long-run Phillips curve has become an important issue in macroeconomics, and the reader is referred to Graham and Snower (2002) and Karanassou et al. (2005) for this problem.

Moreover, Galí et al. (2005), employing different approaches (generalized method of moments (GMM), non-linear instrumental variables and maximum likelihood estimation), estimate the hybrid New Keynesian Phillips curve with the US data and find that the estimation results are robust to the approaches employed. Galí et al. (2001b) estimate the hybrid New Keynesian Phillips curve with more lags of inflation and find that the additional lags of inflation do not greatly affect the results.

The hybrid New Keynesian Phillips curve given by Equation 2.6 is, in fact, similar to the hybrid Phillips curve proposed by Fuhrer and Moore (1995), which reads

$$\pi_t = \phi \pi_{t-1} + (1 - \phi) E_t \pi_{t+1} + \delta y_t. \qquad (2.7)$$

Fuhrer and Moore (1995) derive this hybrid Phillips curve from a model with relative wage hypothesis. Fuhrer and Moore (1995) set $\phi = 0.5$. In case $\beta_2 = 1$, Equation 2.6 looks the same as Equation 2.7 except for a disturbance term in Equation 2.6.

Next, we will estimate the system (Equations 2.5 and 2.6) with the GMM, following Clarida et al. (1998). In the estimation below, we find that $\beta_2$ is always very close to one (0.985 in the case of Germany, 0.990 in France and 0.983 in the US, for example). Therefore, we will assume $\beta_2 = 1$ for simplicity. Thus, the hybrid New Keynesian Phillips curve looks the same as the hybrid Phillips curve derived and employed by Fuhrer and Moore (1995) except that the former has a disturbance term.

Defining $\Omega_t$ as the information available to economic agents when expectations of the output gap and inflation rate are formed, and assuming $\varepsilon_t$ and $\xi_t$ to be iid with zero mean and constant variances for simplicity, one has

$$y_t = \alpha_1 y_{t-1} + (1 - \alpha_1) E[y_{t+1} | \Omega_t] - \alpha_2 (i_t - E[\pi_{t+1} | \Omega_t]) + \varepsilon_t,$$
$$\alpha_i > 0, \quad (2.8)$$

$$\pi_t = \beta_1 \pi_{t-1} + (1 - \beta_1) E[\pi_{t+1} | \Omega_t] + \beta_3 y_t + \xi_t, \quad \beta_i > 0. \quad (2.9)$$

One can rewrite the above two equations as follows:

$$y_t = \alpha_1 y_{t-1} + (1 - \alpha_1) y_{t+1} - \alpha_2 (i_t - \pi_{t+1}) + \eta_t, \qquad (2.10)$$

$$\pi_t = \beta_1 \pi_{t-1} + (1 - \beta_1) \pi_{t+1} + \beta_3 y_t + \varepsilon_t, \qquad (2.11)$$

with

$$\eta_t = (1 - \alpha_1)(E[y_{t+1}|\Omega_t] - y_{t+1}) + \alpha_2 (E[\pi_{t+1}|\Omega_t] - \pi_{t+1}) + \varepsilon_t$$

$$\varepsilon_t = (1 - \beta_1)(E[\pi_{t+1}|\Omega_t] - \pi_{t+1}) + \xi_t.$$

Let $u_t$ ($\in \Omega_t$) denote a vector of variables within the economic agents' information set when expectations of inflation rate and output gap are formed that are orthogonal to $\eta_t$ and $\varepsilon_t$, one has $E[\eta_t|u_t] = 0$ and $E[\varepsilon_t|u_t] = 0$. $u_t$ may contain any lagged variable which can be used to forecast output and inflation, and contemporaneous variables uncorrelated with $\varepsilon_t$ and $\xi_t$.

One now has the following equations:

$$E[y_t - \alpha_1 y_{t-1} - (1 - \alpha_1) y_{t+1} + \alpha_2 (i_t - \pi_{t+1})|u_t] = 0, \quad (2.12)$$

$$E[\pi_t - \beta_1 \pi_{t-1} - (1 - \beta_1) \pi_{t+1} - \beta_3 y_t|u_t] = 0. \qquad (2.13)$$

We will estimate this system by way of the GMM with quarterly data. The data sources are OECD and IMF.[6] The measures of the inflation rate, output gap and short-term interest rate are the same as in the previous section. The estimation results of several Euro-area countries are presented below with *T*-statistics in parentheses. Because the number of instruments used for the estimation is larger than that of the parameters to be estimated,

---

[6] We use the 2SLS to obtain the initial estimates of the parameters and then use these initial estimates to obtain the final estimates by way of the GMM with quarterly data.

we present the J-statistics (J-St.) to illustrate the validity of the overidentifying restriction.[7]

*Germany*: The estimation for Germany is undertaken with the data from 1970.1 to 1998.4. The instruments include the 1–4 lags of the short-term interest rate, inflation rate, output gap, the percentage deviation of the real money supply (M3) from its HP-filtered trend, the log difference of the nominal DM/USD exchange rate, price changes in imports, energy and shares and a constant. Correction for MA(1) autocorrelation is undertaken. J-St. = 0.388 and the residual covariance is $1.11 \times 10^{-10}$.

$$y_t = \underset{(0.883)}{0.002} + \underset{(21.024)}{0.491}\, y_{t-1} + (1 - 0.491)E[y_{t+1}|u_t]$$

$$- \underset{(1.956)}{0.011}\,(i_t - E[\pi_{t+1}|u_t]) + \varepsilon_t$$

$$= 0.002 + 0.491 y_{t-1} + 0.509 E[y_{t+1}|u_t]$$

$$- 0.011(i_t - E[\pi_{t+1}|u_t]) + \varepsilon_t, \quad R^2 = 0.662, \qquad (2.14)$$

$$\pi_t = \underset{(2.236)}{0.001} + \underset{(4.162)}{0.147}\, y_t + \underset{(22.655)}{0.345}\, \pi_{t-1} + (1 - 0.345)E[\pi_{t+1}|u_t] + \xi_t$$

$$= 0.001 + 0.147 y_t + 0.345 \pi_{t-1} + 0.655 E[\pi_{t+1}|u_t] + \xi_t,$$

$$R^2 = 0.954. \quad (2.15)$$

*France*: The estimation of France is undertaken with the data from 1970.1 to 1999.4. The instruments include the 1–4 lags of the interest rate, output gap, inflation rate, log difference of index of unit value of import, log difference of the nominal Franc/USD exchange rate, the unemployment rate and a constant. Correction for MA(1) autocorrelation is undertaken. J-St. = 0.303 and the residual

---

[7] The J-statistic reported here is the minimized value of the objective function in the GMM estimation. Hansen (1982) claims that $n \cdot J \xrightarrow{L} \chi^2(m - s)$, with $n$ being the sample size, $m$ the number of moment conditions and $s$ the number of parameters to be estimated.

covariance is $9.27 \times 10^{-11}$.

$$y_t = \underset{(2.198)}{0.0004} + \underset{(10.725)}{0.361} y_{t-1} + (1 - 0.361)E[y_{t+1}|u_t]$$
$$- \underset{(2.279)}{0.009} (i_t - E[\pi_{t+1}|u_t]) + \varepsilon_t$$
$$= 0.0004 + 0.361 y_{t-1} + 0.639 E[y_{t+1}|u_t]$$
$$- 0.009(i_t - E[\pi_{t+1}|u_t]) + \varepsilon_t, \quad R^2 = 0.615, \qquad (2.16)$$

$$\pi_t = -\underset{(1.075)}{0.0004} + \underset{(6.682)}{0.551} y_t + \underset{(17.865)}{0.709} \pi_{t-1} + (1 - 0.709)E[\pi_{t+1}|u_t] + \xi_t$$
$$= -0.0004 + 0.551 y_t + 0.709 \pi_{t-1} + 0.291 E[\pi_{t+1}|u_t] + \xi_t,$$
$$R^2 = 0.991. \quad (2.17)$$

*Italy*: For Italy we undertake the estimation from 1971.1 to 1999.3. The instruments include the 1–4 lags of the interest rate, inflation rate, output gap, the log difference of index of unit value of import, the log difference of nominal LIRA/USD exchange rate, the unemployment rate and a constant. J-St. is 0.193 and the residual covariance is $1.12 \times 10^{-9}$. Correction for MA(2) autocorrelation is undertaken.

$$y_t = \underset{(7.387)}{0.001} + \underset{(17.788)}{0.357} y_{t-1} + (1 - 0.357)E[y_{t+1}|u_t]$$
$$- \underset{(6.847)}{0.019} (i_t - E[\pi_{t+1}|u_t]) + \varepsilon_t$$
$$= 0.001 + 0.357 y_{t-1} + 0.643 E[y_{t+1}|u_t]$$
$$- 0.019(i_t - E[\pi_{t+1}|u_t]) + \varepsilon_t, \quad R^2 = 0.673, \qquad (2.18)$$

$$\pi_t = -\underset{(1.232)}{0.004} + \underset{(3.138)}{0.106} y_t + \underset{(47.104)}{0.572} \pi_{t-1} + (1 - 0.572)E[\pi_{t+1}|u_t] + \xi_t$$
$$= -0.0004 + 0.106 y_t + 0.572 \pi_{t-1} + 0.428 E[\pi_{t+1}|u_t] + \xi_t,$$
$$R^2 = 0.986. \quad (2.19)$$

*The UK*: The estimation of the UK is undertaken from 1962.4 to 1999.1. The instruments include the 1–4 lags of the interest rate, inflation rate, output gap, price changes in imports, the log difference of the nominal Pound/USD exchange rate, the unemployment rate and a constant. Correction for MA(2) autocorrelation is undertaken. J-St. is 0.214 and the residual covariance is $5.11 \times 10^{-10}$.

$$y_t = \underset{(1.150)}{0.0001} + \underset{(15.840)}{0.363} \, y_{t-1} + (1 - 0.363) E[y_{t+1}|u_t]$$

$$- \underset{(3.443)}{0.007} \, (i_t - E[\pi_{t+1}|u_t]) + \varepsilon_t$$

$$= 0.0001 + 0.363 y_{t-1} + 0.637 E[y_{t+1}|u_t]$$

$$- 0.007 (i_t - E[\pi_{t+1}|u_t]) + \varepsilon_t, \quad R^2 = 0.752, \quad (2.20)$$

$$\pi_t = - \underset{(3.973)}{0.002} + \underset{(3.893)}{0.333} \, y_t + \underset{(22.513)}{0.553} \, \pi_{t-1} + (1 - 0.553) E[\pi_{t+1}|u_t] + \xi_t$$

$$= -0.002 + 0.333 y_t + 0.553 \pi_{t-1} + 0.447 E[\pi_{t+1}|u_t] + \xi_t,$$

$$R^2 = 0.980. \quad (2.21)$$

*The EU4*: As in the previous section we also undertake the estimation with the aggregate data of the Euro-area. The estimation for the EU4 is undertaken from 1979.1 to 1998.3. The instruments include the 1–4 lags of the output gap, inflation rate, interest rate, GDP weighted average price changes in imports, the GDP-weighted unemployment rate, the first difference of the GDP-weighted log of exchange rate and a constant. Correction for MA(1) auto-correlation is undertaken, the residual covariance is $4.59 \times 10^{-11}$ and J-St. $= 0.389$.

$$y_t = \underset{(6.283)}{0.0004} + \underset{(46.290)}{0.811} \, y_{t-1} + (1 - 0.811) E[y_{t+1}|u_t]$$

$$- \underset{(6.310)}{0.018} \, (i_t - E[\pi_{t+1}|u_t]) + \varepsilon_t$$

$$= 0.0004 + 0.811 y_{t-1} + 0.189 E[y_{t+1}|u_t]$$

$$- 0.018 (i_t - E[\pi_{t+1}|u_t]) + \varepsilon_t, \quad R^2 = 0.739, \quad (2.22)$$

$$\pi_t = \underset{(1.715)}{0.0005} + \underset{(6.631)}{0.335 y_t} + \underset{(47.103)}{0.610\,\pi_{t-1}} + (1 - 0.610)E[\pi_{t+1}|u_t] + \xi_t$$

$$= 0.0005 + 0.335 y_t + 0.610\pi_{t-1} + 0.390E[\pi_{t+1}|u_t] + \xi_t,$$

$$R^2 = 0.987. \quad (2.23)$$

*The US*: Next, we undertake the estimation for the US from 1962.1 to 1998.4. For the US we use two lags of the inflation rate in Equation 2.8, since the estimates will have signs opposite to the definition in Equations 2.8 and 2.9 if we just estimate Equation 2.11 with one lag of the inflation rate. The inflation rate of the US is measured by changes in the CPI, the short-term interest rate is the federal funds rate, and the output gap is the percentage deviation of the log of the IPI from its third-order polynomial trend. The instruments include the 1–4 lags of the interest rate, inflation rate, output gap, percentage deviation of the real money supply (M3) from its HP filtered trend, price changes in imports, the log difference of the nominal USD/SDR exchange rate, the unemployment rate and a constant. Correction for MA(1) autocorrelation is undertaken. J-St. is 0.298 and the residual covariance is $2.16 \times 10^{-11}$.

$$y_t = \underset{(2.650)}{0.0004} + \underset{(22.814)}{0.526\,y_{t-1}} + (1 - 0.526)E[y_{t+1}|u_t]$$

$$- \underset{(2.275)}{0.011}(i_t - E[\pi_{t+1}|u_t]) + \varepsilon_t$$

$$= 0.0004 + 0.526 y_{t-1} + 0.474E[y_{t+1}|u_t]$$

$$- 0.011(i_t - E[\pi_{t+1}|u_t]) + \varepsilon_t, \quad R^2 = 0.931, \quad (2.24)$$

$$\pi_t = \underset{(2.217)}{0.0004} + \underset{(2.548)}{0.042\,y_t} + \underset{(19.294)}{0.861\,\pi_{t-1}} - \underset{(7.427)}{0.235\,\pi_{t-2}}$$

$$+ (1 - 0.861 + 0.235)E[\pi_{t+1}|u_t] + \xi_t$$

$$= 0.0004 + 0.042 y_t + 0.861\pi_{t-1} - 0.235\pi_{t-2}$$

$$+ 0.374E[\pi_{t+1}|u_t] + \xi_t, \quad R^2 = 0.990. \quad (2.25)$$

The estimation results above show that the expectations do play some roles in the equations, since the coefficients of the expected variables are usually large enough in comparison with the coefficients of the lagged variables.

## 2.4. CONCLUSION

This chapter presents empirical evidence of the IS- and Phillips-curve. Both backward- and forward-looking behavior has been studied. The results seem to favor the conclusion that there exists some significant relation between inflation rate and output gap, and output gap and real interest rate, no matter whether the forward-looking behavior is considered or not. In the next chapter we will explore evidence for the Phillips curve with the unemployment gap and even with a time-varying NAIRU.

### APPENDIX A2. DERIVATION OF THE NEW KEYNESIAN PHILLIPS CURVE

Below is a brief sketch of Woodford's (1996) derivation of the New Keynesian Phillips and IS curves. The details of the derivation can be found in Woodford (1996, pp. 3–14). The equations are derived from a model of a monopolistically competitive economy.

Let $j \in [0, 1]$ denote a continuum of households which are assumed to be identical and infinite lived, and $z \in [0, 1]$ a continuum of differentiated goods produced by these households, then each household will maximize the following objective function

$$E\left\{\sum_{t=0}^{\infty} \beta^t \langle u(C_t^j + G_t) + v(M_t^J/P_t) - \omega[y_t(j)]\rangle\right\}, \quad (2.26)$$

with $u$ and $v$ being increasing concave functions and $\omega$ an increasing convex function. $0 < \beta < 1$. $E$ is the expectation operator. $y_t(j)$ denotes the product of household $j$. $C_t^j$ is the consumption of household $j$ which reads

$$C_t^j \equiv \left( \int_0^1 c_t^j(z)^{(\theta-1)/\theta} dz \right)^{\theta/(\theta-1)}, \qquad (2.27)$$

with $C_t^j(z)$ denoting household $j$'s consumption of good $z$ and $\theta > 1$ is the constant elasticity of substitution among alternative goods. $G_t$ denotes the public goods. $M_t^j$ denotes the household's money balances at the end of period $t$. $P_t$ is the price index of goods:

$$P_t \equiv \left( \int_0^1 p_t(z)^{1-\theta} dz \right)^{1/(1-\theta)}, \qquad (2.28)$$

with $p_t(z)$ being the price of good $z$ at date $t$.

Let $i_t$ denote the nominal interest rate on a riskless bond and $R_{t,T}$ a stochastic discount factor, it can be shown that

$$1 + i_t \equiv \frac{1}{E_t(R_{t,t+1})}. \qquad (2.29)$$

The consumption of good $z$ and the demand of good $j$ are found to be as follows:

$$c_t^j(z) = C_t^j \left( \frac{p_t(z)}{P_t} \right)^{-\theta} \qquad (2.30)$$

and

$$y_t(j) = Y_t \left( \frac{p_t(j)}{P_t} \right)^{-\theta}, \qquad (2.31)$$

with $Y_t = C_t + G_t$ and $C_t = \int_0^1 C_t^h dh$. Woodford (1996, p. 7) further gives three necessary and sufficient conditions for a household's optimization, two of which are

$$\beta^{T-t} \frac{u'(Y_T)}{u'(Y_t)} \frac{P_t}{P_T} = R_{t,T} \qquad (2.32)$$

$$\frac{v'(M_t/P_t)}{u'(Y_t)} = \frac{i_t}{1 + i_t}. \qquad (2.33)$$

From Equation 2.32 one obtains

$$\beta E_t \frac{u'(Y_{t+1})}{u'(Y_t)} \frac{P_t}{P_{t+1}} = \frac{1}{1 + i_t}. \tag{2.34}$$

Following the Calvo (1983) price-setting model, Woodford (1996, p. 8) shows that the price $p$ must be set to maximize[8]

$$\sum_{k=0}^{\infty} \alpha^k \{ \Lambda_t E_t [R_{t,t+k} p y_{t+k}(p)] - \beta^k E_t [\omega(y_{t+k}(p))] \},$$

with $y_T(p)$ being the demand at date $T$ given by Equation 2.31. $\Lambda_t$ is the marginal utility of holding money. It is shown that the optimal price $\mathcal{P}_t$ must satisfy

$$\sum_{k=0}^{\infty} \alpha^k E_t \{ R_{t,t+k} Y_{t+k} (\mathcal{P}_t / P_{t+k})^{-\theta} [\mathcal{P}_t - \mu S_{t+k,t}] \} = 0, \tag{2.35}$$

where $\mu \equiv \theta/(\theta - 1)$, and $S_{T,t}$ denotes the marginal cost of production at date $T$:

$$S_{T,t} = \frac{\omega'[Y_T(\mathcal{P}_t/P_T)^{-\theta}]}{u'(Y_T)} P_T. \tag{2.36}$$

Employing Equation 2.28, one finds that[9]

$$P_t = [\alpha P_{t-1}^{1-\theta} + (1 - \alpha)\mathcal{P}_t^{1-\theta}]^{1/(1-\theta)}. \tag{2.37}$$

Defining $x_t$ as the percentage deviation of $Y_t$ from its stationary value $Y^*$ (namely, $x_t = (Y_t - Y^*)/Y^*$) and $\hat{\pi}_t$ as the percentage deviation of $\pi_t$ from its stationary value,[10] and linearizing Equation 2.34 at

---

[8] Here $\alpha$ denotes the fraction of producers who keep the old price unchanged.

[9] On the basis of the analysis above, Woodford (1996) then explores how fiscal policy may affect macroeconomic instability. We will not sketch his analysis of this problem here, since this is out of the scope of this chapter.

[10] $\pi_t$ is defined as $P_t/P_{t-1}$, since the stationary value of $\pi_t$ is 1, $\hat{\pi}_t$ is then equal to $(P_t - P_{t-1})/P_{t-1}$.

the stationary values of $Y_t$, $\pi_t$ and $i_t$, one then obtains the following IS curve[11]

$$x_t = E_t x_{t+1} - \sigma(\hat{\imath}_t - E_t \hat{\pi}_{t+1}), \qquad (2.38)$$

with $\hat{\imath}_t$ being the percentage deviation of the nominal interest rate from its stationary value, and

$$\sigma \equiv -\frac{u'(Y^*)}{u''(Y^*)Y^*}.$$

After linearizing Equations 2.35–2.37 around the stationary values of the variables and rearranging the terms, one obtains

$$\hat{\mathcal{P}}_t = \frac{\kappa\alpha}{1-\alpha} \sum_{k=0}^{\infty} (\alpha\beta)^k E_t x_{t+k} + \sum_{k=1}^{\infty} (\alpha\beta)^k E_t \hat{\pi}_{t+k}, \qquad (2.39)$$

$$\hat{\pi}_t = \frac{1-\alpha}{\alpha} \hat{\mathcal{P}}_t, \qquad (2.40)$$

with

$$\kappa \equiv \frac{(1-\alpha)(1-\alpha\beta)}{\alpha} \frac{\varpi+\sigma}{\sigma(\varpi+\theta)} \quad \text{and} \quad \varpi \equiv \frac{\omega'(Y^*)}{\omega''(Y^*)Y^*},$$

where $\hat{\mathcal{P}}_t$ is the percentage deviation of $\mathcal{P}_t/P_t$ from its stationary value, 1. After rearranging Equation 2.39 as

$$\hat{\mathcal{P}}_t = \alpha\beta E_t \hat{\mathcal{P}}_{t+1} + \frac{\kappa\alpha}{1-\alpha} x_t + \alpha\beta E_t \hat{\pi}_{t+1} \qquad (2.41)$$

and substituting Equation 2.40 into Equation 2.41, one finally obtains the following New Keynesian Phillips curve:

$$\hat{\pi}_t = \beta E_t \hat{\pi}_{t+1} + \kappa x_t. \qquad (2.42)$$

---

[11] The stationary value of $i_t$ is found to be $\beta^{-1} - 1$.

# CHAPTER 3

# Time-Varying Phillips Curve

## 3.1. INTRODUCTION

In the previous chapter we have estimated the IS and Phillips curves with both backward- and forward-looking behavior. One crucial assumption is that the coefficients in the equations are invariant. Recently, there has been some discussion on whether there are regime changes in the economy. That is, the parameters in the model might be time varying instead of constant. Cogley and Sargent (2001, 2002), for example, study the inflation dynamics of the US after WWII by way of Bayesian vector autoregression with time-varying parameters and claim to have found regime changes. In this chapter, we will consider this problem and estimate the Phillips curve with time-varying coefficients for several Euro-area countries. This concerns the time-varying reaction of the private sector to the unemployment gap as well as the time variation of what has been called the natural rate of unemployment (or the NAIRU).

There are different approaches to estimate time-varying parameters, among which are the recursive least squares (RLS), flexible least squares (FLS) and the Kalman filter. In this chapter we will apply the Kalman filter because of the drawbacks of the FLS and RLS. By the RLS algorithm, the coefficient usually experiences more significant changes at the beginning than at the end of the sample because earlier observations have larger weights than new ones. Therefore, the RLS estimates may be relatively smooth at the end of the sample, and the real changes in coefficients might not be properly shown.

The FLS assumes that the coefficients evolve slowly. Each choice of an estimate $b = (b_1, ..., b_N)$ for the coefficient vector $b_n$ is connected with two types of errors of model misspecification: (a) the so-called residual measurement error (the difference between dependent variable $y_n$ and the estimated model $x_n^T b_n$), and (b) the so-called residual dynamic error, $(b_{n+1} - b_n)$.[1] One of the most important variables in the FLS estimation is the weight $\mu$ assigned to the dynamic errors. The smaller the $\mu$ is, the larger the changes in the coefficients, and vice versa. In the extreme, when $\mu$ tends to infinity, the coefficients do not change at all. It is quite difficult to assign an appropriate value to $\mu$ and, therefore, it is hard to figure out the real changes of the coefficients. Moreover, there are not only slow but also drastic changes in the coefficients in economic models and, therefore, on the basis of the FLS, Luetkepohl and Herwartz (1996) develop the generalized flexible least squares (GFLS) method to estimate the seasonal changes in coefficients.

In fact, Tucci (1990) finds that the FLS and the Kalman filter are equivalent under some assumptions, that is, under certain conditions there is no difference between these two methods. The Kalman filter undoubtedly has disadvantages too. It is usually assumed that the error terms have Gaussian distributions, which is not necessarily satisfied in practice. A brief sketch of the Kalman filter can be found in the appendix of this chapter.

This chapter is organized as follows. In section 3.2 we estimate the time-varying reaction to the unemployment gap with a constant NAIRU, while in section 3.3 we estimate the time-varying NAIRU with a constant reaction to the unemployment gap.

---

[1] $N$ denotes the number of observations and $x$ is the vector of independent variables. $b$ is the vector of time-varying parameters. The reader is referred to Kalaba and Tesfatsion (1989) for the details of the FLS.

## 3.2. TIME-VARYING REACTION TO THE UNEMPLOYMENT GAP

This section estimates the traditional backward-looking Phillips curve

$$\pi_t = \alpha_0 + \sum_{i=1}^{n} \alpha_i \pi_{t-i} + \alpha_{ut}(U_t - U^N) + \xi_t, \qquad (3.1)$$

$$\alpha_{ut} = \alpha_{ut-1} + \eta_t, \qquad (3.2)$$

where $\pi_t$ is inflation rate, $U_t$ unemployment rate and $U^N$ the so-called NAIRU. $\xi_t$ and $\eta_t$ are shocks subject to normal distributions with zero mean and variance $\sigma_\xi^2$ and $\sigma_\eta^2$, respectively. The $\alpha_{ut}$ is expected to be smaller than zero. The number of lags depends on the $T$-statistics of the corresponding coefficients, that is, lags with insignificant $T$-statistics will be excluded. Equation 3.2 assumes that $\alpha_{ut}$ is time varying and follows a random-walk path. In order to estimate the time-varying path of $\alpha_{ut}$, we employ the maximum likelihood estimation by way of the Kalman filter.[2] The countries to be examined include Germany, France, the UK, Italy and the US. Quarterly data are used. The data sources are OECD and IMF. $T$-statistics of the estimation are shown in parentheses.

The inflation rate of Germany is measured by changes in the CPI. The NAIRU is assumed to be fixed at 6%. This is undoubtedly a simplification, since the NAIRU may change over time too.[3] The data from 1963.4 to 1998.4 generate the following estimation results:

$$\pi_t = \underset{(1.495)}{0.005} + \underset{(9.922)}{1.047}\,\pi_{t-1} - \underset{(2.268)}{0.181}\,\pi_{t-2} + \alpha_{ut}(U_t - U^N).$$

The path of $\alpha_{ut}$ is presented in Figure 3.1A.

---

[2] The reader can also be referred to Hamilton (1994, Chapter 13) for the details of the Kalman filter. In this section, we apply the random-walk model (shown in the appendix) to estimate the time-varying coefficients.

[3] Here we assume that the NAIRU is fixed for all countries, close to the average values of the unemployment rates in these countries. In the next section we will estimate the time-varying NAIRU.

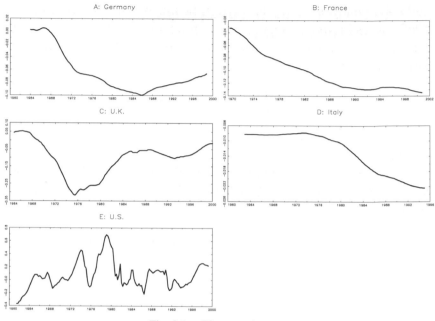

Fig. 3.1:   Time-varying $\alpha_{ut}$.

The inflation rate of France is measured by the log difference of the GDP deflator. The NAIRU is also assumed to be 6%. The data from 1969.1 to 1999.4 generate the following estimation results

$$\pi_t = \underset{(0.566)}{0.008} + \underset{(6.070)}{0.901}\ \pi_{t-1} - \underset{(0.045)}{0.003}\ \pi_{t-2} + \alpha_{ut}(U_t - U^N).$$

The path of $\alpha_{ut}$ is presented in Figure 3.1B.

The inflation rate of the UK is measured by changes in the CPI. The NAIRU is assumed to be 6%. The data from 1964.1 to 1999.4 generate the following estimation results

$$\pi_t = \underset{(2.403)}{0.007} + \underset{(15.845)}{1.384}\ \pi_{t-1} - \underset{(6.695)}{0.491}\ \pi_{t-2} + \alpha_{ut}(U_t - U^N).$$

The path of $\alpha_{ut}$ is presented in Figure 3.1C.

The inflation rate of Italy is also measured by changes in the CPI and the NAIRU is assumed to be 5%. With the data from 1962 to

1999 the changes of $\alpha_{ut}$ are insignificant, but for the period from 1962 to 1994 the changes are significant enough, therefore the estimation is undertaken from 1962.3 to 1994.3 and the result of estimation reads

$$\pi_t = \underset{(0.887)}{0.004} + \underset{(14.111)}{1.409}\,\pi_{t-1} - \underset{(2.870)}{0.448}\,\pi_{t-2} + \alpha_{ut}(U_t - U^N).$$

The path of $\alpha_{ut}$ is presented in Figure 3.1D.

Next, we undertake the estimation for the US. The inflation rate of the US is measured by changes in the CPI and the NAIRU is taken to be 5%. The data from 1961.1 to 1999.4 generate the following estimation results

$$\pi_t = \underset{(2.665)}{0.004} + \underset{(12.242)}{1.198}\,\pi_{t-1} - \underset{(2.119)}{0.298}\,\pi_{t-2} + \underset{(1.589)}{0.203}\,\pi_{t-3}$$

$$- \underset{(2.275)}{0.202}\,\pi_{t-4} + \alpha_{ut}(U_t - U^N).$$

The path of $\alpha_{ut}$ is shown in Figure 3.1E. In Figure 3.1E one finds that for many years $\alpha_{ut}$ is positive, which is inconsistent with the traditional view that there is a negative relation between inflation rate and unemployment rate. One reason may be the value of the NAIRU, which is assumed to be fixed at 5% here. The unemployment rate in the US was quite high in the 1970s and 1980s, attaining 11% around 1983. It experienced significant changes from the 1960s to the 1990s. Therefore, assuming a fixed NAIRU of 5% does not seem to be a good choice.

From the empirical evidence above one finds that the $\alpha_{ut}$ in Equation 3.1 did experience some changes. For the three EU countries of Germany, France and Italy, one finds that the changes of $\alpha_{ut}$ are, to some extent, similar. $\alpha_{ut}$ of France and Italy have been decreasing persistently since the 1960s. In the case of Germany, however, it has been increasing slowly since the middle of the 1980s. As regards the UK, the change of $\alpha_{ut}$ is relatively different from those of the other three countries. It decreased very fast in the 1960s and started to increase in 1975. In order to analyze the causes of the differences of the evolution of $\alpha_{ut}$, we present the inflation and unemployment rates of the four EU countries from 1970 to 1999 in Figures 3.2 and 3.3, respectively. It is obvious that the changes in inflation rates of the four countries are similar. $\pi_t$ attained its highest point around 1975, decreased to a low value in about 4 years, increased to another peak at the end of the 1970s and then continued to go down before 1987, after which it evolved smoothly and stayed below 10%. The evolution of the inflation rate does not seem to be responsible for the differences in the paths of $\alpha_{ut}$ of the four countries. The evolution of the unemployment rates in Figure 3.3, however, may partly explain why the change of $\alpha_{ut}$ in the UK is somewhat different from those of the other three countries. Before 1986 the unemployment rates of the four countries increased almost simultaneously, while after 1986 there existed some differences. The evolution of $U_t$ in the UK was not

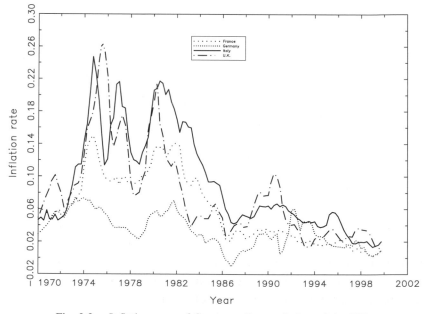

Fig. 3.2:   Inflation rates of Germany, France, Italy and the UK.

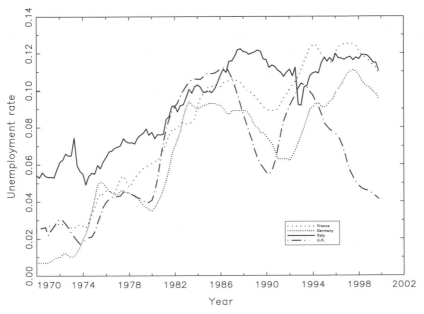

Fig. 3.3:    Unemployment rates of Germany, France, Italy and the UK.

completely consistent with those of the other three countries. After 1992 the $U_t$ of the UK decreased rapidly from about 10 to 4%, while those of the other three countries remained relatively high during the whole of the 1990s and did not begin to go down until 1998.

## 3.3. TIME-VARYING NAIRU WITH SUPPLY SHOCKS

### 3.3.1. Estimate of time-varying NAIRU

In the previous section we have assumed the so-called NAIRU to be fixed. But as mentioned at the beginning of the previous section, there may exist regime changes not only in the Phillips curve but also in the NAIRU. That is, the NAIRU may not be constant but may change with economic environment and this is also a kind of economic uncertainty, which has recently been extensively explored. The uncertainty about economic data such as the NAIRU may greatly influence the decisions of the policy makers. In this section, we assume that the NAIRU follows a random-walk path and estimate the time-varying NAIRU following a model by Gordon (1997). There are of course other papers on the estimation of the time-varying NAIRU and a comprehensive description of how the NAIRU can be estimated can be found in Staiger et al. (1996). In Gordon (1997) the model reads as

$$\pi_t = a(L)\pi_{t-1} + b(L)(U_t - U_t^N) + c(L)z_t + e_t, \qquad (3.3)$$

$$U_t^N = U_{t-1}^N + \eta_t, \qquad (3.4)$$

where $\pi_t$ is inflation rate, $U_t$ the actual unemployment rate and $U_t^N$ denotes the NAIRU which follows a random-walk path indicated by Equation 3.4. $z_t$ is a vector of supply shock variables, $L$ is a polynomial in the lag operator, $e_t$ is a serially uncorrelated error term and $\eta_t$ satisfies the Gaussian distribution with mean zero and variance $\sigma_\eta^2$. Obviously, the variance of $\eta_t$ plays an important role in the estimation. If it is zero, the NAIRU is constant and if it is positive, the NAIRU experiences changes. If $\sigma_\eta^2$ has no constraints, the NAIRU may experience drastic changes.

Gordon (1997) uses $z_t$ to consider supply shocks such as changes of relative prices of imports and the change in the relative price of food and energy. If no supply shocks are taken into account, the NAIRU is referred to as "estimated NAIRU without supply shocks". Though there are no fixed rules on what variables should be included as supply shocks, it seems more reasonable to take supply shocks into account than not, since there are undoubtedly other variables than unemployment rate that may affect inflation rate. In this section the supply shocks considered include mainly price changes of imports ($im_t$), food ($food_t$), and fuel, electricity and water ($fuel_t$). As for which variables should be adopted as supply shocks for the individual countries, we undertake an OLS regression for Equation 3.3 before starting the time-varying estimation, assuming that NAIRU is constant. In most cases we exclude the variables whose *T*-statistics are insignificant. The data source is the same as in the previous subsection.

As mentioned above, the standard deviation of $\eta_t$ plays a crucial role. Gordon (1997) assumes it to be 0.2% for the US for the period of 1955–1996. There is little theoretical background on how large $\eta_t$ should be, but since the NAIRU is usually supposed to be relatively smooth, we constrain the change of the NAIRU within 4%, which is also consistent with Gordon (1997). Therefore, we assume different values of $\eta_t$ for different countries, depending on how large we expect the change of the NAIRU to be.[4]

For Germany, the variance of $\eta_t$ is assumed to be $7.5 \times 10^{-6}$ and the price changes of foods, imports, and fuel, electricity and water are taken as supply shocks. The estimates are presented below with *T*-statistics in parentheses,

$$\pi_t = \underset{(0.056)}{0.004} + \underset{(10.982)}{1.052}\,\pi_{t-1} - \underset{(3.009)}{0.256}\,\pi_{t-2} + \underset{(0.153)}{0.008}\,\pi_{t-3}$$

$$+ \underset{(1.105)}{0.013}\,\text{fuel}_{t-1} + \underset{(1.994)}{0.061}\,\text{food}_{t-1} + \underset{(0.627)}{0.006}\,\text{im}_{t-1}$$

$$- \underset{(0.993)}{0.042}\,(U_t - U_t^N) + e_t,$$

where $\text{fuel}_t$ indicates the price change of fuel, electricity and water, $\text{food}_t$ the price change of food and $\text{im}_t$ the price change of imports. The estimate of the standard deviation of $e_t$ is 0.006 with *T*-statistic being 8.506.

Since the unemployment rates of the four EU countries are presented in Figure 3.3, we present only the estimate of the time-varying NAIRU here. The time-varying NAIRU of Germany is presented in Figure 3.4A.

---

[4] Gordon (1997, pp. 21–22), however, discusses briefly the smoothing problem concerning the estimation of the time-varying NAIRU.

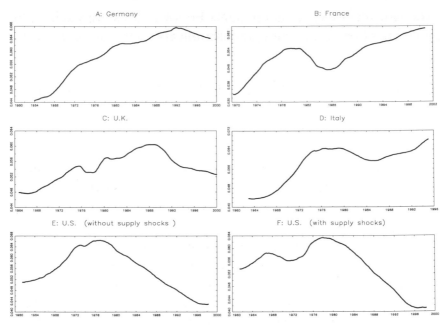

Fig. 3.4:   Time-varying NAIRU of Germany, France, the UK, Italy and the US.

As for France, only one lag of inflation rate is used in the regression, since the coefficient of the unemployment rate gap is almost zero when more lags of inflation are included. The price changes of food and intermediate goods are taken as supply shocks. Three lags of the price changes of intermediate goods are included to smooth the NAIRU. The estimation result reads as

$$\pi_t = \underset{(0.312)}{0.004} + \underset{(27.967)}{0.989}\,\pi_{t-1} - \underset{(2.058)}{0.085}\,\text{food}_{t-1} + \underset{(2.876)}{0.132}\,\text{in}_{t-1}$$

$$- \underset{(1.313)}{0.090}\,\text{in}_{t-2} + \underset{(0.772)}{0.029}\,\text{in}_{t-3} - \underset{(1.889)}{0.054}\,(U_t - U_t^N) + e_t,$$

where $\text{in}_t$ denotes the price change of intermediate goods. The estimate of the standard deviation of $e_t$ is 0.005 with $T$-statistic being 8.808, and the variance of $\eta_t$ is predetermined as $1.3 \times 10^{-5}$. The estimate of the NAIRU of France is presented in Figure 3.4B.

Because of the same reason as for France, one lag of the inflation rate is included in the regression for the UK. The estimation result reads

$$\pi_t = \underset{(0.066)}{0.005} + \underset{(11.063)}{0.818}\,\pi_{t-1} + \underset{(2.768)}{0.130}\,\text{food}_{t-1} + \underset{(0.691)}{0.017}\,\text{fuel}_{t-1}$$

$$- \underset{(0.300)}{0.072}\,(U_t - U_t^N) + e_t.$$

The estimate of the standard deviation of $e_t$ is 0.013 with $T$-statistic being 8.764 and the variance of $\eta_t$ is predetermined as $1.4 \times 10^{-5}$. The estimate of the NAIRU of the UK is presented in Figure 3.4C.

For Italy it seems difficult to get a smooth estimate for the NAIRU if we use only price changes of food, fuel, electricity and water and imports as supply shocks. The main reason seems to be that the inflation rate experienced drastic changes and therefore exerts much influence on the estimate of the NAIRU. Therefore, we try to smooth the estimate of the NAIRU by including the current short-term interest rate ($r_t$) into the regression, which makes the NAIRU more consistent with the actual unemployment rate. The result of estimation is

$$\pi_t = \underset{(0.001)}{0.0035} + \underset{(6.623)}{1.594}\,\pi_{t-1} - \underset{(4.961)}{0.832}\,\pi_{t-2} - \underset{(1.722)}{0.247}\,\text{food}_{t-1}$$

$$+ \underset{(2.255)}{0.322}\,\text{food}_{t-2} - \underset{(1.398)}{0.017}\,\text{fuel}_{t-1} + \underset{(1.599)}{0.030}\,\text{fuel}_{t-2} + \underset{(1.532)}{0.181}\,r_t$$

$$- \underset{(0.902)}{0.304}\,(U_t - U_t^N) + e_t.$$

The estimate of the standard deviation of $e_t$ is 0.010 with $T$-statistic being 8.982, and the variance of $\eta_t$ is assumed to be $2.6 \times 10^{-6}$. The time-varying NAIRU of Italy is presented in Figure 3.4D.

We also undertake the estimation of the NAIRU for the US with and without "supply shocks" for the period of 1962.3–1999.4.

In the estimation without supply shocks, only four lags of inflation rate and unemployment gap are included in the regression and the result of estimation is

$$\pi_t = \underset{(0.002)}{0.002} + \underset{(16.045)}{1.321}\,\pi_{t-1} - \underset{(2.199)}{0.243}\,\pi_{t-2} - \underset{(61.971)}{0.121}\,\pi_{t-3}$$

$$+ \underset{(0.350)}{0.015}\,\pi_{t-4} - \underset{(8.864)}{0.065}\,(U_t - U_t^N) + e_t.$$

The estimate of the standard deviation of $e_t$ is 0.004 with $T$-statistic being 15.651 and the variance of $\eta_t$ is predetermined as $4.5 \times 10^{-6}$. The unemployment rate of the US is presented in Figure 3.5 and the NAIRU without supply shocks is presented in Figure 3.4E, very similar to the result of Gordon (1997).

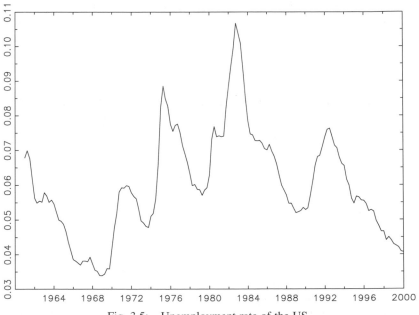

Fig. 3.5:   Unemployment rate of the US.

Considering supply shocks which include price changes in food, energy and imports, we have the following result for the US:

$$\pi_t = \underset{(0.091)}{0.002} + \underset{(10.592)}{0.957}\,\pi_{t-1} - \underset{(1.350)}{0.151}\,\pi_{t-2} - \underset{(0.647)}{0.070}\,\pi_{t-3}$$

$$+ \underset{(1.822)}{0.120}\,\pi_{t-4} + \underset{(4.547)}{0.062}\,\text{food}_t + \underset{(0.468)}{0.007}\,\text{fuel}_{t-1} + \underset{(3.808)}{0.025}\,\text{im}_{t-1}$$

$$- \underset{(3.036)}{0.060}\,(U_t - U_t^N) + e_t.$$

The estimate of the standard deviation of $e_t$ is 0.003 with $T$-statistic being 16.217 and the variance of $\eta_t$ is predetermined as $4 \times 10^{-6}$. The time-varying NAIRU with supply shocks is presented in Figure 3.4F.

### 3.3.2. Why does the NAIRU change over time?

In the previous subsection we have estimated the time-varying NAIRU for several countries. The next question is then, what might have caused changes in the NAIRU.

Stiglitz (1997, pp. 6–8) discusses four factors which may lead to changes in NAIRU: (a) demographics of labor force,[5] (b) the so-called wage-aspiration effect, (c) increased competitiveness of product and labor markets and (d) hysteresis, that is, sustained high actual unemployment rate may raise the NAIRU.[6]

Blanchard and Wolfers (2000) explore how economic shocks, namely the decline in total factor productivity (TFP) growth, shifts in labor demand and the real interest rate, may have affected the

---

[5] To be precise, Stiglitz argues that even if the NAIRU of each demographic group is fixed, the change of the proportion of these groups in the labor force may lead to changes in the average NAIRU.

[6] Taking Europe as an example, Blanchard (2003, Chapter 13) further discusses how technological changes may affect the NAIRU.

NAIRU of OECD countries. They also explore how labor market institutions, namely the replacement rate, unemployment insurance system, duration of unemployment benefits, active labor market policies, employment protection, tax wedge, union contract coverage, union density and coordination of bargaining, have affected the evolution of the unemployment rate in the OECD countries with panel data. The most important argument of Blanchard and Wolfers (2000) is that, shocks and institutions do not influence the evolution of unemployment separately but that they may interact with each other and reinforce the effects on the unemployment rate.

Blanchard (2005) emphasizes the effects of the real interest rate on the change of NAIRU. Taking Europe as an example, Blanchard (2005) argues that the low real interest rates in the 1970s might have led to a low NAIRU in the 1970s and on the contrary, high real rates might have induced the high NAIRU in the 1980s and 1990s. An important mechanism through which the real rate affects the NAIRU is the accumulation of capital.

Next, we will show some preliminary evidence on the effects of the real interest rate on the NAIRU. In Table 3.1 we show the estimation of the following equation from 1982 to the end of the 1990s (*T*-statistics in parentheses)

$$u_{nt} = \tau_0 + \tau_1 \bar{r}, \qquad (3.5)$$

Table 3.1:   Regression results of Equation 3.5 and correlation coefficients of $\bar{r}$ (computed with the ex post real rate) and the NAIRU.

| Parameter | Country | | | |
|---|---|---|---|---|
| | **Germany** | **France** | **UK** | **US** |
| $\tau_0$ | 0.063 (130.339) | 0.051 (24.263) | 0.051 (57.513) | 0.040 (29.076) |
| $\tau_1$ | 0.064 (4.801) | 0.085 (1.986) | 0.128 (6.222) | 0.322 (8.809) |
| $R^2$ | 0.250 | 0.056 | 0.356 | 0.526 |
| Correlation | 0.437 | 0.225 | 0.337 | 0.387 |

where $\bar{r}$ denotes the 8-quarter (backward) average of the real interest rate.[7] The real interest rate is defined as the short-term nominal rate minus the actual inflation rate. The reason that we use the 8-quarter backward average of the real interest rate for estimation is that some researchers argue that the NAIRU is usually affected by the lags of the real rate. The reason that the regression is undertaken only for the period after 1982 is that in the 1970s and at the beginning of the 1980s these countries experienced large fluctuations in the inflation and therefore the real rate also experienced large changes. In Table 3.1 we find that $\tau_1$ is significant enough. We also show the correlation coefficients of the NAIRU and $\bar{r}$ for the same period in Table 3.1.

The real rate above is defined as the gap between the nominal rate and the actual inflation. The real rate defined in this way is usually referred to as the ex post real rate. According to the Fisher equation, however, the real rate should be defined as the nominal rate ($nr_t$) minus the expected inflation, that is

$$r_t = nr_t - \pi_{t|t+1},\tag{3.6}$$

where $\pi_{t|t+1}$ denotes the inflation rate from $t$ to $t+1$ expected by the market at time $t$. The real rate defined above is usually called the ex ante real rate. How to measure $\pi_{t|t+1}$ is a problem. Blanchard and Summers (1986), for example, measure the expected inflation by an autoregressive process of the inflation rate. Below we will measure the expected inflation by assuming that the economic agents forecast the inflation by learning through the RLS. Namely, we assume

$$\pi_{t|t+1} = c_{0t} + c_{1t}\pi_t + c_{2t}y_t,\tag{3.7}$$

where $y_t$ denotes the output gap. This equation implies that the agents predict the inflation in the next period by adjusting the coefficients

---

[7] The interest rates of Germany, France, the UK and the US are the German call money rate, 3-month interbank rate, 3-month treasury bill rate and the Federal funds rate, respectively. Data sources: OECD and IMF.

Table 3.2:   Regression results of Equation 3.5 and correlation coefficients of $\bar{r}$ (computed with the ex ante real rate) and the NAIRU.

| Parameter | Country | | | |
|---|---|---|---|---|
| | **Germany** | **France** | **UK** | **US** |
| $\tau_0$ | 0.063 (162.748) | 0.050 (22.663) | 0.051 (59.251) | 0.040 (31.278) |
| $\tau_1$ | 0.073 (6.817) | 0.097 (2.117) | 0.131 (6.337) | 0.329 (9.579) |
| $R^2$ | 0.410 | 0.065 | 0.371 | 0.574 |
| Correlation | 0.640 | 0.256 | 0.609 | 0.758 |

$c_0$, $c_1$ and $c_2$ period by period. Following Sargent (1999), Orphanides and Williams (2002) and Evans and Honkapohja (2001), we assume that the coefficients evolve in the manner of the RLS

$$C_t = C_{t-1} + t^{-1} V_t^{-1} X_t (\pi_t - X_t' C_{t-1})$$

$$V_t = V_{t-1} + t^{-1} (X_t X_t' - V_{t-1})$$

with $C_t = (c_{0t}\, c_{1t}\, c_{2t})'$ and $X_t = (1\ \pi_{t-1}\ y_{t-1})'$. $V_t$ is the moment matrix of $X_t$.[8] With the output gap measured by the percentage deviation of the industrial production index (IPI) from its HP filtered trend and the $\pi_{t|t+1}$ computed by the equations above, we show the estimation results for Equation 3.5 with the ex ante real rate and the correlation coefficients between the NAIRU and $\bar{r}$ computed with the ex ante real rate in Table 3.2.[9] The results in Table 3.2 are not

---

[8] The reader can be referred to Harvey (1989, Chapter 7) and Sargent (1999) for the RLS.

[9] The IPI has also been used by Clarida et al. (1998) to measure the output for Germany, France, the US, the UK, Japan and Italy. As surveyed by Orphanides and van Norden (2002), there are many methods to measure the output gap. We find that filtering the IPI using the band-pass filter developed by Baxter and King (1995) leaves the measure of the output gap essentially unchanged from the measure with the HP filter. The band-pass filter has also been used by Sargent (1999).

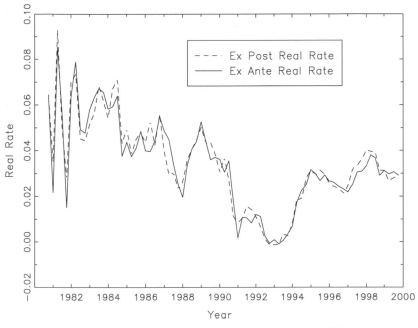

Fig. 3.6:  The ex ante and ex post real rates of the US.

essentially different from those in Table 3.1 except that the correlation coefficients between the NAIRU and $\bar{r}$ in Table 3.2 are larger than those in Table 3.1.

The ex ante and ex post real rates of the US from 1981.1 to 1999.4 are shown in Figure 3.6. It is obvious that the two rates are not significantly different.

The above empirical evidence indicates that real interest rates seem to have affected the NAIRU to some extent, consistent with the statement of Blanchard (2005).

## 3.4. CONCLUSION

This chapter presents the empirical evidence of the time-varying Phillips curve. We first have estimated the state-dependent coefficient of unemployment gap $\alpha_{ut}$ with fixed NAIRU and then estimated the time-varying NAIRU with constant $\alpha_{ut}$. The results indicate that both $\alpha_{ut}$ and NAIRU experience significant changes. The evidence from this chapter raises the question of how to explore monetary policies under uncertainty and regime changes.

We have also explored briefly what might have led to changes in the NAIRU. Effects of economic shocks as well as labor market institutions have been briefly discussed. Based on the estimation of the time-varying NAIRU we have shown some preliminary evidence on the effects of the real interest rate on the NAIRU and found some evidence supporting the statement of Blanchard (2005). Taking the effects of real interest rates into account, Semmler and Zhang (2004) explore monetary policy with an endogenous NAIRU and find that there might exist multiple equilibria in such an economy.

### APPENDIX A3. THE STATE-SPACE MODEL AND KALMAN FILTER

Below is a brief sketch of the State-Space model (SSM) and Kalman filter, following Harvey (1989, 1990) and Hamilton (1994).[10] After arranging a model in a State-Space form, one can use the Kalman filter to estimate the paths of time-varying parameters.

#### A3.1. The State-Space model

$y_t$ is a multivariate time series with $N$ elements. The observations of $y_t$ are related to an $m \times 1$ vector, $\alpha_t$, through the so-called "measurement equation",

$$y_t = Z_t \alpha_t + d_t + \epsilon_t, \tag{3.8}$$

with $t = 1, \ldots, T$. $Z_t$ is an $N \times m$ matrix, $d_t$ an $N \times 1$ vector and $\epsilon_t$ an $N \times 1$ vector of serially uncorrelated disturbances with zero mean

---

[10] Although there are numerous books dealing with the Kalman filter, the framework in this appendix is mainly based on Harvey (1989, 1990).

and covariance matrix $H_t$. $\alpha_t$ is the so-called state vector which is unknown but assumed to follow a first-order Markov process,

$$\alpha_t = T_t\alpha_{t-1} + c_t + R_t\eta_t, \qquad (3.9)$$

with $t = 1, ..., T$. $T_t$ is an $m \times m$ matrix, $c_t$ is an $m \times 1$ vector, $R_t$ is an $m \times g$ matrix and $\eta_t$ is a $g \times 1$ vector of serially uncorrelated disturbances with zero mean and covariance $Q_t$. The model is said to be time invariant if the matrices $Z_t$, $d_t$, $H_t$, $T_t$, $c_t$, $R_t$ and $Q_t$ are constant, otherwise, it is time variant. The equation above is called the "transition equation".

### A3.2. The Kalman filter

The Kalman filter estimates time-varying parameters in three steps. Given all currently available information, the first step forms the optimal predictor of the state vector for the next period through the "prediction equations". The second step updates the estimator by considering the new observation through the "updating equations". These two steps use only the past and current information, disregarding the future information which may also affect the estimation. Therefore, the third step "smooths" the estimators based on all observations.

### A3.2.1. Prediction

Let $a_{t-1}$ denote the optimal estimate of $\alpha_{t-1}$ based on observations from period 1 to period $t - 1$, and $P_{t-1}$ the $m \times m$ covariance matrix of the estimate error, i.e.

$$P_{t-1} = E[(\alpha_{t-1} - a_{t-1})(\alpha_{t-1} - a_{t-1})'].$$

Given $a_{t-1}$ and $P_{t-1}$, the optimal estimate of $\alpha_t$ is given by

$$a_{t|t-1} = T_t a_{t-1} + c_t, \qquad (3.10)$$

while the covariance matrix of the measurement error is

$$P_{t|t-1} = T_t P_{t-1} T_t' + R_t Q_t R_t', \qquad t = 1, \ldots, T. \qquad (3.11)$$

These two equations are called the prediction equations.

### A3.2.2. Updating

Once the new observations of $y_t$ become available, the estimate of $\alpha_t$, $a_{t|t-1}$, can be updated with the following equations

$$a_t = a_{t|t-1} + P_{t|t-1} Z_t' F_t^{-1} v_t, \qquad (3.12)$$

and

$$P_t = P_{t|t-1} - P_{t|t-1} Z_t' F_t^{-1} Z_t P_{t|t-1}, \qquad (3.13)$$

where $v_t = y_t - Z_t a_{t|t-1} - d_t$, which is called the prediction error, and $F_t = Z_t P_{t|t-1} Z_t' + H_t$, for $t = 1, \ldots, T$.

### A3.2.3. Smoothing

The prediction and updating equations estimate the state vector, $\alpha_t$ conditional on information available at time $t$. The step of smoothing takes account of the information available after time $t$.[11] The smoothing algorithms start with the final quantities ($a_T$ and $P_T$) and work backwards. These equations are

$$a_{t|T} = a_t + P_t^*(a_{t+1|T} - T_{t+1} a_t - c_{t+1}), \qquad (3.14)$$

and

$$P_{t|T} = p_t + P_t^*(P_{t+1|T} - P_{t+1|t}) P_t^{*'}, \qquad (3.15)$$

---

[11] Harvey (1989) discusses three smoothing algorithms: (a) fixed-point smoothing, (b) fixed-lag smoothing and (c) fixed-interval smoothing. In this book we use the third one, which is widely used in economic models.

where

$$P_t^* = P_t T_{t+1}' P_{t+1|t}^{-1}, \qquad t = T - 1, ..., 1,$$

with $a_{T|T} = a_T$ and $P_{T|T} = P_T$.

### A3.2.4. The maximum likelihood function

In order to estimate the state vector, one must first estimate a set of unknown parameters ($n \times 1$ vector $\psi$, referred to as "hyperparameters") with the maximum likelihood function. For a multivariate model the maximum likelihood function reads

$$L(y; \psi) = \prod_{t=1}^{T} p(y_t | Y_{t-1}),$$

where $p(y_t | Y_{t-1})$ denotes the distribution of $y_t$ conditional on $Y_{t-1} = (y_{t-1}, y_{t-2}, ..., y_1)$. The likelihood function for a Gaussian model can be written as

$$\log L(\psi) = -(1/2) \left( NT \log 2\pi + \sum_{t=1}^{T} \log|F_t| + \sum_{t=1}^{T} v_t' F_t^{-1} v_t \right), \quad (3.16)$$

where $F_t$ and $v_t$ are the same as those defined in the Kalman filter.

In sum, one has to do the following to estimate the state vector with the Kalman filter. (a) Write the model in a State-Space form of Equations 3.8 and 3.9, run the Kalman filter of Equations 3.10–3.13 and store all $v_t$ and $F_t$ for future use. (b) Estimate the hyperparameters with the maximum likelihood function presented in Equation 3.16. (c) Run the Kalman filter again with the estimates of the hyperparameters to get the non-smoothed estimates of the state vector. (d) Smooth the state vector with the smoothing equations (Equations 3.14 and 3.15).

In order to run the Kalman filter one needs initial values of $a_t$ and $P_t$ ($a_0$ and $P_0$). For a stationary and time invariant transition equation, the starting values are given as follows:

$$a_0 = (I - T)^{-1}c, \tag{3.17}$$

and

$$\text{vec}(P_0) = [I - T \otimes T]^{-1}\text{vec}(RQR'). \tag{3.18}$$

In the case of a non-stationary transition equation, however, the initial values of $a_t$ and $P_t$ must be estimated from the model. There are usually two approaches to deal with this problem. The first approach assumes that the initial state is fixed with $P_0 = 0$ (or a zero matrix) and can then be estimated from the model as unknown parameters. The second approach takes the initial state as random variables subject to a diffuse distribution with the covariance matrix $P_0 = \kappa I$. $\kappa$ is a large number.

### A3.2.5. Time-varying coefficient estimation

Consider a linear model

$$y_t = x_t'\beta_t + \epsilon_t, \qquad t = 1, ..., T,$$

where $x_t$ is a $k \times 1$ vector of exogenous variables and $\beta_t$ the corresponding $k \times 1$ vector of unknown parameters, which are assumed to follow certain stochastic processes. Defining $\beta_t$ as the state vector, one can use the SSM and Kalman filter to estimate the time-varying parameters. There are basically three models which can be used to estimate time-varying coefficients.

*The random-coefficient model.* In this model the coefficients evolve randomly around a fixed mean, $\bar{\beta}$, which is unknown. The State-Space form reads

$$y_t = x_t'\beta_t$$
$$\beta_t = \bar{\beta} + \epsilon_t, \qquad \epsilon_t \sim NID(0, Q),$$

for all $t$.

*The random-walk model.* In the random-walk model the coefficients follow a random-walk path. The State-Space form reads

$$y_t = x'_t \beta_t + \epsilon_t, \qquad t = 1, \dots, T$$

where $\epsilon_t \sim NID(0, H)$ and the vector $\beta_t$ is generated by the process

$$\beta_t = \beta_{t-1} + \eta_t,$$

where $\eta_t \sim NID(0, Q)$.

*The return-to-normality model.* In this model the coefficients are generated by a stationary multivariate AR(1) process. The State-Space form reads

$$y_t = x'_t \beta_t + \epsilon_t, \qquad t = 1, \dots, T, \tag{3.19}$$

$$\beta_t - \bar{\beta} = \phi(\beta_{t-1} - \bar{\beta}) + \eta_t, \tag{3.20}$$

where $\epsilon_t \sim NID(0, H)$, and $\eta_t \sim NID(0, Q)$. The coefficients are stationary and evolve around a mean, $\bar{\beta}$.
In order to apply the Kalman filter one can rewrite the return-to-normality model in the following way. Let $\beta_t^* = \beta_t - \bar{\beta}$, one has

$$y_t = (x'_t x'_t)\alpha_t + \epsilon_t, \qquad t = 1, \dots, T \tag{3.21}$$

and

$$\alpha_t = \begin{bmatrix} \bar{\beta}_t \\ \beta_t^* \end{bmatrix} = \begin{bmatrix} I & 0 \\ 0 & \phi \end{bmatrix} \begin{bmatrix} \bar{\beta}_{t-1} \\ \beta_{t-1}^* \end{bmatrix} + \begin{bmatrix} 0 \\ \eta_t \end{bmatrix}. \tag{3.22}$$

A diffuse prior is assumed for $\bar{\beta}_t$, implying that the starting values are constructed from the first $k$ observations. The starting value of $\beta_t^*$ is given by a zero vector with the starting covariance matrix given in Equation 3.18.

# CHAPTER 4

# Time-Varying Monetary Policy Reaction Function

## 4.1. MONETARY POLICY RULES

There has been extensive discussion on monetary policy rules in macroeconomics. Recently, two important monetary policy rules have been discussed. The first rule takes money supply as the policy instrument and proposes that the growth rate of money supply should be the sum of the target inflation and the desired growth rate of output. The second rule, however, proposes that the short-term interest rate should be taken as the policy instrument and that the interest rate can be determined as a function of the output gap and the deviation of the inflation rate from its target. While the first rule was mainly applied in the 1980s, the second rule began to be adopted at the beginning of the 1990s. In section 4.2, we will briefly discuss these two monetary policy rules with more emphasis on the second one, since it has been proposed to have some advantages over the first one and has been adopted by numerous central banks recently.

Moreover, some researchers, Svensson (2003), for example, distinguish monetary policy rules as "instrument rules" and "targeting rules". As mentioned by Svensson (1999a), most of the literature focuses on instrument rules. By an instrument rule Svensson means that the policy instrument is set as a function of a subset of the central bank's information. The Taylor rule (Taylor, 1993) is a typical instrument rule with the subset of information being the output gap, actual inflation and its target. In the research below we will not explore whether a monetary policy rule is an instrument rule or targeting rule, since this requires much discussion which is out of the scope of this chapter.

An important topic concerning monetary policy rules is whether they are state-dependent or time-invariant. In sections 4.3–4.5 we will explore some empirical evidence of this problem. To be precise, in section 4.3 we will estimate an interest-rate rule with the OLS and explore structural changes in coefficients with the Chow break-point test and in section 4.4 we will estimate the time-varying monetary policy rule with the Kalman filter. While in sections 4.3 and 4.4 only backward-looking behavior is considered, in section 4.5 we will consider coefficient changes in an interest-rate rule with forward-looking behavior.

## 4.2. MONEY-SUPPLY AND INTEREST-RATE RULES

### 4.2.1. The money-supply rule

The money-supply rule originated in the monetarist view of the working of a monetary economy. According to this rule money supply should be taken as the policy instrument and the rate of the nominal money growth should be equal to the target inflation rate plus the desired growth rate of output. To be precise,

$$\hat{m} = \hat{p} + \hat{y},$$

where $\hat{m}$ denotes the nominal money growth rate, $\hat{p}$ the target inflation rate and $\hat{y}$ the desired growth rate of output. This view prevailed during a short period in the 1980s in the US and until recently at the German Bundesbank. Assuming a constant velocity of money, one can derive this money supply rule from the Fisher's quantity theory of money.

This monetary policy rule has been widely applied since the 1980s, but has been given up by numerous central banks in the past decade. The derivation of this rule is based on the assumption of a constant velocity of money. This has, however, been a strong assumption. Mishkin (2003, Chapter 21) shows that the velocity of both $M_1$ and $M_2$ has fluctuated too much to be seen as a constant in the US from 1915 to 2002. Moreover, Mendizábal (2005) explores money velocity in low and high inflation countries by endogenizing the money velocity which may be affected by interest rate. There it is found that there exists a significant correlation between money velocity and inflation if transaction costs are considered.

Another assumption of this rule is that there exists a close relation between inflation and nominal money growth. But this relation has not been found to be robust because money demand may experience a large volatility. Recently, numerous papers have been contributed to this problem and the conclusions differ across countries. Wolters et al. (1998), for example test the stability of money demand in Germany from 1976 to 1994 and find that money demand has been stable except for a structural break around 1990 when the reunification of Germany occurred. Luetkepohl and Wolters (1998) further explore the stability of the German M3 by way of a system estimation rather than a single-equation estimation and find that there does not exist a strong relation between money and inflation and, therefore, money growth should not be used to control inflation. By using different estimation techniques and testing procedures for long-run stability, Scharnagl (1998) claims to have found stability in the German money demand. Tullio et al. (1996), however, claim to have found empirical evidence that money demand in Germany has been unstable after the German reunification. Moreover, Choi and Jung (2003) test for the stability of long-run money demand in the US from 1959 to 2000, and claim that money demand is unstable for the whole sample, but stable in the subperiods of 1959–1974, 1974–1986 and 1986–2000. Vega (1998) explores the stability of money demand in Spain and claims to have found some changes in the long-run properties of money demand.

### 4.2.2. An interest-rate rule

Because of the drawbacks of the money-supply rule mentioned above, another type of monetary policy rule, which takes the short-term interest rate as the policy instrument, has been proposed. The most popular interest-rate rule is the so-called Taylor rule (Taylor, 1993), named after John B. Taylor. The Taylor rule can be written as

$$r_t = \bar{r} + \pi_t + \beta_1(\pi_t - \pi^*) + \beta_2 y_t, \qquad \beta_1, \beta_2 > 0, \qquad (4.1)$$

where $r_t$ denotes the nominal interest rate, $\bar{r}$ the equilibrium real rate of interest, $\pi_t$ the inflation rate, $\pi^*$ the target inflation and $y_t$ denotes the deviation of the actual output from its potential level.[1] $\beta_1$ and $\beta_2$ are reaction coefficients that determine how strongly the monetary authority stresses inflation stabilization and output stabilization.[2]

Taking $\pi^*$ as 2% and using a linear trend of the real GDP to measure the potential output, Taylor (1993) finds that with $\beta_1 = 0.5$, $\bar{r} = 2$ and $\beta_2 = 0.5$ this rule can accurately simulate the short-term

---

[1] There are different approaches to measure the potential output. Orphanides and van Norden (2002), for example argue that output gap should be computed with real-time data. Woodford (2003a), moreover, discusses how to measure output gap at a theoretical level and criticizes Taylor (1993) for his computation of potential output by a deterministic trend of the real GDP. A brief sketch of Woodford's definition of output gap is presented in the appendix of Chapter 6.

[2] Note that $r_t$ in Equation 4.1 denotes the *nominal* rate and $\bar{r}$ the equilibrium *real* rate. One can also express Equation 4.1 as

$$r_t = r^* + (1 + \beta_1)(\pi_t - \pi^*) + \beta_2 y_t,$$

where $r_t$ still denotes the nominal rate, but $r^*$ denotes the equilibrium *nominal* rate rather than the equilibrium *real* rate. Note that the Taylor rule is an "active" monetary policy rule, because its response to the inflation deviation is $1 + \beta_1(>1)$. Leeper (1991) describes a monetary policy as "active" if its response coefficient to the inflation is larger than one, otherwise it is "passive".

nominal interest rate of the US from 1984 to 1992. Taylor (1999c), however, considers an alternative rule with $\beta_1$ maintained at 0.5 and $\beta_2$ raised to 1.0.

Taylor (1999c) describes briefly how the Taylor rule can be derived from the quantity equation of money. In deriving the money-supply rule, the velocity of money ($V$) is assumed to be constant and the money supply ($M$) is assumed to be a variable. In deriving the Taylor rule, however, Taylor assumes money supply to be fixed or growing at a constant rate. The velocity of money, on the contrary, is assumed to depend on the interest rate $r$ and real output or income ($Y$). Under these assumptions he obtains the following linear function

$$r = \pi + gy + h(\pi - \pi^*) + r^f, \qquad (4.2)$$

where $r$ denotes the short-term interest rate, $\pi$ the inflation rate and $y$ the percentage deviation of real output ($Y$) from trend. $g$, $h$, $\pi^*$ and $r^f$ are constants.[3] $\pi^*$ is interpreted as the inflation target and $r^f$ is the central bank's estimate of the equilibrium real rate of interest.

Svensson (2003) states that the idea of a commitment to a simple instrument rule such as the Taylor rule can be considered as a three-step procedure. The first step is to set the monetary policy instrument as a function of a subset of variables of the central bank's information. The instrument is usually determined as a linear function of target variables and the instrument lag.[4] The second step is to assign appropriate values to the parameters in the reaction function, $g$, $h$, $\pi^*$ and $r^f$ in the Taylor rule, for example. The third step is to commit to the instrument rule chosen until a new rule is set.

---

[3] The details can be found in Taylor (1999c, pp. 322–323).

[4] Some Taylor-type rules with interest-smoothing have been proposed in the literature, with the example from Sack and Wieland (2000) being:

$$r_t = \rho r_{t-1} + (1 - \rho)[\bar{r} + \pi_t + \beta_1(\pi_t - \pi^*) + \beta_2 y_t],$$

where $0 < \rho < 1$ is the smoothing parameter. Sack and Wieland (2000) argue that interest-rate smoothing is desirable for at least three reasons: (a) forward-looking behavior, (b) data uncertainty and (c) parameter uncertainty.

### 4.2.3. Comments on the Taylor rule

Svensson (2003, p. 21) points out two advantages of a commitment to an interest-rate rule such as the Taylor rule: simplicity and robustness. As regards robustness, he refers to Levin et al. (1999), who find that a Taylor-type rule with interest-smoothing is robust for different models of the US economy.

Svensson (2003, pp. 22–25) also points out that such a simple instrument rule may have some problems, three of which are: first, other state variables than inflation and output gap might also be important. Asset prices, for instance, might play an important role in an economy. Second, new information about the economy is not sufficiently considered. Third, such a rule does not seem to describe the behavior of current monetary policy accurately.

The recent literature on monetary policy rules, moreover, has proposed two further disadvantages of the Taylor rule. The first one is that it has been mostly concerned with a closed economy. Ball (1999), therefore, extends the closed economy models in Svensson (1997) and Ball (1997) to explore how optimal monetary policies may change in an open economy. There he claims two findings. First, the policy variable is a combination of the short-term interest rate and the exchange rate, rather than the interest rate alone. This seems to be an argument for taking the monetary conditions index (MCI) as the policy instrument, as in the cases of Canada, New Zealand and Sweden.[5] Second, a combination of exchange rate lag and inflation should be used to replace inflation in the Taylor rule.[6] Therefore, different rules are required for closed

---

[5] Deutsche Bundesbank Monthly Report (April 1999, p. 54) describes the MCI as "… the MCI is, at a given time $t$, the weighted sum of the (relative) change in the effective real exchange rate and the (absolute) change in the short-term real rate of interest compared with a base period…". Some research on the MCI can also be found in Gerlach and Smets (2000).

[6] See Ball (1999, p. 131) for details.

and open economies because in open economies monetary policy can influence the economy through the exchange rate channel.

The second disadvantage of the Taylor rule, as explored by Benhabib et al. (2001), is that it may not be able to prevent a deflationary spiral. Benhabib et al. (2001), for example, argue that there might exist infinite trajectories converging to a liquidity trap even if the interest-rate rule is locally active.

A third important issue concerns the interest-rate rule and the price-level (in)determinancy.

This problem is discussed in Wicksell (1898) as follows

> At any moment and in every economic situation there is a certain level of the average rate of interest which is such that the general level of prices has no tendency to move either upwards or downwards. This we call the *normal* rate of interest. Its magnitude is determined by the current level of the natural capital rate, and rises and falls with it.
>
> If, for any reason whatever, the average rate of interest is set and maintained *below* this normal level, no matter how small the gap, prices will rise and will go on rising; or if they were already in process of falling, they will fall more slowly and eventually begin to rise.
>
> If, on the other hand, the rate of interest is maintained no matter how little *above* the current level of the natural rate, prices will fall continuously and without limit (Wicksell, 1898, p. 120).[7]

This problem has been discussed by numerous researchers, see Sargent and Wallace (1975), Carlstrom and Fuerst (2000), Benhabib et al. (2001) and Woodford (2001b, 2003a), for example.

---

[7] Wicksell (1898, p. 102) describes the natural rate of interest as "There is a certain rate of interest on loans which is neutral in respect to commodity prices, and tends neither to raise nor to lower them." Woodford (2003a, p. 248) defines it explicitly as the equilibrium real rate of return in the case of fully flexible prices.

Sargent and Wallace (1975) argue that while money-supply rules lead to a determinate rational-expectations equilibrium, none of the interest-rate rules do. Carlstrom and Fuerst (2000) also show that money-growth rules can produce real determinacy, while interest-rate rules may not do so. As mentioned before, Benhabib et al. (2001) argue that even active interest-rate rules can lead to indeterminacy. Woodford (1994) specify some sufficient conditions for price-level determinacy for both money-supply and interest-rate rules in a cash-in-advance model.

Woodford (2003a) discusses the problem of price-level determinancy in detail and claims that interest-rate rules can lead to price-level determinancy when some conditions are satisfied. Woodford (2003a, Chapter 2) analyzes both *local* and *global* price-level determinacy in a model, assuming that prices are completely flexible and the supply of goods is given by an exogenous endowment. There he specifies different conditions for different interest-rate rules to lead to price-level determinancy *locally*. Moreover, he finds that interest-rate rules can lead to *global* price-level determinancy under certain fiscal-policy regimes. Woodford (2003a, Chapter 4) discusses this problem further in the so-called "neo-Wicksellian" model and specifies conditions under which price-level determinancy can be obtained.[8]

The European Central Bank (ECB) originally followed the money-supply rule. It had been argued that the German Bundesbank had achieved a solid reputation in keeping the inflation rate down with monetary targeting. Interest-rate rules have, however, attracted more attention since the 1990s. The stabilizing properties of these two monetary policy rules are studied in a macroeconometric framework in Flaschel et al. (2001). There it is found that, by and large, the interest-rate rule has better stabilizing properties in both stable and unstable cases. In the medium run, with the Taylor rule,

---

[8] The reader is referred to Woodford (2003a, Chapter 4, propositions 4.2–4.7) for the details of these conditions.

employment, inflation, expected inflation and output experience smaller fluctuations than with the money-supply rule. In line with most recent research on monetary policy rules, this book focuses on the interest-rate rules in the following chapters.

A major recent concern in the literature is how to derive an optimal interest-rate rule from a welfare function, for example of the central bank or the households. In Chapter 6 we will derive an optimal interest-rate rule from a dynamic macroeconomic model with a welfare function of the central bank, a quadratic loss function.[9] There we find that the optimal interest-rate rule is similar to the Taylor rule in the sense that they both are linear functions of inflation and output gap. We will also discuss the derivation of the loss function from a more general welfare function.

### 4.3. THE OLS REGRESSION AND CHOW BREAK-POINT TESTS OF THE INTEREST-RATE RULE

Although we have discussed briefly the two monetary policy rules, we will focus on interest-rate rules in this book. As mentioned by Taylor (1999c), parameter shifts may occur in the Taylor rule. "…shifts in this function would occur when either velocity growth or money growth shifts… (Taylor, 1999c, p. 323)". As will be seen in Chapter 6, the reaction coefficients in the interest-rate rule derived from a dynamic macroeconomic model are functions of parameters in the IS and Phillips curves and the loss function of the central bank. Therefore, if the parameters in the IS and Phillips curves change, the reaction coefficients in the interest-rate rule will also change. The empirical evidence of a time-varying Phillips curve has been explored in the previous chapter. Moreover, as will be seen in Chapter 7, the weight of output stabilization in the central bank's loss function can also be time-varying, and as a result, the monetary

---

[9] Woodford (2003a, Chapter 6) shows that the quadratic loss function of a central bank can be derived from a utility function of households. We will discuss this problem briefly in Chapter 6.

policy rule can be time-varying. In the following sections we will explore some empirical evidence of time-varying interest-rate rules.

Let us write the interest-rate rule as

$$r_t = \beta_c + \beta_\pi \pi_t + \beta_y y_t, \tag{4.3}$$

where $r_t$ is the short-term interest rate, $\pi_t$ is the deviation of inflation rate from its target and $y_t$ denotes output gap. Because the inflation targets are not available, we will take it as a constant and refer to the research of Clarida et al. (1998) (CGG98) who estimate the inflation target for several countries for certain periods. $y_t$ is measured by the percentage deviation of the industrial production index (IPI, base year: 1995) from its HP-filtered trend. There are alternative methods to measure the output gap, a discussion of this problem can be found in Orphanides and van Norden (2002). We find that the potential output measured with the Band-Pass filter is not essentially changed from that computed with the HP filter. The countries to be examined include Germany, Japan, France, Italy, the UK and the US.

### 4.3.1. Germany

CGG98 explore monetary policy rules under the assumption that while making monetary policy the monetary authorities take into account the expected inflation rather than the current inflation rate or the inflation in the past. A by-product of their model is the inflation target. Their estimate of the German target inflation rate from 1979 to 1993 is 1.97%. This seems consistent with the official German target inflation rate, which is usually declared to be 2%. Therefore, in the estimation below we assume the inflation target of Germany to be 2%.[10] The short-term interest rate (3-month treasury bill rate, denoted by $R$), inflation rate (denoted by Inf, measured by changes in the CPI) and output gap (denoted by Gap) of Germany are shown in Figure 4.1 (Data Sources: OECD and IMF).

---

[10] The inflation target does not affect the regression much as long as it is assumed to be a constant.

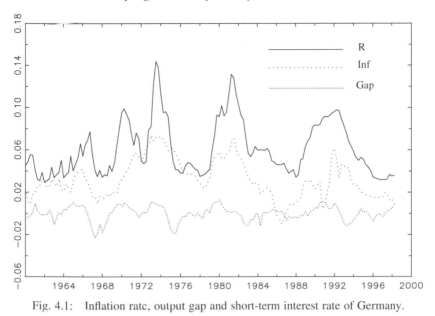

Fig. 4.1: Inflation rate, output gap and short-term interest rate of Germany.

The estimation results of the policy reaction function for Germany from 1960 to 1998 with quarterly data are shown in Table 4.1. We will, for simplicity, not present the estimate of $\beta_c$.

The estimates above indicate some changes in the coefficients for different subperiods. The inflation rate seems to have played a more important role in monetary policy making in the 1970s and 1980s than the output, while in the 1960s and 1990s the output may have

Table 4.1: OLS estimation of the interest-rate rule of Germany.

| Sample | $\beta_\pi$ | | $\beta_y$ | | $R^2$ |
|---|---|---|---|---|---|
| | Estimate | T-statistics | Estimate | T-statistics | |
| 1960.1–1969.4 | 0.052 | 0.181 | 0.372 | 1.300 | 0.070 |
| 1970.1–1979.4 | 1.170 | 6.028 | 1.937 | 5.140 | 0.660 |
| 1980.1–1989.4 | 1.086 | 14.414 | 0.713 | 2.179 | 0.148 |
| 1990.1–1998.2 | 1.201 | 5.905 | 1.766 | 3.723 | 0.579 |
| 1960.1–1998.2 | 0.841 | 10.337 | 0.972 | 4.480 | 0.494 |

had larger effects on the monetary policy. This is consistent with the fact that the inflation rate was relatively low in the 1960s and has been decreasing since the beginning of the 1990s. In order to explore whether there are structural changes in the policy reaction function, we will undertake the Chow break-point test for the regression. We choose 1979 and 1990 as two break-points, when the EMS started and the re-unification of Germany took place. The $F$-statistics of the break-point tests for 1979.4 and 1989.2 are 15.913 and 4.044, respectively, significant enough to indicate structural changes around these two points (the critical value at 5% level of significance lies between 2.60 and 2.68).

### 4.3.2. Japan

The estimate of CGG98 of the inflation target of Japan for the period from 1979.4 to 1994.12 is 2.03%. We will, therefore, assume it to be 2% in the estimation below, since the average inflation rate of the period from 1960 to 1997 is not higher than that of the period of 1979–1994. The short-term interest rate (call money rate), inflation rate (changes in the CPI) and output gap of Japan are presented in Figure 4.2 (Data sources: OECD and IMF).

The estimation for Japan from 1960.1 to 1997.4 with quarterly data is shown in Table 4.2.

The changes in $\beta_\pi$ are not very significant, but the changes in $\beta_y$, however, are significant enough. It was smaller than one before 1980, but higher than one after 1980, especially in the 1980s. Next, we will undertake the Chow break-point test for 1974.4 and 1980.4 around which there were great changes in inflation rate as well as in interest rate. The $F$-statistics are 43.492 and 33.944, respectively, significant enough to indicate structural changes around these two points (the critical value at 5% level of significance lies between 2.60 and 2.68). We have also undertaken the Chow break-point test for 1965.1 and the $F$-statistic is 28.400, significant enough to indicate a structural change at this point.

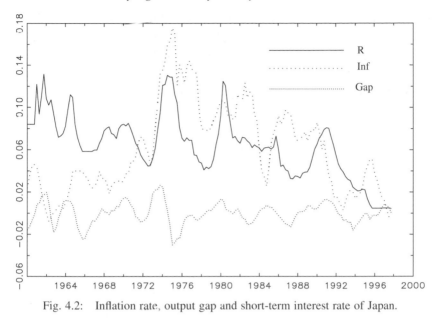

Fig. 4.2:  Inflation rate, output gap and short-term interest rate of Japan.

### 4.3.3. The US

The estimate by CGG98 of the US inflation target is 4.04% for the period of 1979–1994. As stated by the authors, a target of 4% seems to be too high for the US, given a sample average real rate of 3.48%. In the estimation below we, therefore, assume the target inflation to be 2.5%, a little higher than that of Germany. The short-term interest rate

Table 4.2:  OLS estimation of the interest-rate rule of Japan.

| Sample | $\beta_\pi$ | | $\beta_y$ | | $R^2$ |
|---|---|---|---|---|---|
| | Estimate | *T*-statistics | Estimate | *T*-statistics | |
| 1960.1–1964.4 | 0.075 | 0.377 | 0.740 | 2.493 | 0.269 |
| 1965.1–1969.4 | 0.334 | 1.206 | 0.738 | 4.576 | 0.560 |
| 1970.1–1979.4 | 0.430 | 4.825 | 0.344 | 1.234 | 0.376 |
| 1980.1–1989.4 | 0.598 | 4.676 | 2.171 | 4.976 | 0.472 |
| 1990.1–1997.4 | 0.405 | 2.128 | 1.398 | 2.541 | 0.494 |
| 1960.1–1997.4 | 0.216 | 4.055 | 0.657 | 3.008 | 0.131 |

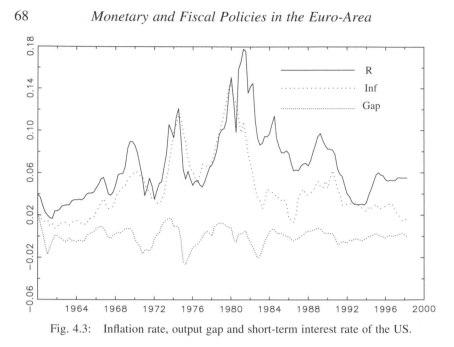

Fig. 4.3: Inflation rate, output gap and short-term interest rate of the US.

(the federal funds rate), inflation rate (changes in the CPI) and output gap of the US are presented in Figure 4.3 (Data Sources: OECD and IMF) and the estimation results of the policy reaction function with quarterly data for different periods are shown in Table 4.3.

One can observe some significant changes in the coefficients. In the middle of the 1980s the coefficient of the inflation rate

Table 4.3: OLS estimation of the interest-rate rule of the US.

| Sample | $\beta_\pi$ | | $\beta_y$ | | $R^2$ |
|---|---|---|---|---|---|
| | **Estimate** | **T-statistics** | **Estimate** | **T-statistics** | |
| 1960.1–1969.4 | 1.047 | 14.913 | 0.443 | 2.965 | 0.903 |
| 1970.1–1979.4 | 0.643 | 9.975 | 0.808 | 5.245 | 0.825 |
| 1980.1–1984.4 | 0.489 | 3.152 | 0.723 | 1.053 | 0.493 |
| 1985.1–1989.4 | −0.027 | 0.097 | 2.230 | 2.439 | 0.481 |
| 1990.1–1998.2 | 0.854 | 5.034 | 2.389 | 3.965 | 0.556 |
| 1960.1–1998.2 | 0.772 | 13.117 | 0.527 | 2.333 | 0.562 |

changed even from positive to negative. In the first half of the 1980s, $\beta_\pi$ was much larger than $\beta_y$ with a significant $T$-statistic, but in the second half of the 1980s $\beta_\pi$ became negative with an insignificant $T$-statistic of 0.097. This indicates that the inflation rate may have played a more important role in monetary policy making in the first half than in the second half of the 1980s. This should not be surprising, since the US experienced very high inflation rate in the first half of the 1980s and the interest rate was raised to deal with this problem after Volcker was appointed the chair of the Fed.

Next, we undertake the Chow break-point test for 1982.1 because there were significant changes in the inflation rate and interest rate around this point. The $F$-statistic is 18.920, significant enough to indicate a structural change at this point (the critical value at 5% level of significance lies between 2.60 and 2.68).

### 4.3.4. France

CGG98 fail to obtain a reasonable estimate of the inflation target for France and it is then assumed it to be 2% for the period of 1983–1989. Since the data used here cover a much longer period (1970–1996) than that of CGG98, we assume the inflation target to be 2.5% for France, since France experienced a high inflation rate from the beginning of the 1970s to the middle of the 1980s, with the average rate higher than 8%. The inflation rate (changes in the CPI), short-term interest rate (3-month treasury bill rate) and output gap of France are presented in Figure 4.4 (Data Sources: OECD and IMF). The output gap was quite smooth during the whole period except a relatively significant change in the middle of the 1970s. The inflation rate was quite high before the middle of the 1980s and decreased to a relatively lower level around 1985. The results of regression with quarterly data are shown in Table 4.4.

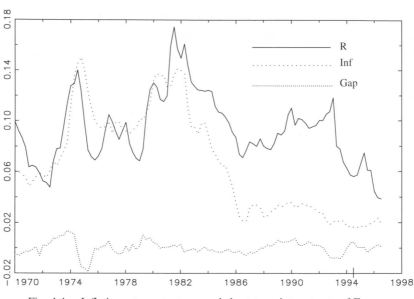

Fig. 4.4:   Inflation rate, output gap and short-term interest rate of France.

One can observe a significant change in the $\beta_\pi$. It was about 0.60 before 1990, but rose to 2.345 in the 1990s. Unfortunately, the estimate of $\beta_y$ has insignificant $T$-statistics most of the time. This may suggest either model misspecification or problems in the output gap measurement. The Chow break-point test for 1979.4 has an $F$-statistic of 29.143, significant enough to indicate a structural change at this point (the critical value at 5% level of significance is

Table 4.4:   OLS estimation of the interest-rate rule of France.

| Sample | $\beta_\pi$ | | $\beta_y$ | | $R^2$ |
|---|---|---|---|---|---|
| | **Estimate** | **$T$-statistics** | **Estimate** | **$T$-statistics** | |
| 1970.1–1979.4 | 0.603 | 6.257 | 0.835 | 2.391 | 0.523 |
| 1980.1–1989.4 | 0.570 | 12.842 | 0.180 | 0.280 | 0.822 |
| 1990.1–1996.3 | 2.345 | 4.142 | 0.778 | 0.832 | 0.507 |
| 1970.1–1996.3 | 0.425 | 8.207 | 0.365 | 0.930 | 0.395 |

about 2.70). One can observe some large changes in the interest rate and inflation rate around this point in Figure 4.4.

### 4.3.5. The UK

CGG98 are also unable to obtain a reasonable estimate of the inflation target for the UK. We assume it to be 2.5% in the estimation for the period from 1960.1 to 1997.4. The short-term interest rate (3-month treasury bill rate), inflation rate (changes in the CPI) and output gap of the UK are presented in Figure 4.5 (Data Sources: OECD and IMF). The regression results of the interest-rate rule with quarterly data are shown in Table 4.5.

It is surprising that $\beta_y$ was negative with a significant *T*-statistic in the 1990s. This may be due to model misspecification or the computation of the output gap. The $\beta_y$ seems to have experienced more significant changes than the $\beta_\pi$. We undertake the Chow break-point test for 1979.1 and obtain an *F*-statistic of 72.900,

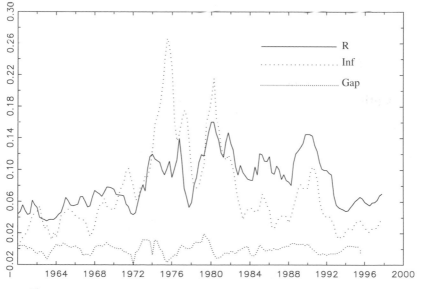

Fig. 4.5: Inflation rate, output gap and short-term interest rate of the UK.

Table 4.5:    OLS estimation of the interest-rate rule of the UK.

| Sample | $\beta_\pi$ | | $\beta_y$ | | $R^2$ |
|---|---|---|---|---|---|
| | Estimate | T-statistics | Estimate | T-statistics | |
| 1960.1 – 1969.4 | 0.440 | 4.072 | 0.644 | 2.045 | 0.409 |
| 1970.1 – 1979.4 | 0.322 | 5.496 | 1.790 | 4.812 | 0.520 |
| 1980.1 – 1989.4 | 0.453 | 10.075 | 0.886 | 2.319 | 0.745 |
| 1990.1 – 1997.4 | 1.144 | 16.596 | − 1.252 | 2.858 | 0.910 |
| 1960.1 – 1997.4 | 0.358 | 9.151 | 0.802 | 2.391 | 0.363 |

significant enough to indicate a structural change at this point (the critical value at 5% level of significance lies between 2.60 and 2.68).

### 4.3.6. Italy

CGG98 explore the monetary policy of Italy for the period from 1981 to 1989 and fail to obtain a reasonable inflation target. Our estimation covers the period from 1970 to 1998. The inflation rate was quite high during this period, evolving between 1.18 and 24.75% with the average value being 9.72%. Therefore, we assume the target inflation to be 3.0%, a little higher than those of the other European countries. We present the short-term interest rate (official discount rate), inflation rate (changes in the CPI) and output gap of Italy in Figure 4.6 (Data Sources: OECD and IMF) and the results of estimation with quarterly data in Table 4.6.

The *F*-statistic of the Chow break-point test for 1979.4 is 67.473, significant enough to indicate a structural change at this point (the critical value at 5% level of significance is about 2.50).

### 4.4. ESTIMATION OF THE TIME-VARYING INTEREST-RATE RULE WITH THE KALMAN FILTER

From the OLS regression and Chow break-point tests one finds that there are some structural changes in the monetary reaction function.

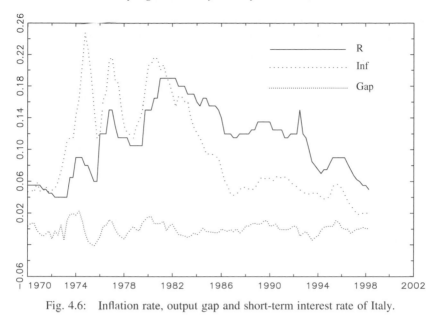

Fig. 4.6: Inflation rate, output gap and short-term interest rate of Italy.

The drawback of the Chow break-point test is that one can only explore structural changes at some predetermined points. This approach is not of much help if one wants to explore all possible structural changes or wants to obtain the path of a time-varying parameter. In order to explore how the coefficients in the monetary policy reaction function may have changed over time, we will estimate the time-varying interest-rate rule with the Kalman filter in this section. In Chapter 3, we have estimated the time-varying

Table 4.6: OLS estimation of the interest-rate rule of Italy.

| Sample | $\beta_\pi$ | | $\beta_y$ | | $R^2$ |
|---|---|---|---|---|---|
| | **Estimate** | **$T$-statistics** | **Estimate** | **$T$-statistics** | |
| 1970.1–1979.4 | 0.401 | 5.937 | 0.468 | 1.294 | 0.513 |
| 1980.1–1989.4 | 0.354 | 8.120 | 0.073 | 0.184 | 0.707 |
| 1990.1–1998.2 | 1.361 | 7.730 | 0.696 | 1.593 | 0.729 |
| 1970.1–1998.2 | 0.340 | 5.889 | 0.301 | 0.700 | 0.248 |

Phillips curve with the Kalman filter, assuming that the coefficient in the Phillips curve follows a random-walk path.

Somewhat different from the estimation in Chapter 3, however, we will employ the so-called "Return-to-Normality" (mean-reversion) model in this section, i.e. we assume that the time-varying parameters are stationary and evolve around a mean. If the parameter is found to be non-stationary, we will give up the mean-reversion model and resort to the random-walk model as in Chapter 3. A brief introduction to the "Return-to-Normality" model is shown in the appendix of Chapter 3.

### 4.4.1. Empirical evidence

Let us define the variables as follows:

$$x_t = \begin{pmatrix} 1 \\ \pi_t \\ y_t \end{pmatrix} \qquad \text{and} \qquad \beta_t = \begin{pmatrix} \beta_{ct} \\ \beta_{\pi t} \\ \beta_{yt} \end{pmatrix}.$$

In the "Return-to-Normality" model the time-varying coefficients are assumed to be generated by a stationary multivariate AR(1) process. The interest-rate rule can then be written in the following State-Space form

$$r_t = x_t' \beta_t + \epsilon_t, \qquad t = 1, \ldots, T,$$

$$\beta_t - \bar{\beta} = \phi(\beta_{t-1} - \bar{\beta}) + \eta_t,$$

where $\epsilon_t \sim NID(0, H)$, and $\eta_t \sim NID(0, Q)$. The coefficients are stationary and evolve around the mean, $\bar{\beta}$. After arranging the interest-rate rule in an SSM one can use the Kalman filter to estimate $\phi \bar{\beta}$, $\beta_t$ and, as a result, obtains a path of $\alpha_t$. The estimation results of Germany, France, Italy, Japan, the UK and the US are presented below. If the elements of the matrix $\phi$ are larger than one in absolute value, the "Return-to-Normality" model has to be abandoned and the random-walk model should be employed.

### 4.4.1.1. Germany

The German quarterly data of 1960–1998 generate the $\phi$ as

$$\begin{pmatrix} 0.935 & 0 & 0 \\ 0 & 0.892 & 0 \\ 0 & 0 & 0.925 \end{pmatrix}.$$

All elements of $\phi$ are smaller than one, indicating that the coefficients are stationary. $\bar{\beta}$ is

$$\begin{pmatrix} 0.052 \\ 0.260 \\ 0.294 \end{pmatrix},$$

indicating that $\beta_c$ evolves around 0.052, $\beta_\pi$ around 0.260 and $\beta_y$ around 0.294.

The paths of $\beta_\pi$ and $\beta_y$ are shown in Figure 4.7A and B. The path of $\beta_c$ is not shown here just for simplicity.

As shown in Figure 4.7A, $\beta_\pi$ experiences significant changes. Comparing Figure 4.7A with Figure 4.1, one finds that the switching of $\beta_\pi$ was similar to that of $\pi_t$, except in the 1960s. That is, when the inflation rate was high, $\beta_\pi$ was also high, and vice versa. In 1970, 1974 and 1981, $\beta_\pi$ reached some peaks, when the interest rate

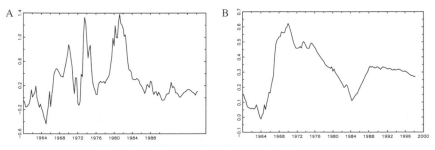

Fig. 4.7: Time-varying $\beta_\pi$ and $\beta_y$ of Germany.

and inflation rate were also at their peaks. In the 1960s $\beta_\pi$ and $\pi_t$ evolved in opposite directions most of the time, especially from 1965 to 1970. The fact that the changes of $\beta_\pi$ and $\pi_t$ are inconsistent with each other in the 1960s may be caused by the initial start-up idiosyncrasies of the Kalman filter algorithm. From 1960 to 1965 $\beta_\pi$ was below zero most of the time, consistent with the OLS regression ($\beta_\pi = -0.804$ from 1960.1 to 1964.4). Figure 4.7A shows that $\beta_\pi$ experienced a significant structural change around 1979 and a small change around 1989, consistent with the Chow break-point tests in the previous section, $\beta_y$ experienced significant changes around 1970 and 1984.

### 4.4.1.2. *France*

The French quarterly data from 1970 to 1996 generate the $\phi$ as

$$\begin{pmatrix} 0.967 & 0 & 0 \\ 0 & 0.826 & 0 \\ 0 & 0 & 0.575 \end{pmatrix}$$

with all elements smaller than one, indicating that the return-to-normality model is the right choice. $\bar{\beta}$ equals

$$\begin{pmatrix} 0.064 \\ 0.631 \\ 0.091 \end{pmatrix},$$

indicating that $\beta_c$, $\beta_\pi$ and $\beta_y$ evolve around 0.064, 0.631 and 0.091, respectively. The paths of the $\beta_\pi$ and $\beta_y$ are presented in Figure 4.8A and B.

Figure 4.8A shows that $\beta_\pi$ experienced significant changes in the 1970s and has been staying at a relatively stable level since the middle of the 1980s. It decreased to the lowest point in 1979 and reached the highest point in 1981, when the interest rate also

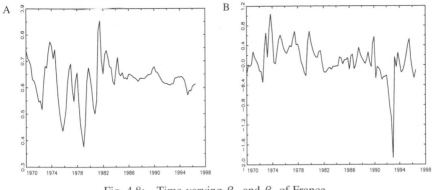

Fig. 4.8: Time-varying $\beta_\pi$ and $\beta_y$ of France.

reached the highest point. $\beta_\pi$ remained at a relatively high level after the 1980s, even if the inflation rate has been quite low since the middle of the 1980s, which may indicate the effect of the EMS on the monetary policies of member countries, $\beta_y$ also experienced a change in 1979. This is consistent with the conclusion of the Chow break-point test in the previous section. Note that $\beta_y$ had a negative mean ($-0.153$) in the 1990s and decreased to the lowest point of $-1.867$ in 1993, consistent with the fact that $\beta_y$ in the OLS regression was negative in the 1990s.

### 4.4.1.3. The UK

The UK quarterly data from 1960 to 1997 generate the $\phi$ as

$$\begin{pmatrix} 0.956 & 0 & 0 \\ 0 & 0.931 & 0 \\ 0 & 0 & 0.049 \end{pmatrix}$$

with all elements smaller than one. Note that the last element is very small (0.049), indicating that $\beta_y$ may have not experienced

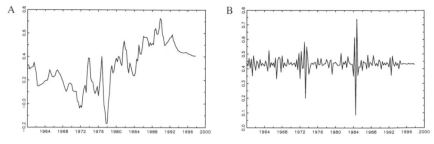

Fig. 4.9:   Time-varying $\beta_\pi$ and $\beta_y$ of the UK.

significant structural changes. $\bar{\beta}$ is

$$\begin{pmatrix} 0.069 \\ 0.353 \\ 0.330 \end{pmatrix},$$

indicating that $\beta_c$, $\beta_\pi$ and $\beta_y$ evolve around 0.069, 0.353 and 0.330, respectively. The paths of $\beta_\pi$ and $\beta_y$ are presented in Figure 4.9A and B, respectively.

Figure 4.9A shows that $\beta_\pi$ experienced significant changes in the 1970s and remained at a relatively high and stable level afterwards. Note that the switching of $\beta_\pi$ is similar in France and the UK: it experienced similar changes in the 1970s and then stayed at a relatively high level without significant changes after the 1980s.

Figure 4.9B shows that $\beta_y$ did not experience such significant changes as those of the other European countries. This is consistent with the fact that the last element in $\phi$ is not large (0.049).

### 4.4.1.4. Italy

The Italian quarterly data from 1970 to 1998 generate the $\phi$ as

$$\begin{pmatrix} 0.992 & 0 & 0 \\ 0 & 1.021 & 0 \\ 0 & 0 & 0.400 \end{pmatrix}$$

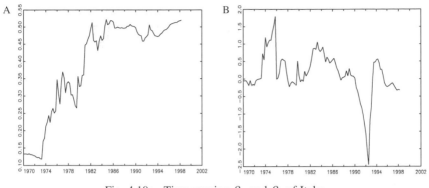

Fig. 4.10:   Time-varying $\beta_\pi$ and $\beta_y$ of Italy.

and $\bar\beta$ as

$$\begin{pmatrix} 0.066 \\ 0.059 \\ 0.238 \end{pmatrix}.$$

Because the second diagonal element of $\phi$ is larger than one, $\beta_\pi$ is therefore non-stationary and we have to employ the random-walk model instead of the "Return-to-Normality" model. The paths of $\beta_\pi$ and $\beta_y$ estimated with the random-walk model are presented in Figure 4.10A and B.

Figure 4.10A shows that $\beta_\pi$ has been increasing since the middle of the 1970s. It experienced a structural change in 1979 and then increased to a relatively stable and high level, similar to the cases of France and the UK. $\beta_y$ of Italy also experienced a large decrease around 1993, similar to the case of France.

### 4.4.1.5. *Japan*

The quarterly data of Japan from 1960 to 1997 generate the $\phi$ as

$$\begin{pmatrix} 1.013 & 0 & 0 \\ 0 & 0.935 & 0 \\ 0 & 0 & 0.715 \end{pmatrix}.$$

One element of $\phi$ is larger than one and the other two are smaller than one. This implies that $\beta_c$ is non-stationary, but $\beta_\pi$ and $\beta_y$ are stationary. Because the intercept is not of much interest, we stick to the "Return-to-Normality" model, $\bar{\beta}$ is

$$
\begin{pmatrix}
-0.258 \\
0.177 \\
0.674
\end{pmatrix},
$$

implying that $\beta_c$ evolves around $-0.258$, $\beta_\pi$ around 0.177 and $\beta_y$ around 0.674. The paths of $\beta_\pi$ and $\beta_y$ are presented in Figure 4.11A and B. $\beta_\pi$ experienced large changes around 1974 and 1980, attaining the highest point of about 0.55. This is consistent with the switching of the interest rate and inflation rate, which also attained their highest values around these two points.

In the previous section, we have undertaken the Chow break-point test for 1974.4 and 1980.4 when there were great changes in the interest rate and conclude that there are indeed structural changes in the model. Figure 4.11A and B confirms this conclusion: $\beta_\pi$ attained its second highest value around 1974 and $\beta_y$ also increased to a high value. Figure 4.11A and B also shows that there were structural changes in both coefficients between 1980 and 1981,

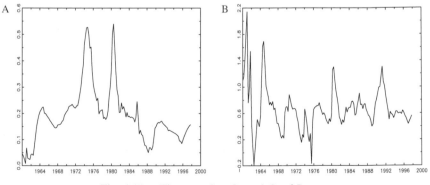

Fig. 4.11:   Time-varying $\bar{\beta}_\pi$ and $\beta_y$ of Japan.

when the interest rate and inflation increased to some large values. In 1964, there were also break-points in both $\beta_\pi$ and $\beta_y$, consistent with the conclusion of the Chow break-point test.

### 4.4.1.6. The US

The US quarterly data from 1960 to 1998 generate the $\phi$ as

$$\begin{pmatrix} 0.991 & 0 & 0 \\ 0 & 0.893 & 0 \\ 0 & 0 & 0.674 \end{pmatrix}.$$

$\bar{\beta}$ is

$$\begin{pmatrix} 0.050 \\ 0.448 \\ 0.705 \end{pmatrix},$$

indicating that $\beta_c$ evolves around 0.050, $\beta_\pi$ around 0.448 and $\beta_y$ around 0.705. The paths of $\beta_\pi$ and $\beta_y$ are presented in Figure 4.12A and B, respectively.

Figure 4.12A shows that the switching of $\beta_\pi$ is very similar to that of the inflation rate and interest rate. That is, when the inflation rate was high $\beta_\pi$ was also high.

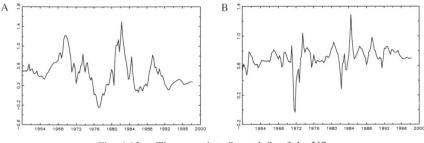

Fig. 4.12: Time-varying $\beta_\pi$ and $\beta_y$ of the US.

We have estimated the time-varying coefficients in the interest-rate rule and find that there do exist some structural changes. One may propose that the policy reaction coefficients of the inflation rate and output gap are state-dependent. That is, the changes of the economic environment may have caused the changes in the coefficients. One observes that the changes in the coefficients seem to have been more or less consistent with the changes in the corresponding economic variables, the inflation rate and output gap. In order to explore empirical evidence for this argument, we will estimate the following two equations, taking the US as an example:

$$\beta_\pi = c_1 + c_2 \pi_t, \tag{4.4}$$

$$\beta_y = \tau_1 + \tau_2 y_t. \tag{4.5}$$

The estimation results for different subperiods are shown in Tables 4.7 and 4.8.

The state-dependent evidence of $\beta_\pi$ seems more obvious than that of $\beta_y$, since the estimates of Equation 4.4 usually have more significant $T$-statistics and higher $R^2$ than those of Equation 4.5. In fact, comparing Figures 4.12 and 4.3 one can find some similar evidence. The change of the $\beta_\pi$ seems to be more consistent with the change of the inflation rate than the $\beta_y$ with the output gap.

Table 4.7:   State-dependent evidence of the US $\beta_\pi$.

| Sample | $c_1$ | | $c_2$ | | $R^2$ |
|---|---|---|---|---|---|
| | **Estimate** | **T-statistics** | **Estimate** | **T-statistics** | |
| 1960.1–1969.4 | 0.615 | 41.781 | 13.989 | 13.790 | 0.833 |
| 1970.1–1974.4 | 0.584 | 6.799 | 1.468 | 0.765 | 0.032 |
| 1975.1–1979.4 | −0.217 | 2.474 | 5.528 | 3.932 | 0.462 |
| 1980.1–1989.4 | 0.423 | 5.651 | 4.180 | 2.385 | 0.130 |
| 1990.1–1998.2 | 0.255 | 15.458 | 6.575 | 4.750 | 0.414 |
| 1960.1–1998.2 | 0.428 | 14.278 | 1.303 | 1.584 | 0.016 |

Table 4.8:   State-dependent evidence of the US $\beta_y$.

| Sample | $\tau_1$ | | $\tau_2$ | | $R^2$ |
|---|---|---|---|---|---|
| | Estimate | *T*-statistics | Estimate | *T*-statistics | |
| 1960.1–1969.4 | 0.667 | 52.160 | 3.217 | 1.728 | 0.073 |
| 1970.1–1979.4 | 0.654 | 21.442 | 4.821 | 1.854 | 0.083 |
| 1980.1–1989.4 | 0.768 | 33.552 | 11.201 | 3.353 | 0.228 |
| 1990.1–1994.4 | 0.772 | 38.250 | 3.586 | 0.679 | 0.025 |
| 1995.1–1998.2 | 0.716 | 56.978 | 5.363 | 0.648 | 0.034 |
| 1960.1–1998.2 | 0.650 | 36.000 | 4.500 | 1.600 | 0.070 |

## 4.4.2. Comparison of E3-countries

CGG98 refer to France, Italy and the UK as the E3 countries, in contrast to the so-called G3 countries of Germany, Japan and the US whose central banks have virtually autonomous control over the domestic monetary policies. Above we have presented the estimation results of the time-varying coefficients in the interest-rate rule of the E3 countries. As mentioned before, the changes in the coefficients in the monetary reaction function in the case of these three countries are, to some extent, similar. We will analyze this problem briefly below. $\beta_\pi$ of the three countries are shown in Figure 4.13. The $\beta_\pi$ of the UK is presented from 1970 to 1998, so that it is consistent with the time period of the estimation of the other two countries.

Figure 4.13 shows that the $\beta_\pi$ of the three countries experienced some significant changes in the 1970s and then remained at a relatively stable and high level after the middle of the 1980s. This indicates that the inflation deviation may have played an important role in the three countries' policy making after 1980. Moreover, the switching of $\beta_\pi$ in the cases of the UK and France was very similar before 1985, though the $\beta_\pi$ of France stayed at a higher level than that of the UK in this period. We also present the inflation rates of the three countries in Figure 4.14.

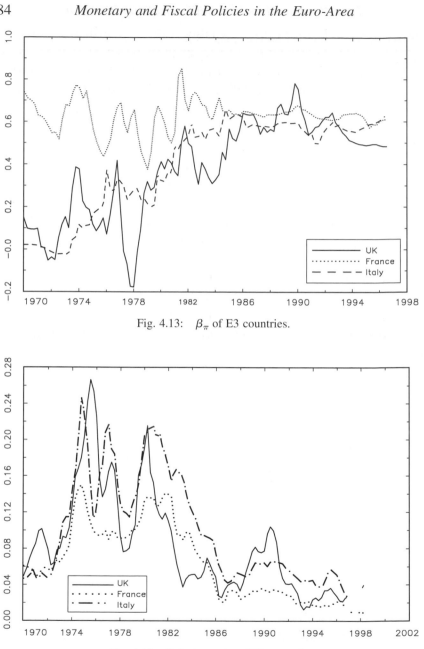

Fig. 4.13:    $\beta_\pi$ of E3 countries.

Fig. 4.14:    Inflation rates of E3 countries.

Figure 4.14 shows that the inflation rates of the three countries also experienced some similar changes: they increased to the highest value around 1975, went down at the end of the 1970s, increased to another high point at the beginning of the 1980s and then decreased persistently with some small increases around 1990 and 1995. The similarity of the inflation rates among the three countries may, to some extent, explain the consistency of $\beta_\pi$. But the EMS may also have some common effects on the monetary policy of the three countries. We present $\beta_y$ of the three countries in Figure 4.15.

The switching of the $\beta_y$ in Italy and France is also similar most of the time. That is, both decreased to the lowest point between 1992 and 1993 when the crisis of the EMS occurred. The $\beta_y$ of the UK is very smooth, as mentioned before. The output gaps for the three countries are presented in Figure 4.16.

Figure 4.16 shows that the output gaps of the three countries also experienced some similar changes, especially in the cases of the UK and France. This evidence seems to indicate some consistency

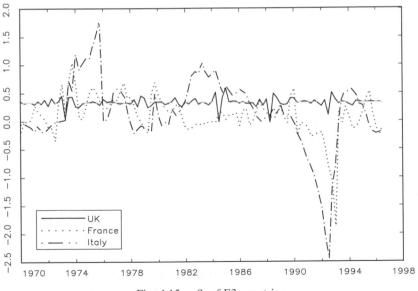

Fig. 4.15: $\beta_y$ of E3 countries.

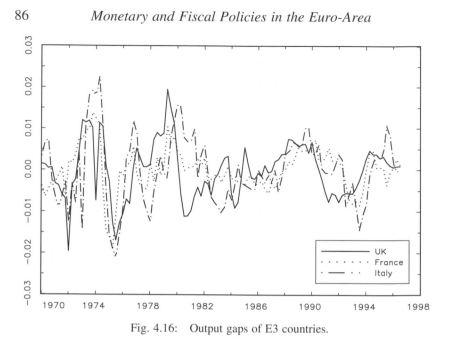

Fig. 4.16:    Output gaps of E3 countries.

between the monetary policies of the E3 countries. One can observe that for all three countries the response coefficient of the inflation deviation moved up and stayed high in the 1990s and that the response coefficient of the output gap is almost constant except when Germany raised the interest rate after the German reunification and the other countries had to raise the interest rate too, in spite of a negative output gap.

## 4.5.  PARAMETER CHANGES IN A FORWARD-LOOKING MONETARY POLICY RULE

In the last two sections, we have estimated the simple Taylor rule (1993) with the OLS and Kalman filter to explore the changes of the coefficients. Note that, up to now we have just explored the simple Taylor rule considering only the current or past inflation rate and output gap, ignoring the roles that may have been played by expectations. A monetary policy rule considering expectations can be found in CGG98. Similar models can also be found in Bernanke and Gertler (1999). This section is to estimate the CGG98 model for Germany, France, Italy, the UK and the US. CGG98 estimate the mode for these countries for only a certain period; we will estimate the model for two periods to see the changes of the coefficients. We will also undertake a statistic test to explore structural stability in the parameters.

CGG98 assume the short-term interest rate follows the following path:

$$R_t = (1 - \rho)R_t^* + \rho R_{t-1} + v_t, \qquad (4.6)$$

where $R_t$ denotes the short-term interest rate, $R_t^*$ the interest rate target, $v_t$ an iid with zero mean and constant variance, and $\rho \in [0, 1]$ denotes the degree of interest-rate smoothing. The target interest rate is assumed to be formed in the following way:

$$R_t^* = \bar{R} + \beta(E[\pi_{t+n}|\Omega_t] - \pi^*) + \gamma(E[Y_t|\Omega_t] - Y_t^*), \qquad (4.7)$$

where $\bar{R}$ is the long-run equilibrium nominal interest rate, $\pi_{t+n}$ the rate of inflation between periods of $t$ and $t + n$, $Y_t$ is real output and $\pi^*$ and $Y_t^*$ are, respectively, targets of the inflation rate and output. $E$ is the expectation operator and $\Omega_t$ the information available to the central bank at the time it sets interest rates. If we define $\alpha = \bar{R} - \beta\pi^*$ and $y_t = Y_t - Y_t^*$, Equation 4.7 can be rewritten as

$$R_t^* = \alpha + \beta E[\pi_{t+n}|\Omega_t] + \gamma E[y_t|\Omega_t]. \qquad (4.8)$$

After substituting Equation 4.8 into Equation 4.6, we have the following path for $R_t$:

$$R_t = (1 - \rho)\alpha + \beta E[\pi_{t+n}|\Omega_t] + \gamma E[y_t|\Omega_t]$$
$$+ \rho R_{t-1} + v_t. \qquad (4.9)$$

One can rewrite the above equation as

$$R_t = (1 - \rho)\alpha + (1 - \rho)\beta\pi_{t+n} + (1 - \rho)\gamma y_t$$
$$+ \rho R_{t-1} + \eta_t, \qquad (4.10)$$

where $\eta_t = -(1 - \rho)\beta(\pi_{t+n} - E[\pi_{t+n}|\Omega_t]) + \gamma(y_t - E[y_t|\Omega_t]) + v_t$. Let $u_t(\in \Omega_t)$ be a vector of variables within the central bank's information set when it sets the interest rate that are orthogonal to $\eta_t$. $u_t$ may contain any lagged variable that can be used to forecast inflation and output, and contemporaneous variables uncorrelated with $v_t$. Since $E[\eta_t|u_t] = 0$, Equation 4.10 implies the following orthogonality conditions:

$$E[R_t - (1 - \rho)\alpha - (1 - \rho)\beta\pi_{t+n} - (1 - \rho)\gamma y_t - \rho R_{t-1}|u_t] = 0.$$

$$(4.11)$$

The generalized method of moments (GMM) is employed to undertake the estimation with quarterly data. We will undertake the estimation for Germany, France, Italy, the US and the UK. In order to explore structural stability in the parameters, we will undertake some tests discussed in Hamilton (1994, p. 425). Let $T$ denote the total number of observations, we want to test whether the estimates of the parameters with the first $T_1$ observations are significantly different from those with the rest $T - T_1$ observations.

Let $\hat{\Theta}_1$ denote the estimate of the vector of parameter in the first $T_1$ observations, $\Theta_1$, and $\hat{\Theta}_2$ the estimate of the vector of parameter in the rest $T - T_1$ observations, $\Theta_2$, Hamilton (1994, p. 414, proposition 14.1) then shows that

$$\sqrt{T_1}(\hat{\Theta}_1 - \Theta_1) \xrightarrow{L} N(0, V_1)$$

$$\sqrt{T - T_1}(\hat{\Theta}_2 - \Theta_2) \xrightarrow{L} N(0, V_2).$$

Define $\tau = T_1/T$ and

$$\lambda_T = T(\hat{\Theta}_1 - \hat{\Theta}_2)'\{\tau^{-1}\hat{V}_1 + (1 - \tau)^{-1}\hat{V}_2\}^{-1}(\hat{\Theta}_1 - \hat{\Theta}_2),$$

then $\lambda_T \xrightarrow{L} \chi^2(a)$ under the null hypothesis that $\Theta_1 = \Theta_2$, with $\hat{\Theta}_1$ and $\hat{\Theta}_2$ being the estimates of $\Theta_1$ and $\Theta_2$, respectively, and $a$ being the number of the parameters to be estimated. $\hat{V}_1$ and $\hat{V}_2$ denote

Table 4.9:    Germany 1971.1–1999.1.

| Parameter | Sample | | |
|---|---|---|---|
| | **1971–1979** | **1979–1999** | **1971–1999** |
| $\rho$ | 0.624 (163.105) | 0.856 (51.223) | 0.910 (49.289) |
| $\alpha$ | −0.008 (1.920) | 0.029 (7.561) | 0.043 (6.160) |
| $\beta$ | 1.441 (21.649) | 0.584 (4.986) | 0.024 (0.095) |
| $\gamma$ | 0.209 (12.368) | 0.755 (6.753) | 1.279 (4.760) |
| $R^2$ | 0.775 | 0.937 | 0.885 |
| $J$-statistics | 0.251 | 0.117 | 0.104 |

the estimators of $V_1$ and $V_2$, respectively.[11] The data sources in this section are the same as in the previous sections, namely, OECD and IMF.

### 4.5.1. Germany

The estimation for Germany is undertaken from 1971.1 to 1999.1 with quarterly data. The instruments used include 1–4 lags of inflation rate, output gap, real effective exchange rate, changes in import prices, short-term interest rate, growth rate of broad money supply M3 and a constant. We will test whether there are structural changes in the parameters around 1979 when the EMS started. The estimation results with $T$-statistics in parentheses are shown in Table 4.9.

It is found that $\lambda_T = 383.851$. With $a = 4$ it is clear that Prob$[\chi^2 \leq 14.86] = 0.995$. Therefore, we should deny the null hypothesis that $\Theta_1 = \Theta_2$. From Table 4.9 we find that $\beta$ has insignificant $T$-statistic for the whole sample 1971–1999, but has significant $T$-statistics for the two subsamples 1971–1979 and 1979–1999. This may also, to some extent, imply that there is structural instability in the parameters.

---

[11] The reader is referred to Hamilton (1994, Chapter 14) for the estimation of $V_1$ and $V_2$.

Table 4.10:    France 1971.1–2000.4.

| Parameter | Sample | | |
|---|---|---|---|
| | 1971–1979 | 1979–2000 | 1971–2000 |
| $\rho$ | 0.662 (29.622) | 0.921 (44.480) | 0.943 (47.915) |
| $\alpha$ | −0.023 (4.933) | 0.038 (4.433) | 0.032 (1.926) |
| $\beta$ | 1.023 (23.021) | 1.091 (6.254) | 0.439 (1.423) |
| $\gamma$ | 0.529 (10.418) | 2.793 (3.294) | 3.193 (2.567) |
| $R^2$ | 0.835 | 0.953 | 0.937 |
| $J$-statistics | 0.210 | 0.126 | 0.126 |

### 4.5.2.  France

The estimation results of France undertaken with quarterly data from 1971.1 to 2000.4 are shown in Table 4.10, with $T$-statistics in parentheses. The instrument variables include 1–4 lags of real effective exchange rate, inflation rate, output gap, short-term interest rate, changes in the share price and a constant. Data of M3 and import price index are not available. The estimation is undertaken for two subsamples, 1971–1979 and 1979–2000, to explore whether there were structural changes in the parameters before and after the EMS started.

It is found that $\lambda_T = 380.815$, much larger than the critical value 14.86, indicating that the parameters with data before 1979 can be significantly different from those thereafter. Although $\beta$ did not change much, the ratio of $\beta$ to $\gamma$ changed greatly.

### 4.5.3.  Italy

The estimation results for Italy with quarterly data from 1971.1 to 1998.4 are shown in Table 4.11, with $T$-statistics in parentheses. The instrument variables include 1–4 lags of real effective exchange rate, output gap, changes in import price, short-term interest rate, inflation rate and a constant. We test structural stability in the parameters for 1979 and find that $\lambda_T = 276.380$, this implies

Table 4.11:   Italy 1971.1–1998.4.

| Parameter | Sample | | |
|---|---|---|---|
| | **1971–1978** | **1979–1998** | **1971–1998** |
| $\rho$ | 0.831 (157.339) | 0.791 (60.986) | 0.952 (135.884) |
| $\alpha$ | 0.038 (4.928) | 0.026 (0.996) | −0.000 (0.001) |
| $\beta$ | 0.364 (7.316) | 0.686 (5.784) | 0.946 (3.926) |
| $\gamma$ | 0.746 (12.801) | 2.882 (2.865) | 6.878 (2.552) |
| $R^2$ | 0.851 | 0.953 | 0.942 |
| $J$-statistics | 0.175 | 0.121 | 0.084 |

structural changes around 1979 when the EMS started. $\gamma$, for instance, changed from 0.746 to 2.882.

### 4.5.4. The UK

The estimation results for the UK with quarterly data from 1965.1 to 1999.4 are shown in Table 4.12, with $T$-statistics in parentheses. The instrument variables used include 1–4 lags of nominal exchange rate (pound/US dollar, the data of real effective exchange rate of pound are not available), output gap, inflation rate, short-term

Table 4.12:   The UK 1965.1–1999.4.

| Parameter | Sample | | |
|---|---|---|---|
| | **1965–1978** | **1979–1999** | **1965–1999** |
| $\rho$ | 0.592 (12.961) | 0.926 (50.837) | 0.920 (68.032) |
| $\alpha$ | 0.056 (17.793) | 0.035 (2.830) | 0.052 (4.954) |
| $\beta$ | 0.159 (5.912) | 0.723 (3.858) | 0.481 (3.847) |
| $\gamma$ | 0.113 (1.849) | 2.517 (3.580) | 2.075 (3.813) |
| $R^2$ | 0.760 | 0.926 | 0.893 |
| $J$-statistics | 0.146 | 0.114 | 0.055 |

Table 4.13:  The US 1971.1–2002.1.

| Parameter | Sample | | |
| --- | --- | --- | --- |
| | **1971–1981** | **1982–2002** | **1971–2002** |
| $\rho$ | 0.660 <br> (60.725) | 0.791 <br> (35.252) | 0.976 <br> (77.962) |
| $\alpha$ | 0.052 <br> (6.716) | 0.029 <br> (3.071) | −0.016 <br> (0.302) |
| $\beta$ | 0.113 <br> (1.313) | 0.752 <br> (3.117) | 2.731 <br> (2.019) |
| $\gamma$ | 0.633 <br> (12.325) | 0.522 <br> (5.538) | 2.709 <br> (1.608) |
| $R^2$ | 0.789 | 0.922 | 0.896 |
| $J$-statistics | 0.232 | 0.152 | 0.113 |

interest rate, changes in import price and a constant. The $\lambda_T$ turns out to be 89.754, much larger than the critical value 14.86, indicating that the parameters in the first subsample of 1965.1–1978.4 can be significantly different from those in the second subsample of 1979.1–1999.4. In fact, one can see that the parameters experienced relatively large changes. $\gamma$, for example, is only 0.113 in the first subsample but increased to 2.517 in the second subsample.

### 4.5.5. The US

The estimation results for the US with quarterly data from 1971.1 to 2002.1 are shown in Table 4.13, with $T$-statistics in parentheses. The instrument variables are the 1–4 lags of real effective exchange rate, output gap, changes in import price, inflation rate, federal funds rate, growth rate of M3 and a constant. We undertake the estimation for the two subsamples of 1971–1981 and 1982–2002. The $\lambda_T = 70.013$, much larger than the critical value 14.86, implying a structural change in the parameters around 1982, when the Fed changed its chairmanship.

### 4.6. CONCLUSION

This chapter presents some empirical evidence for the time-varying monetary policy reaction function. We have first explored the parameter changes in the simple Taylor rule with OLS regression and Chow break-point tests, which indicate that there are really structural changes in $\beta_\pi$ and $\beta_y$. Because the Chow break-point test can only explore structural changes at predetermined points, we resort to the Kalman filter to explore all possible structural changes of the coefficients.[12] The time-varying estimation indicates that the response coefficients have experienced some structural changes and are more or less state-dependent. We have also estimated an amended Taylor rule of CGG98 with forward-looking behavior. In order to observe the possible changes in the parameters, we estimate the model for different periods with the GMM, and the results also indicate that the parameters have experienced some significant changes. All evidence seems to favor the conclusion that the monetary policy reaction function is state-dependent and is significantly influenced by the economic environment.

---

[12] The OLS and time-varying-parameter estimations show that $\beta_\pi$ may be smaller than one in practice. This seems to be inconsistent with the optimal interest-rate rule that will be derived from the dynamic model shown in Chapter 6 and the original Taylor rule discussed in footnote 2 in this chapter. This problem has been briefly discussed by Woodford (2003a, p. 93).

# CHAPTER 5

# Euro-Area Monetary Policy Effects Using US Monetary Policy Rules

## 5.1. INTRODUCTION

It is well known that in the 1990s the economy of the Euro-area performed worse than that of the US. The difference in the growth and unemployment performance of the Euro-area and the US may have been caused by differences in monetary policies. Difference in the interest rates can be seen in Figure 5.1. Similar to Peersman and Smets (1999), we use the German call money rate to study the monetary policy in the Euro-area. The aggregate inflation rate and output gap of the Euro-area are measured, respectively, by the GDP weighted sums of the inflation rates and output gaps of Germany, France and Italy. A similar aggregation of the data can be found in Taylor (1999b). In particular, before 1994 the interest rate of the US was much lower (4.9% on average) than that of the Euro-area (8.5% on average). For the whole decade of the 1990s the average rate of the US was 5.1%, while that of the Euro-area was 6.1%. We find similar results for the real interest rate. The real interest rate of the US in the 1990s was 1.8%, while that of the Euro-area was 3.2%.

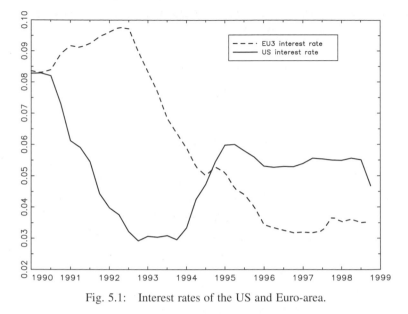

Fig. 5.1:   Interest rates of the US and Euro-area.

So an interesting question is: what would have happened if the Euro-area had followed the monetary policy rule of the US in the 1990s? This chapter tries to answer this question.

On the basis of the theoretical and empirical research in the previous chapters, we will simulate the inflation rate and output gap for the Euro-area for the period of 1990–1998, assuming that the Euro-area had followed the monetary policy of the US. Section 5.2 undertakes simulations under the assumption that the Taylor rule has changing response coefficients and section 5.3 assumes that the Taylor rule has fixed coefficients. A similar counterfactual study has been undertaken by Taylor (1999c) using the pre-Volcker policy interest rate reaction function to study the macroeconomic performance of the Volcker and post-Volcker periods. Therefore, in section 5.4 we undertake the simulations with the two rules suggested by Taylor.

## 5.2. SIMULATION USING THE TIME-VARYING COEFFICIENT TAYLOR RULE OF THE US

Let us write the Taylor rule with time-varying response coefficients as

$$R_t = \bar{R} + \beta_{\pi t}(\pi_t - \pi^*) + \beta_{yt}y_t, \qquad (5.1)$$

where $R_t$ is the short-term interest rate, $\bar{R}$ is the long-run equilibrium interest rate, and other variables are interpreted the same as in Chapter 4.[1] The paths of $\beta_\pi$ and $\beta_y$ of the US are presented in Figure 4.12.

Next, we assume that the Euro-area follows the monetary policy of the US by determining the interest rate according to the HP-filtered trends of $\beta_{\pi t}$ and $\beta_{yt}$ of the US instead of the exact paths of $\beta_{\pi t}$ and $\beta_{yt}$ since we assume that the Euro-area had followed only approximately the US monetary policy rule. We simulate the Euro-area interest rate with Equation 5.1 by defining $\bar{R}$ as the average interest rate of the Euro-area of the 1990s and substituting the $\beta_{\pi t}$ and $\beta_{yt}$ trends for $\beta_{\pi t}$ and $\beta_{yt}$. The inflation target is assumed to be 2.5%. The simulated Euro-area interest rate is presented in Figure 5.2, together with the actual Euro-area interest rate. The simulated rate is much lower (3.56% on average before 1995) than the actual rate in the first half of the 1990s and close to the actual rate after 1994. The average value of the simulated rate is 3.39% for the period of 1990–1998.

The simulations of the Euro-area inflation rate and output gap will be undertaken with the IS-Phillips curves[2]:

$$\pi_t = a_1 + a_2\pi_{t-1} + a_3\pi_{t-2} + a_4\pi_{t-3} + a_5y_{t-1}, \qquad (5.2)$$

$$y_t = b_1 + b_2y_{t-1} + b_3y_{t-2} + b_4(R_{t-1} - \pi_{t-1}), \qquad (5.3)$$

---

[1] Output gap is computed in the same way as in the previous chapter. *Data sources*: OECD and IMF.

[2] The number of lags of variables included depend on the $T$-statistics of the OLS estimates, namely, the lags with insignificant $T$-statistics are excluded. This model is similar to that employed in Rudebusch and Svensson (1999).

where all variables have the same interpretations as in Equation 5.1. In order to simulate the $\pi_t$ and $y_t$ from Equations 5.2 and 5.3, we need to know the values of the coefficients, $a_i$ and $b_i$, which will be generated by estimating Equations 5.2 and 5.3 with the SUR with Euro-area data from 1990 to 1998. The estimation results for this system are presented as follows, with $T$-statistics in parentheses[3]:

$$\pi_t = \underset{(0.254)}{-0.0006} + \underset{(6.165)}{0.984}\,\pi_{t-1} - \underset{(1.307)}{0.291}\,\pi_{t-2} + \underset{(1.743)}{0.286}\,\pi_{t-3} + \underset{(1.014)}{0.149}\,y_{t-1},$$

$$R^2 = 0.852,$$

$$y_t = \underset{(0.277)}{0.0002} + \underset{(7.841)}{1.229}\,y_{t-1} - \underset{(2.467)}{0.403}\,y_{t-2} - \underset{(0.334)}{0.008}\,(R_{t-1} - \pi_{t-1}),$$

$$R^2 = 0.799.$$

The determinant residual covariance is $6.82 \times 10^{-11}$. After substituting the simulated interest rate into these equations, we have the simulations of $\pi_t$ and $y_t$.[4] The simulated output gap is presented in Figure 5.3. We find that the simulated output gap declines very

---

[3] The $T$-statistics of the last terms of these two equations are unfortunately insignificant. The results seem sensitive to the period covered and how potential output is computed. If we use the linear quadratic trend of the log value of the industrial production index as the potential output, for example, we can have the following results with the data from 1986 to 1998:

$$\pi_t = \underset{(1.806)}{0.004} + \underset{(8.150)}{1.117}\,\pi_{t-1} - \underset{(1.719)}{0.341}\,\pi_{t-2} + \underset{(0.556)}{0.072}\,\pi_{t-3} + \underset{(1.934)}{0.184}\,y_{t-1}, \quad R^2 = 0.830,$$

$$y_t = \underset{(1.772)}{0.001} + \underset{(9.376)}{1.254}\,y_{t-1} - \underset{(1.835)}{0.275}\,y_{t-2} - \underset{(1.714)}{0.045}\,(R_{t-1} - \pi_{t-1}), \quad R^2 = 0.909$$

with determinant residual covariance being $6.44 \times 10^{-11}$. The $T$-statistics of the last terms are now more significant. Since the $T$-statistics of these terms do not have great effects on our simulations, we do not discuss how output gap should be defined here.

[4] As for the three initial lags of inflation and two initial lags of output gap, we just take the actual inflation rate from 1989.2 to 1989.4 and output gap from 1989.3 to 1989.4.

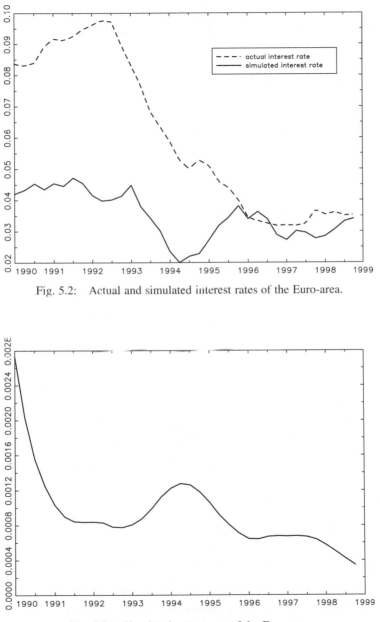

Fig. 5.2:   Actual and simulated interest rates of the Euro-area.

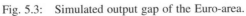

Fig. 5.3:   Simulated output gap of the Euro-area.

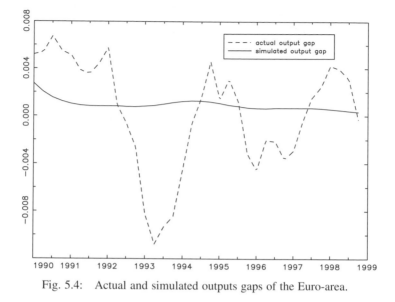

Fig. 5.4:    Actual and simulated outputs gaps of the Euro-area.

fast at the beginning of the 1990s and increases a little in 1994. The simulated and actual output gaps are presented in Figure 5.4. Unlike the actual output gap, which experienced significant decreases during 1992–1994 and 1995–1997, the simulated output gap is always positive and smoother than the actual one. The simulated and actual inflation rates are presented in Figure 5.5. We find that the simulated inflation rate looks similar to the linear trend of the actual inflation rate and lower than the actual inflation most of the time.

## 5.3. SIMULATION USING THE FIXED COEFFICIENT TAYLOR RULE OF THE US

In the last section we have simulated the inflation and output gap of the Euro-area under the assumption that the coefficients of output gap and inflation are changing in the Taylor rule. In this section, we assume that these coefficients are fixed. Using the US data of

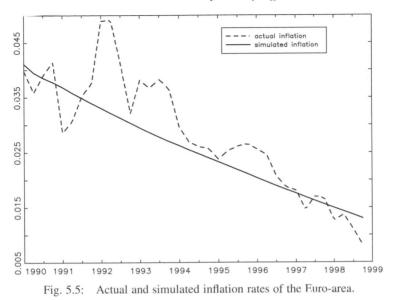

Fig. 5.5: Actual and simulated inflation rates of the Euro-area.

1990.1 – 1998.4, we get the following estimate (*T*-statistics in parentheses)

$$R_t = \underset{(26.970)}{0.049} + \underset{(5.077)}{0.735}\,(\pi_t - \pi^*) + \underset{(5.469)}{0.703}\,y_t, \quad R^2 = 0.520.$$

With these coefficients we can get the simulated interest rate of the Euro-area, as presented in Figure 5.6, together with the actual Euro-area interest rate and the simulated interest rate from the last section (denoted by simulated interest rate 1). The simulated interest rate from this section is denoted by simulated interest rate 2. We find that the simulated interest rate under the assumption of fixed coefficients is higher than the simulated rate with the time-varying coefficient assumption most of the time and experiences more significant changes, but it is still much lower than the actual interest rate.

We can now get the simulated inflation rate and output gap with the simulated interest rate by way of Equations 5.2 and 5.3. The simulated inflation rate (denoted by simulated inflation 2) is

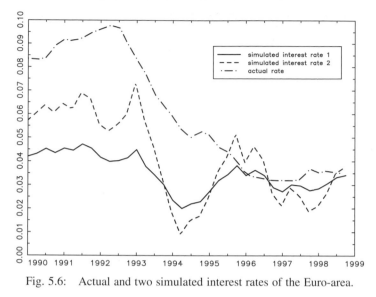

Fig. 5.6:   Actual and two simulated interest rates of the Euro-area.

presented here together with the actual inflation rate (denoted by actual inflation) and the simulated inflation from the previous section (denoted by simulated inflation 1) in Figure 5.7. The figure shows that the simulated inflation from this section is slightly lower than the simulated inflation from the last section. This is consistent with the fact that the simulated interest rate of this section is higher than that from the last section most of the time.

The simulated output gap (denoted by simulated output gap 2) is presented in Figure 5.8 together with the simulated output gap from the previous section (denoted by simulated output gap 1) and actual output gap. We find that the output gap simulated here is also very smooth and close to the simulation from the previous section.

## 5.4. SIMULATION USING THE SUGGESTED TAYLOR RULES AND ACTUAL INTEREST RATE

In the last two sections, we have undertaken simulations for the Euro-area economy with time-varying and fixed $\beta_\pi$ and $\beta_y$ chosen as

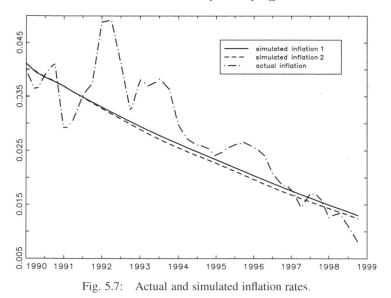

Fig. 5.7:   Actual and simulated inflation rates.

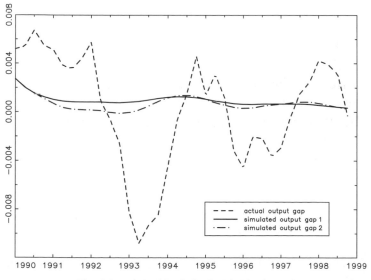

Fig. 5.8:   Actual and simulated output gaps.

the estimates from the monetary reaction function for the 1990s with the US data. In Taylor (1999c), however, a counterfactual study was undertaken with the pre-Volcker policy interest rate reaction function to explore the macroeconomic performance of the post-Volcker period. Two suggested rules can be found there. In this section we will undertake simulations for the Euro-area with the two suggested Taylor rules and make a comparison with the simulations above.

The first rule, which was first stated in Taylor (1993), suggests $\beta_\pi$ to be 1.5 and $\beta_y$ 0.5, namely,

$$R_t = \bar{R} + 1.5(\pi - \pi^*) + 0.5y_t.$$

An alternative rule keeps $\beta_\pi$ at 1.5 but raises $\beta_y$ to 1.0, namely

$$R_t = \bar{R} + 1.5(\pi - \pi^*) + y_t.$$

The interest rates simulated with these two suggested rules are presented in Figure 5.9, together with the actual interest rate and

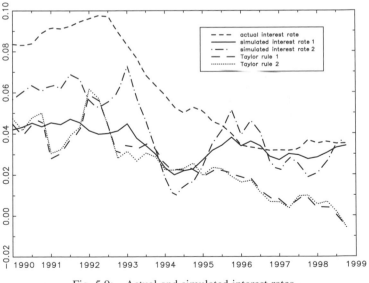

Fig. 5.9:   Actual and simulated interest rates.

the interest rates simulated in the previous two sections. The two rules simulated here (denoted by Taylor rule 1 and Taylor rule 2) are close to each other, lower than the interest rates simulated in the last two sections most of the time and much lower than the actual rate.

The simulated output gaps with the suggested Taylor rules are presented in Figure 5.10. They are positive all the time, decrease to the lowest points in 1992 and then increase slowly. In Figure 5.11 we present the four simulated output gaps together, from which we can see the difference obviously. Before 1995 the simulated output gaps with the two suggested Taylor rules are very close to the simulation with the time-varying response coefficient interest rate rule, but after 1995 there is an obvious difference: the former increases slowly, while the latter decreases.

The inflation rates simulated with the two suggested Taylor rules (denoted by simulated inflation 3 and 4, respectively) are very close to each other. They are presented in Figure 5.12 together with

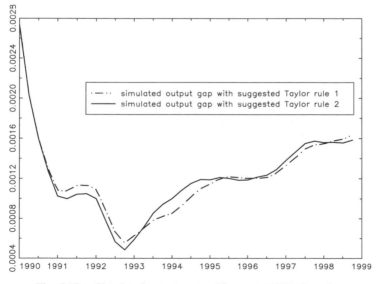

Fig. 5.10:    Simulated output gaps with suggested Taylor rules.

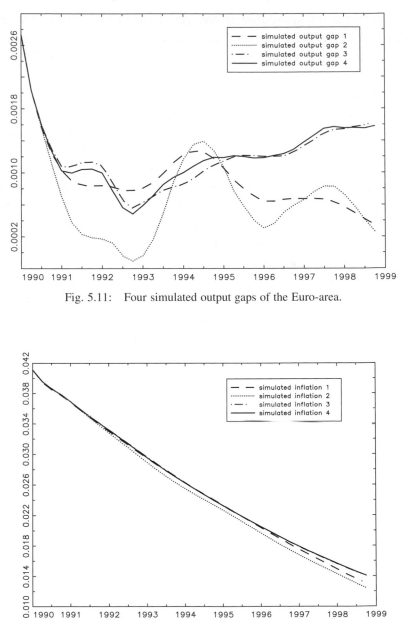

Fig. 5.11:   Four simulated output gaps of the Euro-area.

Fig. 5.12:   Four simulated inflation rates of the Euro-area.

the simulated inflation rates from the last two sections (denoted by simulated inflation 1 and simulated inflation 2). It is obvious that the four simulations are all very similar to a linear trend of the actual inflation rate.

Up to now we have simulated the inflation rate and output gap for the Euro-area, assuming that different interest rate rules of the US had been followed in the 1990s. The simulations above favor the conclusion that if the Euro-area economy had followed the interest rate rule of the US, the output gap would have been much smaller and smoother than the actual one, while the inflation rate was very similar to a linear trend of the actual one. Note that we have used the German call money rate as the interest rate of the Euro-area and assumed that the actual output and inflation rate are really generated by this interest rate, which was higher than the US rate most of the time in the 1990s. So the question arising here is, what will happen if simulations are undertaken with the actual Euro-area

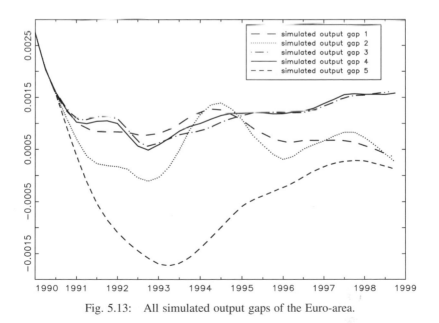

Fig. 5.13: All simulated output gaps of the Euro-area.

rate? Will the simulated output gap really experience drastic changes like the actual one? To answer this question, we will do the simulations with the actual Euro-area rate (German call money rate) below. The output gap simulated with the actual Euro-area rate is presented in Figure 5.13 together with all the other simulated output gaps. It is obvious that the output gap simulated with actual interest rate (denoted by simulated output gap 5 in Figure 5.13) is lower and experiences more obvious changes than the others. Moreover, like the actual output gap (which experienced a large decrease during 1991 and 1995), it is negative from 1991 to 1996. The simulated inflation rate with the actual Euro-area interest rate is presented in Figure 5.14, denoted by simulated inflation 5, together with the other four simulations, it is slightly lower than the others.

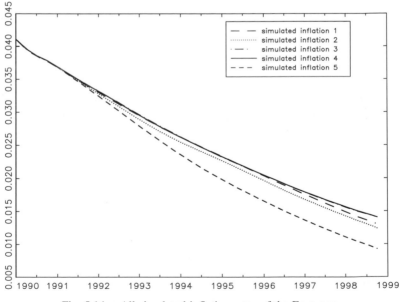

Fig. 5.14:   All simulated inflation rates of the Euro-area.

## 5.5. CONCLUSION

Based on the evidence of the previous chapters, this chapter explores whether the Euro-area interest rate was too high in the 1990s. We have undertaken some simulations of the inflation rate and output gap for the Euro-area using the following interest rate rules: estimated time-varying and fixed coefficient Taylor rules and the two rules of the US as suggested by Taylor. In order to undertake a comparison with the simulations undertaken with the four US interest rate rules, we have also undertaken simulations with the actual Euro-area interest rate. All of the simulations seem to favor the conclusion that if the Euro-area had followed the interest rate rules of the US in the 1990s, the output gap would not have experienced such a fall. It would have been higher and smoother, while the inflation rate would have been similar to the linear trend of the actual one. Of course, many observers of the monetary policy of the Euro area would argue that lowering the interest rate would not have been a feasible policy since this would have led to an accelerated depreciation of European currencies and later of the Euro. As, however, shown in Semmler and Wöhrmann (2004) the Euro-area has large net foreign assets and thus large foreign currency reserves, so that an accelerated depreciation would not have occurred. Moreover, as has been shown by Corsetti and Pesenti (1999) the high value of the dollar in the 1990s was strongly positively correlated with the growth differentials of the US and Euro-area economies. One might conjecture that a lower interest rate and thus higher expected growth rate of the Euro-area would have attracted capital inflows into the Euro-area and this would have prevented the Euro from being depreciated.

CHAPTER 6

# *Optimal Monetary Policy and Adaptive Learning*

## 6.1. INTRODUCTION

In Chapters 4 and 5 we have presented some empirical evidence on monetary policy reaction functions with constant or time-varying coefficients. This chapter presents some theoretical background on how monetary policy rules may be derived from a monetary optimal control model. Assuming that there exists an objective function for some economic agents (central banks or households), the main problem is to find a policy rule, which maximizes or minimizes the given objective function. By optimal monetary policy rule we mean a monetary policy rule, which optimizes an objective function. In the case of intertemporal models, two methods usually applied to solve these problems are optimal control theory using the Hamiltonian and dynamic programming. We will apply the latter in this chapter. Another interesting problem concerning monetary policy is how to deal with uncertainty when economic models or some parameters in economic models are unknown to economic agents. This problem will also be discussed in this chapter.

This chapter is organized as follows. We present a short introduction to discrete deterministic dynamic programming in section 6.2. In section 6.3 we derive a monetary policy rule from a dynamic model. Sections 6.4 and 6.5 explore monetary policy rules under uncertainty with adaptive learning and robust control.

## 6.2. DISCRETE-TIME DETERMINISTIC DYNAMIC PROGRAMMING

The dynamic programming literature is based on Bellman (1957). Recent elaborations on this topic can be found in many papers and books, see Sargent (1987), Stokey and Lucas (1996) and Ljungvist and Sargent (2000), for example.

A typical discrete-time deterministic dynamic programming problem can be written as

$$\underset{\{u_t\}_0^\infty}{\text{Max}} \sum_{t=0}^{\infty} \rho^t r(x_t, u_t)$$

subject to

$$x_{t+1} = g(x_t, u_t),$$

where $\rho \in (0, 1)$ is a discount factor, $x_t$ an $n \times 1$ vector of state variables with $x_0$ given, and $u_t$ a $k \times 1$ vector of controls. Under the assumption that $r(x_t, u_t)$ is a concave function and that the set $\{(x_{t+1}, x_t) : x_{t+1} \leq g_t(x_t, u_t), \ u_t \in R^k\}$ is convex and compact, dynamic programming seeks a response function $u_t = h(x_t)$ which solves the above dynamic optimization problem.

By the way of dynamic programming the above problem is usually recursively written in the form of the Bellman equation

$$V(x) = \underset{u}{\text{Max}} \{r(x, u) + \rho V[g(x, u)]\},$$

where $V(\cdot)$ is the so-called value function. In case that $h(x)$ maximizes the right-hand side of the above equation, this problem can be rewritten as

$$V(x) = r[x, h(x)] + \rho V\{g[x, h(x)]\}.$$

Though there are many algorithms to solve the Bellman equation, we will not discuss them, since this is out of the scope of this book.[1]

Next, we will sketch a special case of dynamic programming, the linear-quadratic (LQ) problem, which has a quadratic return function and a linear-transition equation. The discounted LQ problem (usually also referred to as the optimal linear-regulator problem) reads

$$\underset{\{u_t\}_0^\infty}{\text{Max}} \sum_{t=0}^{\infty} \rho^t \{x_t' R x_t + u_t' Q u_t\}$$

subject to

$$x_{t+1} = A x_t + B u_t,$$

where $R$ is a negative semi-definite symmetric matrix, $Q$ a negative definite symmetric matrix, $A$ an $n \times n$ matrix and $B$ an $n \times k$ matrix. $x_0$ is given. The optimal policy rule for this problem turns out to be

$$u_t = -F x_t, \tag{6.1}$$

where $F = \rho(Q + \rho B' P B)^{-1} B' P A$, with $P$ being the limiting value of $P_j$ from the following Riccati equation

$$P_{j+1} = R + \rho A' P_j A - \rho^2 A' P_j B (Q + \rho B' P_j B)^{-1} B' P_j A. \tag{6.2}$$

An interesting feature of the LQ problem is that, if one considers stochastic transition equations, one has the same optimal policy rule. That is, if the problem is changed to

$$\underset{\{u_t\}_0^\infty}{\text{Max}} E_0 \sum_{t=0}^{\infty} \rho^t \{x_t' R x_t + u_t' Q u_t\}$$

---

[1] For the review up to 1989, see Taylor and Uhlig (1990). Recent development can be found in Judd (1998), Ljungvist and Sargent (2000), Marimon and Scott (1999), Grüne (1997, 2001) and Grüne and Semmler (2004a).

subject to

$$x_{t+1} = Ax_t + Bu_t + \eta_{t+1},$$

where $\eta_{t+1}$ is an $n \times 1$ vector of random variables, $\eta_t \sim N(0, \sigma^2)$ and $E$ the expectation operator. The optimal policy rule also turns out to be

$$u_t = -Fx_t$$

with $F$ defined by Equation 6.1 and $P$ by Equation 6.2. This feature is known as the *certainty equivalence principle*.

## 6.3. DERIVING AN OPTIMAL MONETARY POLICY RULE

In this section we will derive a monetary policy rule from a simple model on the basis of the discussion above. As will be seen, the interest-rate rule derived below is similar to the Taylor rule in the sense that they both are linear functions of inflation and output gap. Before deriving this monetary policy rule, we will discuss briefly the goal of monetary policy. There are usually two types of objective functions in monetary policy models. Some researchers claim that monetary policy should be pursued with reference to households' welfare functions. This type of objective function is usually employed by the New Classical economists. Other researchers have traditionally studied monetary policy by applying a loss function of the monetary authority. But even if it is agreed that monetary policy should be pursued to minimize a loss function of the central bank, there is still disagreement on what kind of loss functions should be minimized. This problem has been explored by Woodford (2003a) in detail. There he finds that the maximization of a utility function of the households can be shown to be consistent with the minimization of loss functions of the central bank. Next, we will give a brief sketch of his analysis, the details can be found in Woodford (2003a, Chapter 6).

### 6.3.1. The goal of monetary policy

In the basic analysis Woodford (2003a) assumes that there are no monetary frictions. The representative household's expected utility is

$$E\left\{\sum_{t=0}^{\infty} \rho^t U_t\right\}, \tag{6.3}$$

where $\rho$ denotes the discount factor between 0 and 1, and $U_t$ the utility function in period $t$ of the specific form

$$U_t = u(C_t; \xi_t) - \int_0^1 v(h_t(i); \xi_t)di, \tag{6.4}$$

where $C_t$ denotes the Dixit–Stiglitz consumption

$$C_t \equiv \left[\int_0^1 c_t(i)^{\theta-1/\theta} di\right]^{\theta/\theta-1}$$

with $c_t(i)$ denoting the consumption of differentiated goods $i$ in period $t$. $\theta(> 1)$ is the constant elasticity of substitution among goods. $\xi_t$ is a vector of preferences shocks and $h_t(i)$ is the supply of labor used in sector $i$. Let $G_t$ denote the public goods and $y_t(i)$ the production of goods $i$ in period $t$, using $C_t + G_t = Y_t$ and $y_t(i) = A_t f(h_t(i))$, one can rewrite the utility function above as

$$U_t = \tilde{u}(Y_t; \tilde{\xi}_t) - \int_0^1 \tilde{v}(y_t(i); \tilde{\xi}_t)di, \tag{6.5}$$

where $A_t$ ($>0$) is the exogenous technology factor which may change over time, and

$$\tilde{u}(Y; \tilde{\xi}) \equiv u(Y - G; \xi), \tag{6.6}$$

$$\tilde{v}(y; \tilde{\xi}) \equiv v(f^{-1}(y/A); \xi) \tag{6.7}$$

with $\tilde{\xi}_t$ denoting the vector of disturbances ($\xi_t$, $G_t$ and $A_t$) and

$$Y_t \equiv \left[ \int_0^1 y_t(i)^{\theta-1/\theta} \, di \right]^{\theta/\theta-1}. \tag{6.8}$$

Assuming small fluctuations in production, small disturbances and small value of distortion in the steady-state output level and applying the Taylor series expansion, Woodford (2003a) finds that $U_t$ can be approximately written as

$$U_t = -\frac{\bar{Y}u_c}{2} \{ (\sigma^{-1} + \omega)(x_t - x^*)^2 + \theta(1 + \omega\theta)\text{var}_i \log p_t(i) \}$$

$$+ \text{t.i.p.} + o(\|\cdot\|^3), \tag{6.9}$$

where $x_t$ denotes the output gap.[2] $p_t(i)$ is the price level of goods $i$ and $x^*$ denotes the efficient level of output gap. t.i.p. denotes the terms independent of policy. o(·) denotes higher-order terms.[3] Woodford (2003a, p. 396) further claims that the approximation above "applies to any model with no frictions other than those due to monopolistic competition and sticky prices".

Considering alternative types of price-setting, Woodford (2003a) finds that the approximation of the utility function above can be written as a quadratic function of the inflation rate and output gap. Examples considered are[4]

(1) *Case 1.* A fraction of goods prices are fully flexible, while the remaining fraction must be fixed a period in advance. In this

---

[2] The definitions of output gap of Woodford (2003a) are shown in Appendix A6.
[3] This is Equation 2.13 in Woodford (2003a, p. 396). The reader is referred to Woodford (2003a, Chapter 6) for the details of the other parameters and variables in Equation 6.9.
[4] The reader is referred to Woodford (2003a, Chapter 6) for the details of the derivation of these results.

case $U_t$ can be approximated as

$$U_t = -\Omega L_t + \text{t.i.p.} + \text{o}(\|\cdot\|^3),$$

where $\Omega$ is a positive constant and $L_t$ is a quadratic loss function of the form

$$L_t = (\pi_t - E_{t-1}\pi_t)^2 + \lambda(x_t - x^*)^2 \qquad (6.10)$$

with $\pi_t$ denoting inflation and $E$ the expectations operator. $\lambda$ is the weight of output-gap stabilization.

(2) *Case 2.* Discrete-time version of the Calvo (1983) pricing model. It turns out that

$$\sum_{t=0}^{\infty} \rho^t U_t = -\Omega \sum_{t=0}^{\infty} \rho^t L_t + \text{t.i.p.} + \text{o}(\|\cdot\|^3), \qquad (6.11)$$

where $L_t$ is given by

$$L_t = \pi_t^2 + \lambda(x_t - x^*)^2. \qquad (6.12)$$

(3) *Case 3.* Inflation Inertia. Equation 6.11 now holds with $L_t$ given by

$$L_t = (\pi_t - \gamma\pi_{t-1})^2 + \lambda(x_t - x^*)^2.$$

In the basic analysis Woodford (2003a) also considers the case of habit persistence in the preferences of the representative household and finds that Equation 6.9 can be modified to incorporate $x_{t-1}$.[5] He further shows that the modified equation can also be written in the form of quadratic functions of inflation rate and current and lagged output gaps.

While the models above are discussed in a cashless economy, in the extensions of analysis Woodford (2003a) considers the effect

---

[5] The reader is referred to Woodford (2003a, Chapter 5, pp. 332–335) for the discussion of habit persistence.

of transaction frictions. Therefore, in the extended models interest rates will be taken into account. The approximation of the representative household's utility function is, as a result, correspondingly modified. Under certain assumptions, for example, the approximation in Equation 6.11 is changed with $L_t$ defined as

$$L_t = \pi_t^2 + \lambda_x(x_t - x^*)^2 + \lambda_i(i_t - i^*)^2,$$

where $i_t$ denotes the nominal rate and $i^*$ is an optimal nominal interest rate. Woodford (2003a) extends the basic analysis by considering not only transaction frictions, but also the zero-interest-rate bound, asymmetric disturbances, sticky wages and prices and time-varying tax wedges or markups. In all cases he finds that the utility function of the representative household can be approximated with the Taylor-series expansion and, as a result, be written in alternative forms of a quadratic loss function of the inflation rate, output gap and interest rate.

In Woodford (2003a, Chapter 4) the IS equation[6]

$$x_t = E_t x_{t+1} - \sigma(i_t - E_t \pi_{t+1} - r_t^n),$$

and the interest-rate rule[7]

$$i_t = \bar{\imath}_t + \phi_\pi(\pi_t - \bar{\pi}) + \phi_x(x_t - \bar{x})/4$$

with the natural rate of output, $Y_t^n$, and the natural rate of interest, $r_t^n$, are impacted by real shocks determining the natural magnitudes of $Y_t^n$ and $r_t^n$. Although, Woodford, following Wicksell and Friedman, would like to formulate them as natural magnitudes, as benchmarks, they are not, as Blanchard (2005) has recently argued, and as discussed in Chapter 3, independent of the persistent effects

---

[6] $x_t$ denotes the output gap $Y_t - Y_t^n$, with $Y_t$ being the actual output and $Y_t^n$ the natural rate of output. $i_t$ denotes the nominal interest rate and $r_t^n$ the natural rate of interest.

[7] Here $\bar{\imath}_t$ is an exogenous term, $\bar{\pi}$ is the inflation target, and $\bar{x}$ is the steady-state value of output gap.

of monetary policy on output and employment. Because of the ambiguity of what the natural rate $r^n$ represents, we rather have preferred in our book, and will prefer, to define the output gap as actual output relative to some detrended output as Taylor (1993, 1999c) has suggested.[8]

Returning to the traditional loss function, some researchers, Nobay and Peel (2003), for example, argue that the loss function of the central bank may be asymmetric rather than symmetric. Therefore, the quadratic loss functions proposed above may not appropriately express the central bank's preferences. Therefore, some research has been done in the framework of an asymmetric loss function. A typical asymmetric loss function is the so-called LINEX function.[9] To be precise, the central bank may suffer lower loss when inflation is under its target than when it is above its target, and the opposite is true of output gap. Dolado et al. (2001) show that most central banks show a stronger reaction to the positive inflation deviation than to the negative one, but no asymmetric behavior with respect to output gap is found except for the Federal Reserve.

Another issue is the shape of the Phillips curve and monetary policy. Tambakis (1998) explores monetary policy with a convex Phillips curve and an asymmetric loss function and finds that "for parameters estimates relevant to the United States, the symmetric loss function dominates the asymmetric alternative" (Tambakis, 1998, abstract). Chadha and Schellekens (1998) also explore monetary policy with an asymmetric loss function and argue that

---

[8] Although, the Woodford concept of natural interest rate and natural output is theoretically more elaborate, the deficient classification of what is "natural" and of how to accurately empirically measure them leads us to prefer the traditional definition of output gap. Also, recent literature on RBC models have shown, see Hornstein and Uhlig (2000) and Grüne and Semmler (2004b), that there is currently no consensus of what preference should explain the natural interest rate. Since the risk-free interest rate, a proxy for the natural interest rate, is an asset return, preferences have a decisive impact on the natural interest rate.

[9] The graph of this function is shown in Figure 8.3.

asymmetries affect the optimal rule under both additive and multiplicative uncertainty, but the policy rule is shown to be similar or equivalent to that obtained in the case of a quadratic loss function. Moreover, they further claim that the assumption of quadratic loss functions may not be so drastic in monetary policy-making. Svensson (2002, p. 5) also claims that a symmetric loss function is undesirable because too low inflation can be as great a problem as too high inflation, since the former may lead to liquidity trap and deflationary spirals, as has happened in Japan. He further argues that "asymmetric loss functions are frequently motivated from a descriptive rather than prescriptive point of view", and that central banks should make decisions from a prescriptive point of view (Svensson, 2002, p. 5).

Overall, our discussion of the literature discussed above may justify that we take a short cut and assume, as a reasonable first approximation, that the central bank pursues monetary policy to minimize a quadratic loss function.

### 6.3.2. Derivation of an interest-rate rule

Next, we show how to derive an interest-rate rule from a dynamic macroeconomic model with a loss function of the monetary authority. The simple model reads

$$\underset{\{r_t\}_0^\infty}{\text{Min}} \sum_{t=0}^{\infty} \rho^t L_t \tag{6.13}$$

with[10]

$$L_t = (\pi_t - \pi^*)^2 + \lambda y_t^2, \qquad \lambda > 0$$

subject to

$$\pi_{t+1} = \alpha_1 \pi_t + \alpha_2 y_t, \qquad \alpha_i > 0, \tag{6.14}$$

$$y_{t+1} = \beta_1 y_t - \beta_2 (r_t - \pi_t), \qquad \beta_i > 0, \tag{6.15}$$

---

[10] If $\lambda = 0$, the model is referred to as "strict inflation targeting", here we assume $\lambda > 0$, therefore, it is "flexible inflation targeting".

where $\pi_t$ denotes the deviation of the inflation rate from its target $\pi^*$ (assumed to be zero in the model), $y_t$ is the output gap, $r_t$ denotes the gap between the short-term nominal rate $R_t$ and its long-run equilibrium level, $\bar{R}$, namely $r_t = R_t - \bar{R}$. $\rho$ is the discount factor between 0 and 1. Equation 6.14 is the Phillips curve and Equation 6.15 is the IS curve.[11]

Following Svensson (1997, 1999b), we will derive the optimal monetary policy rule from the above model.[12] Let us ignore the state equation of $y_t$ at the moment. The problem now turns out to be

$$V(\pi_t) = \underset{y_t}{\text{Min}} \left[ (\pi_t^2 + \lambda y_t^2) + \rho V(\pi_{t+1}) \right] \qquad (6.16)$$

subject to

$$\pi_{t+1} = \alpha_1 \pi_t + \alpha_2 y_t. \qquad (6.17)$$

Equation 6.16 is the so-called Hamilton–Jacobi–Bellman (HJB) equation and $V(\pi_t)$ is the value function, with $y_t$ being the control variable now. For a linear-quadratic control problem above, it is clear that the value function must be quadratic. Therefore, we assume that the value function takes the form

$$V(\pi_t) = \Omega_0 + \Omega_1 \pi_t^2, \qquad (6.18)$$

where $\Omega_0$ and $\Omega_1$ remain to be determined. The first-order condition turns out to be

$$\lambda y_t + \rho \alpha_2 \Omega_1 \pi_{t+1} = 0$$

[11] In order for consistent expectations to exist, $\alpha_1$ is usually assumed to be 1. The loss function here is similar to that in the second case of Woodford (2003a) shown above with $x^*$ being zero. The discussion about $x^* = 0$ can be found in Woodford (2003a, p. 407).

[12] The reader can also be referred to Svensson (1997) and the appendix of Svensson (1999b) for the derivation below.

from which one has

$$\pi_{t+1} = -\frac{\lambda}{\rho\alpha_2\Omega_1}y_t. \tag{6.19}$$

Substituting Equation 6.19 into Equation 6.15 gives

$$y_t = -\frac{\rho\alpha_1\alpha_2\Omega_1}{\lambda + \rho\alpha_2^2\Omega_1}\pi_t, \tag{6.20}$$

and after substituting this equation back into Equation 6.19, one has

$$\pi_{t+1} = \frac{\alpha_1\lambda}{\lambda + \rho\alpha_2^2\Omega_1}\pi_t. \tag{6.21}$$

By applying Equations 6.16, 6.18 and 6.20, the envelop theorem gives us the following equation:

$$V_\pi(\pi_t) = 2\left(1 + \frac{\alpha_1^2\rho\lambda\Omega_1}{\lambda + \rho\alpha_2^2\Omega_1}\right)\pi_t,$$

and from Equation 6.18, one has

$$V_\pi(\pi_t) = 2\Omega_1\pi_t,$$

these two equations tell us that

$$\Omega_1 = 1 + \frac{\alpha_1^2\rho\lambda\Omega_1}{\lambda + \rho\alpha_2^2\Omega_1}.$$

The right-hand side of this equation has the limit

$$1 + \frac{\alpha_1^2\lambda}{\alpha_2^2}$$

as $\Omega_1 \to \infty$. The root of $\Omega_1$ larger than one can, therefore, be solved from the equation

$$\Omega_1^2 - \left[1 - \frac{(1 - \rho\alpha_1^2)\lambda}{\rho\alpha_2^2}\right]\Omega_1 - \frac{\lambda}{\rho\alpha_2^2} = 0,$$

which gives the solution of $\Omega_1$:

$$\Omega_1 = \frac{1}{2}\left(1 - \frac{\lambda(1 - \rho\alpha_1^2)}{\rho\alpha_2^2} + \sqrt{\left(1 - \frac{\lambda(1 - \rho\alpha_1^2)}{\rho\alpha_2^2}\right)^2 + \frac{4\lambda}{\rho\alpha_2^2}}\right).$$

(6.22)

By substituting $t + 1$ for $t$ into Equation 6.20, one has

$$y_{t+1} = -\frac{\rho\alpha_1\alpha_2\Omega_1}{\lambda + \rho\alpha_2^2\Omega_1}\pi_{t+1}.$$

(6.23)

Substituting Equations 6.14 and 6.15 into Equation 6.23 with some computation, one obtains the optimal decision rule for the short-term interest rate:

$$R_t = \bar{R} + f_1\pi_t + f_2 y_t$$

(6.24)

with

$$f_1 = 1 + \frac{\rho\alpha_1^2\alpha_2\Omega_1}{(\lambda + \rho\alpha_2^2\Omega_1)\beta_2},$$

(6.25)

$$f_2 = \frac{\beta_1}{\beta_2} + \frac{\rho\alpha_2^2\alpha_1\Omega_1}{(\lambda + \rho\alpha_2^2\Omega_1)\beta_2}.$$

(6.26)

Equation 6.24 shows that the optimal short-term interest rate should be a linear function of the inflation rate and output gap. This is similar to the Taylor rule presented before in the sense that the short-term interest rate is a linear function of the output gap and inflation deviation. Note that $f_1 > 1$, indicating that the optimal monetary policy should be "active". That is, there is a more than one-for-one increase in the nominal interest rate with the increase in inflation.

### 6.3.3. Simulation of the model

Next, we undertake some simulations with the US quarterly data from 1961.1 to 1999.4. The seemingly uncorrelated regression (SUR) estimation of the IS and Phillips curves reads[13]

$$\pi_{t+1} = \underset{(0.800)}{0.0007} + \underset{(59.406)}{0.984}\,\pi_t + \underset{(3.948)}{0.066}\,y_t, \quad R^2 = 0.958, \qquad (6.27)$$

$$y_{t+1} = \underset{(0.529)}{-0.0006} + \underset{(20.203)}{0.960}\,y_t - \underset{(2.662)}{0.157}\,\{(R_t - \pi_t) - \bar{R}\},$$

$$R^2 = 0.788. \qquad (6.28)$$

With the parameters estimated above and $\lambda = 0.1, \rho = 0.985$, one obtains $\Omega_1 = 4.93$ and the following optimal policy reaction function

$$R_t = \bar{R} + 17.50\pi_t + 7.22y_t. \qquad (6.29)$$

Let both $\pi_0$ and $y_0$ be 0.03, the simulations with $\lambda = 0.1$ are presented in Figure 6.1. Next, we undertake the simulation with a larger $\lambda$. Let $\lambda = 10$, one obtains $\Omega_1 = 22.76$ and the following optimal interest-rate reaction function

$$R_t = \bar{R} + 1.92\pi_t + 6.18y_t \qquad (6.30)$$

with the simulations presented in Figure 6.2. The response coefficients of the inflation deviation and output gap are relatively large, because the estimate of $\beta_1$ is relatively larger than that of $\beta_2$.

Figures 6.1A and 6.2A represent the path of the optimal interest rate, Figures 6.1B,C and 6.2B,C are the optimal trajectories of $\pi_t$ and $y_t$, and Figures 6.1D and 6.2D are the phase diagrams of the inflation deviation and output gap with starting values $(0.03, 0.03)$. Both Figures 6.1 and 6.2 show that the optimal trajectories of the inflation

---

[13] We assume $\bar{R}$ to be zero for simplicity. The inflation rate is measured by changes in the CPI, the output gap is measured by the percentage deviation of the log of the introduction production index (base year: 1995) from its HP filtered trend. $R_t$ is the federal funds rate. *Data sources*: OECD and IMF.

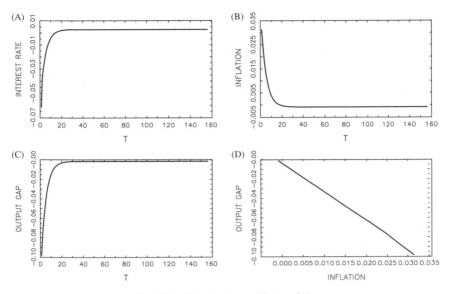

Fig. 6.1: Simulations with $\lambda = 0.1$.

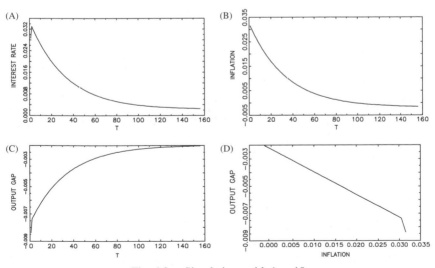

Fig. 6.2: Simulations with $\lambda = 10$.

deviation and output gap converge to zero over time. As the inflation deviation and output gap converge to zero, the optimal feedback rule converges to the long-run equilibrium interest rate $\bar{R}$. From Equation 6.15 one knows that as $\pi_{t+1}$, $\pi_t$, $y_{t+1}$ and $y_t$ converge to zero, $R_t \to \bar{R}$.

Next, we explore how the relative weight of output stabilization, $\lambda$, influences the optimal monetary policy rule. Denoting $f = f_1/f_2$, one has

$$f = \frac{1}{\Theta}[(\lambda + \rho\alpha_2^2\Omega_1)\beta_2 + \rho\alpha_1^2\alpha_2\Omega_1] \tag{6.31}$$

with $\Theta = (\lambda + \rho\alpha_2^2\Omega_1)\beta_1 + \rho\alpha_2^2\alpha_1\Omega_1$, and

$$\frac{df}{d\lambda} = \frac{1}{\Theta^2}[\rho\alpha_1\alpha_2\Omega_1(\alpha_2\beta_2 - \alpha_1\beta_1)]. \tag{6.32}$$

It is clear that $df/d\lambda < 0\ (>0)$ if $\alpha_2\beta_2 - \alpha_1\beta_1 < 0\ (>0)$. As long as the inflation and output are greatly influenced by their lags, as is usually true in estimations, one has $\alpha_2\beta_2 - \alpha_1\beta_1 < 0$. This implies that if $\lambda$ increases, namely, if more emphasis is put on the output stabilization than on the inflation, the ratio of the reaction coefficient on the output gap and that on the inflation in the optimal monetary policy rule is correspondingly relatively larger. In the simulation above $f = 0.41$ if $\lambda = 0.1$, and $f = 3.22$ if $\lambda = 10$.

Recently, some researchers, Woodford (2001b), for example, argue that central banks are not only concerned with the stabilization of the inflation and output, but also concerned with the stabilization of the short-term interest rate. If the interest-rate stabilization is also taken as a target and included into the return function, the problem can be simply written as

$$\operatorname*{Min}_{\{R_t\}_0^\infty} \sum_{t=0}^\infty \rho^t U_t, \quad U_t = (\pi_t - \pi^*)^2 + \lambda_1 y_t^2 + \lambda_2(R_t - \bar{R})^2, \quad \lambda_1, \lambda_2 > 0$$

$$\tag{6.33}$$

subject to Equations 6.14 and 6.15. Let $r_t = R_t - \bar{R}$ be the control, this problem can be solved by the way of standard LQ optimal control method.[14]

With the same parameters as in the previous section, and let $\lambda_1 = 0.1$, and $\lambda_2 = 1$, we get

$$P = -\begin{pmatrix} 25.61 & 11.99 \\ 11.99 & 6.89 \end{pmatrix} \qquad \text{and} \qquad F = -(1.73 \quad 1.00),$$

and, therefore, we have

$$R_t = \bar{R} + 1.73\pi_t + y_t \tag{6.34}$$

with value function $V(\pi_t, y_t) = 25.61\pi_t^2 + 6.89y_t^2 + 24.00\pi_t y_t$. If we change $\lambda_1$ from 0.1 to 10, we have

$$P = -\begin{pmatrix} 32.81 & 10.42 \\ 10.42 & 24.88 \end{pmatrix} \qquad \text{and} \qquad F = -(1.38 \quad 2.38),$$

and

$$R_t = \bar{R} + 1.38\pi_t + 2.38y_t, \tag{6.35}$$

and

$$V(\pi_t, y_t) = 32.81\pi_t^2 + 24.88y_t^2 + 20.84\pi_t y_t.$$

It is obvious that the monetary reaction functions are still linear combinations of inflation and output gaps, similar to that derived from last section. But the coefficients on inflation and output gaps are smaller than when no interest-rate stabilization is considered. Namely, in Equation 6.29, the coefficients of the inflation deviation and output gap are 17.50 and 7.22, respectively, while in Equation 6.34 they are 1.73 and 1.00, and in Equation 6.30 they are 1.92 and 6.18, respectively, while in Equation 6.35 they are

---

[14] The Matlab program OLRP.m by Ljungvist and Sargent (2000) is applied here for the simulation.

1.38 and 2.38. Since this is a typical LQ problem, the state variables will converge to their equilibria (zero) over time.

## 6.4. MONETARY POLICY RULES WITH ADAPTIVE LEARNING

Up to now we have explored monetary policy rules assuming that economic agents (central banks, for example) know the specification of models. But in reality this may not be true. Zhang and Semmler (2005) explore both parameter and shock uncertainties in the US economy by way of a State-Space model with Markov-Switching. They find that there have been great uncertainties in the US IS and Phillips curves. It is clear that the optimal monetary policy rule derived in the previous section is largely affected by the parameters in the IS and Phillips curves, that is, if the IS and Phillips curves are uncertain, it is difficult to define accurately the monetary policy rule.

Facing such uncertainties, what can central banks do? Recently, numerous papers have been contributed to this problem. Svensson (1999b), Orphanides and Williams (2002), Tetlow and von zur Muehlen (2003), Söderström (2002), and Beck and Wieland (2002), for example, explore optimal monetary policy rules under the assumption that the economic agents learn the parameters in the model in a certain manner. One assumption is that the economic agents may learn the parameters using the Kalman filter. This assumption has been taken by Tucci (1997) and Beck and Wieland (2002). Another learning mechanism which is also applied frequently is recursive least squares (RLS). This kind of learning mechanism has been applied by Sargent (1999) and Orphanides and Williams (2002). By intuition we would expect that economic agents reduce uncertainty, and therefore, improve economic models by learning with all information available. Of course, there is the possibility that economic agents do not improve model specification but seek a monetary policy rule robust to uncertainty. This is what robust control theory aims at.

In this section we will explore monetary policy rules under uncertainty under the assumption that the central banks reduce uncertainty by way of learning. As mentioned above, some researchers, Beck and Wieland (2002) and Orphanides and Williams (2002), for example, have explored this problem. Besides the difference in the learning algorithm, another difference between Beck and Wieland (2002) and Orphanides and Williams (2002) is that the former do not consider the role of expectations in the model, while the latter take into account expectations in the Phillips curve. Unlike Beck and Wieland (2002), Orphanides and Williams (2002) do not employ an intertemporal framework. They provide a learning algorithm with constant gain but do not use a discounted loss function. Moreover, Orphanides and Williams (2002) assume that the government knows the true model, but the private agents do not know the true model and have to learn the parameters with the RLS algorithm. In their case the government and the private agents are treated differently. Sargent (1999) employs both a learning algorithm as well as a discounted loss function but in a linear-quadratic model. This implies that after one step of learning the learned coefficient is presumed to hold forever when the LQ problem is solved. In our model below, however, both the central bank and the private agents are learning the parameters, that is, they are not treated differently.

The difference of our model from that of Beck and Wieland (2002) can be summarized as follows. First, we take into account expectations. This is consistent with the model of Orphanides and Williams (2002). Second, we employ the RLS learning algorithm instead of the Kalman filter. In fact, Harvey (1989) and Sargent (1999) prove that RLS is a specific form of the Kalman filter. Evans and Honkapohja (2001) analyze expectations and learning mechanisms in macroeconomics in detail. The difference from Sargent (1999) is that we can, in fact, allow for coefficient drift through learning by RLS and solve a non-linear optimal control model using a dynamic programming algorithm.

Orphanides and Williams (2002) assume that the current inflation rate is not only affected by the inflation lag but also by inflation expectations. Following Orphanides and Williams (2002), we assume that the linear Phillips curve has the following form:

$$\pi_t = \gamma_1 \pi_{t-1} + \gamma_2 \pi_t^e + \gamma_3 y_t + \epsilon_t, \qquad \epsilon_t \sim \text{iid}(0, \sigma_\epsilon^2), \quad (6.36)$$

where $\pi_t^e$ denotes the agents' (including the central bank) expected inflation rate based on the time $t - 1$ information, $\gamma_1$, $\gamma_2 \in (0, 1)$, $\gamma_3 > 0$ and $\epsilon_t$ is a serially uncorrelated shock. We further assume the IS equation reads[15]

$$y_t = -\theta r_{t-1} + \eta_t, \qquad \theta > 0, \eta_t \sim \text{iid}(0, \sigma_\eta^2) \quad (6.37)$$

with $r_t$ denoting the deviation of the short-term real interest rate from its equilibrium level. Substituting Equation 6.37 into Equation 6.36, we have

$$\pi_t = \gamma_1 \pi_{t-1} + \gamma_2 \pi_t^e - \gamma_3 \theta r_{t-1} + \varepsilon_t, \ \varepsilon_t \sim \text{iid}(0, \sigma_\varepsilon^2) \quad (6.38)$$

with $\varepsilon_t = \gamma_3 \eta_t + \epsilon_t$ and $\sigma_\varepsilon^2 = \gamma_3^2 \sigma_\eta^2 + \sigma_\epsilon^2$.

In the case of rational expectations, namely, $\pi_t^e = E_{t-1} \pi_t$, we get

$$E_{t-1} \pi_t = \gamma_1 \pi_{t-1} + \gamma_2 E_{t-1} \pi_t - \gamma_3 \theta r_{t-1},$$

that is,

$$E_{t-1} \pi_t = \bar{a} \pi_{t-1} + \bar{b} r_{t-1}$$

with

$$\bar{a} = \frac{\gamma_1}{1 - \gamma_2}, \tag{6.39}$$

$$\bar{b} = -\frac{\gamma_3 \theta}{1 - \gamma_2}. \tag{6.40}$$

With these results we get the rational expectations equilibrium (REE)

$$\pi_t = \bar{a} \pi_{t-1} + \bar{b} r_{t-1} + \varepsilon_t. \tag{6.41}$$

---

[15] This is the same as Orphanides and Williams (2002).

Now suppose that the agents believe the inflation rate follows the process

$$\pi_t = a\pi_{t-1} + br_{t-1} + \varepsilon_t$$

corresponding to the REE, but that $a$ and $b$ are unknown and have to be learned. Suppose that the agents have data on the economy of periods $i = 0, \ldots, t - 1$. Thus the time $t - 1$ information set is $\{\pi_i, r_i\}_{i=0}^{t-1}$. Further, suppose that agents estimate $a$ and $b$ by a least squares regression of $\pi_i$ on $\pi_{i-1}$ and $r_{i-1}$. The estimates will be updated over time as more information is collected. Let $(a_{t-1}, b_{t-1})$ denote the estimates through time $t - 1$, the forecast of the inflation rate is then given by

$$\pi_t^e = a_{t-1}\pi_{t-1} + b_{t-1}r_{t-1}. \tag{6.42}$$

The least squares formula gives the equations

$$\begin{pmatrix} a_t \\ b_t \end{pmatrix} = \left( \sum_{i=1}^{t} z_i' z_i \right)^{-1} \left( \sum_{i=1}^{t} z_i' \pi_i \right), \tag{6.43}$$

where $z_i = (\; \pi_{i-1} \quad r_{i-1} \;)'$.

Defining $c_t = \begin{pmatrix} a_t \\ b_t \end{pmatrix}$, we can also compute Equation 6.43 using the stochastic approximation of the RLS equations

$$c_t = c_{t-1} + \kappa_t V_t^{-1} z_t(\pi_t - z_t' c_{t-1}), \tag{6.44}$$

$$V_t = V_{t-1} + \kappa_t(z_t z_t' - V_{t-1}), \tag{6.45}$$

where $c_t$ and $V_t$ denote the coefficient vector and the moment matrix for $z_t$ using data $i = 1, \ldots, t$. $\kappa_t$ is the gain. To generate the least squares values, one must set the initial values of $c_t$ and $V_t$ approximately.[16]

---

[16] Evans and Honkapohja (2001, Chapter 2, footnote 4) explain how to set the starting values of $c_t$ and $V_t$ as follows. Assuming $Z_k = (z_1, \ldots z_k)'$ is of full rank and letting $\pi^k$ denote $\pi^k = (\pi_1, \ldots, \pi_k)'$, the initial value $c_k$ is given by $c_k = Z_k^{-1}\pi^k$ and the initial value $V_k$ is given by $V_k = k^{-1}\sum_{i=1}^{k} z_i z_i'$.

The gain $\kappa_t$ is an important variable. According to Evans and Honkapohja (2001), the assumption that $\kappa_t = t^{-1}$ (decreasing gain) together with the condition $\gamma_2 < 1$ ensures the convergence of $c_t$ as $t \to \infty$. That is, as $t \to \infty$, $c_t \to \bar{c}$ with probability 1, with $\bar{c} = \begin{pmatrix} \bar{a} \\ \bar{b} \end{pmatrix}$, and therefore, $\pi_t^e \to \text{REE}$.

As indicated by Sargent (1999) and Evans and Honkapohja (2001), if $\kappa_t$ is a constant, however, there might be difficulties of convergence to the REE. If the model is non-stochastic and $\kappa_t$ sufficiently small, $\pi_t^e$ converges with probability 1 under the condition $\gamma_2 < 1$. However, if the model is stochastic with $\gamma_2 < 1$, the belief does not converge to REE, but to an ergodic distribution around it. Here we follow Orphanides and Williams (2002) and assume that agents are constantly learning in a changing environment. The assumption of a constant gain indicates that the agents believe the Phillips curve may experience structural changes over time. Orphanides and Williams (2002) denote the case of $\kappa_t = 1/t$ as infinite memory and the case of constant $\kappa_t$ as finite memory. Similar to many papers on monetary policy (Svensson, 1997; 1999a, for example) we assume that the central bank pursues a monetary policy by a Quadratic loss function. The problem reads as

$$\underset{\{r_t\}_0^\infty}{\text{Min}} \, E_0 \sum_{t=0}^{\infty} \rho^t L(\pi_t), \qquad L(\pi_t) \equiv (\pi_t - \pi^*)^2 \qquad (6.46)$$

subject to Equations 6.38, 6.42, 6.44 and 6.45. $\pi^*$ is the target inflation rate, which will be assumed to be zero just for simplicity.

Note that the difference of our model from that of Sargent (1999) is obvious, although, he also applies the RLS learning algorithm and an optimal control framework with infinite horizon. Yet, Sargent (1999) constructs his results in two steps. First, following the RLS with a decreasing or constant gain, the agents estimate a model of the economy (the Phillips curve) using the latest available data, updating parameter estimates from period to period. Second, once the parameter is updated, the government pretends that the updated parameter will govern the dynamics forever and derives an optimal policy from an LQ control model. These two steps are repeated over and over. As remarked by Tetlow and von zur Muehlen (2003), however, these two steps are inconsistent with each other. Our model, however, treats the changing parameters as endogenous variables in a non-linear optimal control problem. This is similar to the methodology used by Beck and Wieland (2002).

As mentioned above, if the unknown parameters are adaptively estimated with RLS with a small and constant gain, they will converge in distributions in a stochastic model and converge w.p.1 in a non-stochastic model. But in an optimal control problem such as Equation 6.46 with non-linear state equation the model will not necessarily converge even if the state equations are non-stochastic.

Next, we undertake some simulations for the model. Though the return function is quadratic and the Phillips curve linear, the problem falls outside the scope of LQ optimal control problems, since some parameters in the Phillips curve are time-varying and follow non-linear paths. Therefore, the problem cannot be solved analytically and numerical solutions have to be employed. In the simulations below we resort to the algorithm developed by Grüne (1997), who applies adaptive instead of uniform grids. A less technical description of this algorithm can be found in Grüne and Semmler (2004a). The simulations are undertaken for the deterministic case. In order to simplify the simulations, we assume that $a_t$ is known and equals $\bar{a}$. Therefore, only $b_t$ has to be learned in the model. In this case, we have $c_t = b_t$ and $z_i = r_{i-1}$. As mentioned by Beck and Wieland (2002, p. 1361), the reason for focusing on the unknown parameter $b$ is that "this parameter is multiplicative to the decision variable $r_t$ and, therefore, central to the trade-off between current control and estimation".

### 6.4.1. Numerical study

In the numerical study, undertaken by the above mentioned dynamic programming algorithm, we assume $\gamma_1 = 0.6$, $\gamma_2 = 0.4$, $\gamma_3 = 0.5$, $\theta = 0.4$, $\rho = 0.985$ and $\kappa_t = 0.05$. The initial values of $\pi_t$, $b_t$ and $V_t$ are 0.2, $-0.6$ and 0.04. The paths of $\pi_t$, $b_t$, $V_t$, and $r_t$ are shown in Figure 6.3A–D, respectively. Figure 6.3E is the phase diagram of $\pi_t$ and $r_t$. Neither the state variables nor the control variable converges. In fact, they fluctuate cyclically. We try the simulations with different initial values of the state variables and smaller $\kappa_t$ (0.01, for example) and find that in no case do the variables converge. Similar results are obtained with different values for $\gamma_1$ (0.9 and 0.3, for example) and $\gamma_2$ (0.1 and 0.7, for example).

With the parameters above, we have $\bar{a} = 1$, $\bar{b} = 0.33$, therefore, the REE in the stochastic version is

$$\pi_t = \pi_{t-1} - 0.33 r_{t-1} + \varepsilon_t. \tag{6.47}$$

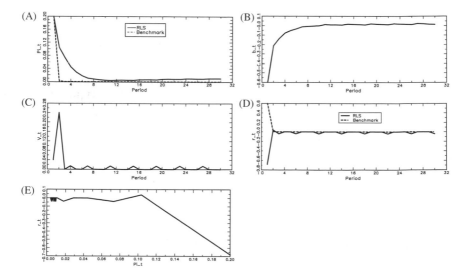

Fig. 6.3:   Simulations of RLS learning (solid) and benchmark model (dashed).

In the case of RLS learning, however, we have

$$\pi_t = \pi_{t-1} + \tilde{b}_t r_{t-1} + \varepsilon_t,$$

with

$$\tilde{b}_t = \gamma_2 b_{t-1} - \gamma_3 \theta.$$

If there is perfect knowledge with rational expectation, $\pi_t$ can converge to its target value $\pi^*$ (zero here), since the model then becomes a typical LQ control problem which has converging state and control variables in a non-stochastic model. We define this case as the benchmark model. The results of the benchmark model are shown in Figure 6.3A and D (dashed line). Note that in the benchmark model there is only one state variable, namely $\pi_t$ with dynamics denoted by Equation 6.47. In the non-stochastic benchmark model the optimal monetary policy rule turns out to be $r_t = 3.00\pi_t$ and substituting this into the non-stochastic version of Equation 6.47 generates the optimal trajectory of $\pi_t$, that is, $\pi_t = 0.01\pi_{t-1}$. It is obvious that in the steady state we have $\pi_t = \pi_{t-1} = 0$. From Figure 6.3A and D we observe that $\pi_t$ and $r_t$ converge to zero in the benchmark model.

## 6.5. MONETARY POLICY RULES WITH ROBUST CONTROL

Facing uncertainties, economic agents can improve their knowledge of economic models by learning with all information available. This is what has been explored above. A disadvantage of the adaptive learning analyzed in the previous section is that we have considered only parameter uncertainty. Other uncertainties such as shock uncertainty may also exist. Moreover, as studied in some recent literature, there is the possibility that economic agents resort to a strategy robust to uncertainty instead of learning. This problem has recently been largely explored with the robust control theory. Robust control induces the economic agents to seek an optimal policy rule in the "worst case". The robust control theory assumes that there is some model misspecfication—not only the uncertainty of the parameters like $\alpha$ and $\beta$ in the IS- and Phillips curves, but also other kinds of uncertainties. Therefore, robust control might deal with more general uncertainty than adaptive learning. Robust control is now given more and more attention in the field of macroeconomics, because the classic optimal control theory can hardly deal with model misspecification. On the basis of some earlier papers (see Hansen and Sargent, 1999; 2001a,b), Hansen and Sargent (2002) explore robust control in macroeconomics in details. Cagetti et al. (2002) also employ the robust control in macro-economics. Svensson (2000) analyzes the idea of robust control in a simpler framework. Giordani and Söderlind (2002), however, extend robust control by including forward-looking behavior.

In this section we will also explore monetary policy rules using robust control. Before starting empirical research we will briefly sketch the framework of robust control, following Hansen and Sargent (2002). Let the loss function be $L(y, u) = -(x'Qx + u'Ru)$, with $Q$ being positive semi-definite and $R$ being positive definite matrices, respectively. The optimal linear-regulator problem without model misspecification is

$$\underset{\{u_t\}_{t=0}^{\infty}}{\text{Max}} \ E_0 \sum_{t=0}^{\infty} \rho^t L(x_t, u_t), \qquad 0 < \rho < 1 \qquad (6.48)$$

subject to the so-called approximating model[17]

$$x_{t+1} = Ax_t + Bu_t + C\breve{\epsilon}_{t+1}, \qquad x_0 \text{ given}, \qquad (6.49)$$

where $\{\breve{\epsilon}\}$ is an iid vector process subject to normal distribution with mean zero and identity covariance matrix. In case there is model misspecification which cannot be depicted by $\breve{\epsilon}$, Hansen and Sargent (2003) take a set of models surrounding Equation 6.49 of the form

---

[17] The matrices $A$, $B$, $Q$ and $R$ are assumed to satisfy the assumptions stated in Hansen and Sargent (2003, Chapter 3).

(the so-called distorted model)

$$x_{t+1} = Ax_t + Bu_t + C(\epsilon_{t+1} + \omega_{t+1}), \qquad (6.50)$$

where $\{\epsilon_t\}$ is another iid process subject to normal distribution with mean zero and identity covariance matrix, and $\omega_{t+1}$ is a vector process that reads

$$\omega_{t+1} = g_t(x_t, x_{t-1}, \ldots) \qquad (6.51)$$

with $\{g_t\}$ being a measurable function. Hansen and Sargent (2003) restrain the approximation errors by

$$E_0 \sum_{t=0}^{\infty} \rho^{t+1} \omega_{t+1}' \omega_{t+1} \leq \eta_0 \qquad (6.52)$$

to show that Equation 6.49 is a reasonable approximation when Equation 6.50 generates the data. In order to solve the robust control problem Equation 6.48 subject to Equations 6.50 and 6.52, Hansen and Sargent (2003) consider two kinds of robust control problems, the constraint problem and the multiplier problem, which differ in how the constraint Equation 6.52 is dealt with. The constraint problem reads

$$\underset{\{u_t\}_{t=0}^{\infty}}{\text{Max}} \ \underset{\{\omega_{t+1}\}_{t=0}^{\infty}}{\text{Min}} \ E_0 \sum_{t=0}^{\infty} \rho^t U(x_t, u_t) \qquad (6.53)$$

subject to Equations 6.50 and 6.52. Given $\theta \in (\underline{\theta}, +\infty)$ with $\underline{\theta} > 0$, the multiplier problem reads as

$$\underset{\{u_t\}_{t=0}^{\infty}}{\text{Max}} \ \underset{\{\omega_{t+1}\}_{t=0}^{\infty}}{\text{Min}} \ E_0 \sum_{t=0}^{\infty} \rho^t \{U(x_t, u_t) + \rho\theta\omega_{t+1}'\omega_{t+1}\} \qquad (6.54)$$

subject to Equation 6.50. Hansen and Sargent (2003, Chapter 6) prove that under certain conditions the two problems have the same outcomes. Therefore, solving one of the two problems is sufficient.

The robustness parameter $\theta$ plays an important role in the problem's solution. If $\theta$ is $+\infty$, the problem then becomes the usual optimal control without model misspecification. In order to find a reasonable value for $\theta$, Hansen and Sargent (2003, Chapter 13) design a detection error probability function by a likelihood ratio. Assume that there is a sample of observations from $t = 0$ to $T - 1$, and define $L_{ij}$ as the likelihood of this sample for model $j$ provided that the data are generated by model $i$, the likelihood ratio is then

$$r_i \equiv \log \frac{L_{ii}}{L_{ij}}. \qquad (6.55)$$

Note that $r_i$ should be larger than zero if the data are generated by model $i$. Define

$$p_i = \text{Prob}(\text{mistake}|i) = \text{freq}(r_i \leq 0),$$

$$p_j = \text{Prob}(\text{mistake}|j) = \text{freq}(r_j \leq 0).$$

Assuming equal prior weights to both models, the detection error probability can be defined as

$$p(\theta) = \tfrac{1}{2}(p_i + p_j). \qquad (6.56)$$

When a reasonable value of $p(\theta)$ is chosen, a corresponding value of $\theta$ can be determined by inverting the probability function defined in Equation 6.56. Hansen and Sargent (2003, Chapter 7) find that $\theta$ can be defined as the negative inverse value of the so-called risk-sensitivity parameter $\sigma$, that is $\theta = -1/\sigma$.

Note the interpretation of the detection error probability. The larger the detection error probability, the more difficult it is to tell the two models apart. In case $p = 0.5$ ($\theta = +\infty$), the two models cannot be told apart from each other. So a central bank can choose a $\theta$ according to how large a detection error probability it wants. Note that the higher the $\theta$, the lower is the robustness, not the opposite. In the research below we can see that a larger detection error probability corresponds to a larger $\theta$. Gonzalez and Rodriguez

(2003) explore how the robust parameter $\theta$ affects the control variable and prove that in a one-state, one-control model, the response is a hyperbolic function with a discontinuity at $\underline{\theta}$. Such a response is concave on the right side of the discontinuity and convex on the left. In the research below we will explore whether this is true of a two-state and one-control model.

$$\mathcal{D}(P) = P + PC(\theta I - C'PC)^{-1}C'P, \qquad (6.57)$$

$$\mathcal{F}(\Omega) = \rho[R + \rho B'\Omega B]^{-1}B'\Omega A, \qquad (6.58)$$

$$\mathcal{T}(P) = Q + \rho A(P - \rho PB(R + \rho B'PB)^{-1}B'P)A. \qquad (6.59)$$

Let $P$ be the fixed point of iterations on $T \circ \mathcal{D}$ :

$$P = T \circ \mathcal{D}(P),$$

then the solution of the multiplier problem 6.54 is

$$u = -Fx, \qquad (6.60)$$

$$\omega = Kx \qquad (6.61)$$

with

$$F = \mathcal{F} \circ \mathcal{D}(P), \qquad (6.62)$$

$$K = \theta^{-1}(I - \theta^{-1}C'PC)^{-1}C'P[A - BF]. \qquad (6.63)$$

It is obvious that in case $\theta = +\infty$, $\mathcal{D}(P) = P$ and the problem above then becomes the traditional LQ problem.

### 6.5.1. Simulations

Following Rudebusch and Svensson (1999) we obtain the following OLS estimates with the US data from 1962 to 1999 of the backward-looking IS- and Phillips curves (*T*-statistics in parentheses):

$$\pi_t = \underset{(1.961)}{0.002} + \underset{(17.408)}{1.380} \pi_{t-1} - \underset{(2.967)}{0.408} \pi_{t-2} + \underset{(1.570)}{0.214} \pi_{t-3}$$

$$- \underset{(2.836)}{0.221} \pi_{t-4} + \underset{(3.024)}{0.045} y_{t-1}, \qquad R^2 = 0.970, \qquad (6.64)$$

$$y_t = \underset{(1.050)}{0.002} + \underset{(19.486)}{1.362} y_{t-1} - \underset{(7.083)}{0.498} y_{t-2} - \underset{(1.360)}{0.074} (R_{t-1} - \pi_{t-1}),$$

$$R^2 = 0.843. \quad (6.65)$$

Let $A_{11}$ be the sum of the coefficients of the inflation lags in the Phillips curves (0.965) and $A_{22}$ be the sum of the coefficients of the output gap lags in the IS curve (0.864), we define

$$A = \begin{pmatrix} 0.965 & 0.045 \\ 0.074 & 0.864 \end{pmatrix}, \qquad B = \begin{pmatrix} 0 \\ -0.074 \end{pmatrix}, \qquad x_t = \begin{pmatrix} \pi_t \\ y_t \end{pmatrix}.$$

The problem to solve turns out to be

$$\underset{\{R_t\}_{t=0}^{\infty}}{\text{Max}} \quad \underset{\{\omega_{t+1}\}_{t=0}^{\infty}}{\text{Min}} \quad E_0 \sum_{t=0}^{\infty} \rho^t [-(\pi_t^2 + \lambda y_t^2) + \rho\theta\omega'_{t+1}\omega_{t+1}]$$

subject to

$$x_{t+1} = Ax_t + BR_t + C(\epsilon_{t+1} + \omega_{t+1}).$$

With the parameters above and the starting values of $\pi_0$ and $y_0$ both being 0.02, $\lambda = 1$, $\rho = 0.985$ and

$$C = \begin{pmatrix} 0.01 & 0 \\ 0 & 0.01 \end{pmatrix},$$

we present the detection error probability in Figure 6.4.[18] If we want a detection error probability of about 0.15, $\sigma = -33$, that is $\theta = 0.03$.

---

[18] $T$ (number of periods) is taken as 150. 5000 simulations are undertaken here.

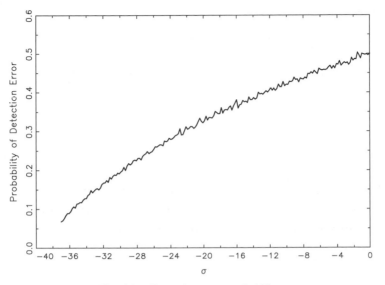

Fig. 6.4: Detection error probability.

With $\theta = 0.03$, we obtain

$$F = (10.462 \quad 12.117), \quad K = \begin{pmatrix} 5.291 & 0.247 \\ 4.737 \times 10^{-7} & 5.486 \times 10^{-7} \end{pmatrix},$$

and the value function turns out to be $V(\pi, y) = 16.240\pi^2 + 1.033y^2 + 1.421\pi y + 0.113$. If one wants a higher detection error probability, 0.40, for example, one has $\sigma = -11$ ($\theta = 0.091$), and

$$F = (7.103 \quad 11.960), \quad K = \begin{pmatrix} 1.173 & 0.055 \\ 1.072 \times 10^{-7} & 1.805 \times 10^{-7} \end{pmatrix},$$

and $V(\pi, y) = 11.134\pi^2 + 1.022y^2 + 0.945\pi y + 0.080$. In case $\theta = +\infty$,[19] one has $F = (6.438 \ 11.929)$ and $V(\pi, y) = 10.120\pi^2 + 1.020y^2 + 0.850\pi y + 0.073$. Comparing the elements in $F$ obtained

---

[19] In the simulation we just take $+\infty = 10,000$. In fact, the changes in the simulation results are too small to be observed if $\theta$ is a large number. Therefore, taking $\theta = 10,000$ can capture the simulation results of $\theta = +\infty$.

with different values of $\theta$, one finds that the lower the $\theta$, the higher is the coefficients of the inflation rate and output gap in the interest-rate rule, that is, the farther the distorted model stays away from the approximating one, the stronger is the response of the interest rate to the inflation and output gap. This is consistent with the conclusion of Giannoni (2002) who shows that uncertainty does not necessarily require caution in a forward-looking model with robust control.

We present the paths of the inflation rate, output gap and interest rate with different values of $\theta$ in Figure 6.5A–C. One finds that the lower the $\theta$, the larger the volatility of the state and control variables. The standard deviations of the state and control variables are shown in Table 6.1, which indicates that the standard deviations of the state and control variables increases if $\theta$ decreases.[20]

Next, we come to a special case, namely the case of zero shocks. What do the state and control variables look like and how can the robustness parameter $\theta$ affect the state variables and the value function? According to the certainty equivalence principle, the optimal rules of robust control with zero shocks are the same as when there are non-zero shocks, that is, $F$ and $K$ in Equations 6.62 and 6.63 do not change no matter whether there are shocks or not. The difference lies in the value function. The simulations for zero shocks and with the same parameters as in the case of non-zero shocks are shown in Figure 6.6. Figure 6.6A–C presents the paths of the state and control variables with different $\theta$. In Figure 6.6 one finds that the state variables converge to their equilibria zero no matter whether the robustness parameter is small or large. But in the case of a small robustness parameter, the state variables evolve at a higher level and converse more slowly to zero than when the robustness parameter is large. The simulations tell us that the larger

---

[20] Some researchers, Orphanides and Williams (2002), for example, assume that the loss function of central bank is the weighted sum of the variances of output gap and inflation. In this case the results numerical computation above implies that the smaller the $\theta$, the higher the loss function.

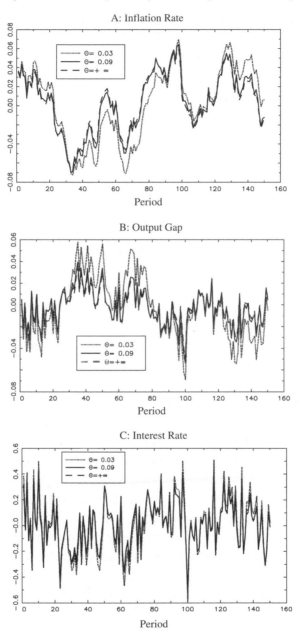

Fig. 6.5: Simulation of the robust control with $\pi_0 = 0.02$ and $y_0 = 0.02$.

Table 6.1:   Standard deviations of state and control variables with different values of $\theta$.

| $\theta$ | SD of $\pi_t$ | SD of $y_t$ | SD of $r_t$ |
|---|---|---|---|
| 0.03 | 0.038 | 0.028 | 0.223 |
| 0.09 | 0.032 | 0.017 | 0.186 |
| $+\infty$ | 0.030 | 0.015 | 0.179 |

the robustness parameter $\theta$, the lower are the $\pi_t$, $y_t$ and $r_t$, and moreover, the faster the state variables converge to their equilibria. And in case $\theta = +\infty$, the state variables reach their lowest values and attain the equilibria at the highest speed.

In sum, we have shown that uncertainty with respect to model misspecification might not necessarily require caution. Though robust control can deal with problems that cannot be solved with the classical optimal control theory, some researchers have cast doubt on robust control. Chen and Epstein (2000) and Epstein and Schneider (2001), for example, criticize the application of the robust control theory for problems of time-inconsistency in preferences. Therefore, Hansen and Sargent (2001b) discuss the time-consistency of the alternative representations of preferences that underlie the robust control theory. An important criticism of robust control comes from Sims (2001a). He criticizes the robust control approach on conceptual grounds. As pointed out by Sims (2001a), there are major sources of more fundamental types of uncertainties that the robust control theory does not address. One major uncertainty is the extent to which there is a medium run trade-off between inflation and output. This refers, as discussed in Chapter 3, to the impact of monetary policy on the NAIRU. Sims (2001a) also shows that long-run effects of inflation on output may not need to be completely permanent in order to be important. On the other hand, deflation may exhibit strong destabilizing effects while interest rates are already very low. Thus, there may, in fact, be a long-run non-vertical Phillips curve.[21]

---

[21] See Graham and Snower (2002) and Blanchard (2005), for example.

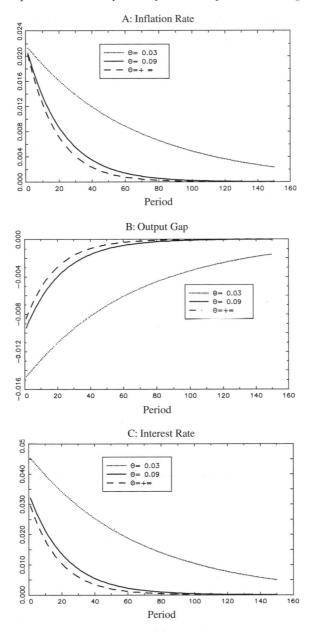

Fig. 6.6: Results of the robust control with zero shocks.

Yet, the robust control approach developed so far seems to follow the neutrality postulate, implying a vertical long-run Phillips curve.

## 6.6. CONCLUSION

This chapter presents some theoretical background of how optimal monetary policy rules and the central bank's interest-rate reaction functions may be derived. We have first presented a brief introduction to dynamic programming and then derived an optimal monetary policy rule from a simple model. As mentioned and explored in the previous chapters, economic agents are often faced with uncertainty in economic modeling. Therefore, we have also explored monetary policy rules under uncertainty with adaptive learning and robust control. We find that the state and control variables do not converge with the RLS learning algorithm of constant gain even in a non-stochastic model. The simulations of the robust control indicate that the robust parameter affects not only the state variables and value function, but also the central bank's reaction to inflation and output gaps. To be precise, the central bank may have a stronger response to the state variables when there exists uncertainty than when no uncertainty exists.

### APPENDIX A6. IMPORTANT OUTPUT CONCEPTS

The output gap defined by Woodford (2001b, 2003a) is the gap between actual output and the natural rate of output, not the same as in Taylor (1993). In Taylor (1993) the output gap is measured by the real GDP relative to a deterministic trend. Woodford (2001b, p. 234) defines "the natural rate of output as the equilibrium level of output that would obtain in the event of perfectly flexible prices". Moreover, the natural level of output could be, due to distortions such as monopolistic competition and tax rates, different from the efficient level of output with no distortions. Yet, it is likely to move in tandem with the efficient level of output. Concerning the output gap, he further suggests that "in general, this will not grow with a smooth trend, as a result of real disturbances of many kinds". Three other concepts concerning output are the steady-state level of output, the efficient level of output and the equilibrium level of output. Below is a brief sketch of Woodford's definitions of these concepts.

Let $w_i$ denote the nominal wage of labor type $i$ in period $t$, we know the variable cost of supplying a quantity $y_t(i)$ of good $i$ is given by

$$w_t(i)f^{-1}(y_t(i)/A_t),$$

then the nominal marginal cost of supplying good $i$ can be written as

$$S_t(i) = \frac{w_t(i)}{A_t} \Psi(y_t(i)/A_t)$$

with

$$\Psi(y) = \frac{1}{f'(f^{-1}(y))}.$$

The real marginal cost can then be written as

$$s_t(i) = S_t(i)/P_t = s(y_t(i), Y_t; \bar{\xi}_t).$$

Woodford (2003a, pp. 393–394) defines the first two concepts as follows. The steady-state level of output is the quantity $\bar{Y}$ that satisfies $s(\bar{Y}, \bar{Y}; 0) = (1 - \tau)/\mu$ with $\tau$ being the constant proportional tax rate on sales proceeds and $\mu$ the desired markup. The efficient level of output is the quantity $Y^*$ that satisfies $s(Y^*, Y^*; 0) = 1$. Woodford (2003a, p. 151) defines the equilibrium level of output $Y_t^n$ as the quantity that satisfies $s(Y_t^n, Y_t^n; \tilde{\xi}_t) = \mu^{-1}$. The efficient level of output gap $x^*$ is the difference between the efficient level of output and the natural rate of output (see also Woodford, 2001b). As for the details of the economic models, the reader is referred to Chapter 3 and Chapter 6 of Woodford (2003a).

# CHAPTER 7

# Time-Varying Optimal Monetary Policy

## 7.1. INTRODUCTION

As discussed earlier, the current research on monetary policy rules generally presumes that the central bank follows some discretionary monetary policy responding to output variability as well as inflation variability. Yet recent research also has shown that central banks, in particular since the beginning of the 1980s, have shifted their emphasis toward giving a stronger weight to inflation targeting. Underlying the discretionary monetary policy of central banks is, as above discussed, the Phillips-curve. The central bank is posited to minimize a loss function, which is quadratic both in production and inflation or in unemployment and inflation respectively. The weights for the inflation and output gaps are, however, mostly fixed. As shown in Chapter 6, in the use of the linear quadratic control problem for modeling central bank's behavior, usually the steady state is uniquely determined.[1] The typical monetary control framework was introduced in the previous chapter.

---

[1] Examples of such central banks preferences can be found in Svensson (1997) and Kierman and Lippi (1999), and the numerous contributions in the recently edited book by Taylor (1999a).

As also mentioned earlier, in other recent approaches a more general welfare function has been taken as a starting point to evaluate policy actions of monetary authorities. This is pursued by Rotemberg and Woodford (1999) and Woodford (2003a) who postulate a household's welfare function[2] and then undertake a second-order Taylor series expansion about a steady state. This gives a quadratic loss function about possible steady states of the model. They then study the impact of different variants of monetary policy rules on the household's welfare. Yet, under mild non-concavity of the households' welfare function[3] there are likely to arise multiple steady states.

An explicit model with multiple steady-state equilibria is given in Benhabib et al. (1998, 2001). They also use a framework with a household's utility function where consumption and money balances affect household's welfare positively and labor effort and inflation rates negatively. In their model multiple steady-state equilibria arise due to a specific (but rather simple) policy rule (Taylor rule) and certain cross-derivatives between consumption and money balances in the household's utility function. Their inflation path is a perfect foresight path and thus they do not need to use a Phillips-curve as in the traditional literature that builds on the linear quadratic control problem. They study the local and global dynamics about the steady states.[4]

In this chapter we also want to study a monetary policy model with multiple equilibria but, because of heuristic reasons, stay in the tradition of the literature on quadratic loss functions that has been discussed in Chapter 6, rather than using a representative

---

[2] See also Christiano and Gust (1999).

[3] One can show that in case of assets entering the households' welfare or in case of the existence of externalities multiple steady states may easily emerge, see Semmler and Sieveking (2000) and Grüne, Semmler and Sieveking (2004).

[4] Yet, they do not undertake a welfare evaluation (neither with respect to the equilibrium path for different policy rules).

household's welfare function. We will slightly depart from the quadratic loss function as described in Chapter 6. There are other recent papers that have also departed from the standard quadratic objective function. Nobay and Peel (2003) for example, suppose that a Linex function, that is a combination of a linear and exponential function, is more appropriate in order to model the deviation of inflation and output from their desired levels. This holds because a Linex functions implies that an inflation rate (output level) above (below) the desired level goes along with higher disutility compared to an inflation rate (output level) below (above) the desired value. Orphanides and Wilcox (1996) postulate non-quadratic preferences where output only is stabilized if the inflation rate is within a certain bound. Moreover, Orphanides and Wieland (2000) argue that the loss function is flat for a certain range of inflation rates and output levels. This implies that the central bank takes discretionary policy measures only when certain threshold levels are reached. As long as inflation and unemployment remain within certain bands the central bank will not become active.

We too will slightly depart from a quadratic loss function and demonstrate that the (intertemporal) optimization problem faced by a central bank may lead—or contribute—to history dependence and hysteresis effects on the labor market.[5] Following our results of Chapter 4 we suppose an endogenously changing weighting function which makes output stabilization more important relative to inflation control for low levels of output compared to high levels. On the other hand inflation stabilization will become more

---

[5] The idea of hysteresis effects on the labor markets has originally been introduced by Blanchard and Summers (1986, 1988). In the recent literature, see Stiglitz (1997), this argument has been used to explain why the US economy has experienced a persistent low level of unemployment and Europe a persistent high level of unemployment. We do not want to argue that monetary policy is the sole cause for hysteresis but rather can significantly contribute to it. This is a line of research that Blanchard (2003) also has pursued. Further discussions are given below.

important at high levels of inflation. Recent literature has introduced a non-linearity in the interest rate feedback rule, the Taylor rule, to also take account of such considerations. It has been stated that a central bank is likely to pursue an active monetary policy at high inflation rates and a passive policy at low inflation rates.[6] Similar to the model by Benhabib et al. (1998, 2001) our model too is likely to give rise to multiple steady state equilibria and history dependence. We show that such a model can be solved by applying either Pontryagin's maximum principle and the Hamiltonian as well as the Hamilton–Jacobi–Bellman (HJB) equation. In contrast to Rotemberg and Woodford (1999), Christiano and Gust (1999) and Benhabib et al. (1998, 2001) our approach allows us to evaluate the welfare function also outside the steady state equilibria.

Appendix A7 of the current chapter contains a discussion of solution techniques for models with multiple equilibria, namely the Hamiltonian function and the HJB equation, and derives the optimal Taylor rule for our model.

## 7.2. THE CENTRAL BANK'S CONTROL PROBLEM

The monetary authority can control the level of aggregate output $x(t)$ by its policy variable $u(t)$ (in the short run). For simplicity we assume that the change in aggregate output is a linear function of $u(t)$,

$$\dot{x}(t) = u(t). \tag{7.1}$$

$u(t) > 0$ $(<0)$ implies that the central bank conducts an expansionary (contractionary) monetary policy. This means that it expands the money supply, for example, or that it reduces the interest rate in order to stimulate output. Appendix A7 studies the problem when

---

[6] In Benhabib et al. (1998, 2001) this takes the form of a state dependent interest rate feedback rule of the central bank.

the central bank sets the interest rate according to an interest rate reaction function.[7]

The deviation of the inflation rate $\pi(t)$ from its core level $\pi^*$ depends on both $u(t)$ and the deviation of aggregate output $x(t)$ from the exogenously given long-run output level, $x_n$ which implies a constant inflation rate, whereby $x_n$ corresponds to be the NAIRU which we take in the current model as fixed. If $x(t) > x_n$ we have an inflationary pressure tending to raise the inflation rate above its core level $\pi^*$ and vice versa. This assumption implies that a high level of output corresponds to a high level of employment tending to raise inflation. Note that hereby we could view the core inflation as being given by a medium-run expected price change where the central bank's desired inflation rate may also play an important role. The core inflation rate $\pi^*$ could be viewed as summarizing medium-run competitive pressures on the product and labor markets, medium-run money growth and price expectations extracted from product and labor markets as well as financial and commodity markets.[8] This inflation rate is also often taken as the medium-run target rate of inflation for the monetary authority.[9] The German Bundesbank, for example, has in its $\pi^*$ concept defined such a core inflation rate which it then attempted to adhere to. Recently, the concept of core inflation has been restated in Deutsche Bundesbank (2000). Inflation expectations is captured in $\pi^*$ in the sense that the central bank's view on

---

[7] Assuming a dynamic IS equation relating the change in output to the interest rate, one can derive a central bank interest rate reaction function, the Taylor rule, describing the optimal interest rate. This is undertaken in Appendix A7, see also Svensson (1997), and Greiner and Semmler (2003) for more details.

[8] See also Stiglitz (1997).

[9] The core inflation could also be perceived as forward looking target rate of inflation that is consistent with saddle path dynamics of our optimal control model. To avoid those complicated numerical computations we keep the core rate $\pi^*$ fixed.

acceptable or desirable rates of inflation play an important role for private inflation expectations, see Gerlach and Svensson (2002). Of course, the inflation rate $\pi^*$ might be seen to be influenced by actual inflation rates as well, for example, as Gerlach and Svensson (2002) argue, if the private agents are disappointed by the central bank's target and thus the rate $\pi^*$ might be assumed to move over time.[10] For analytical purposes, however, in order to avoid a two state variable model, it is here presumed to be fixed. Note that by using the concept of core inflation we refrain from explicitly modeling the private sector expectations formation as in Sargent (1999) in order to simplify the model.[11]

As concerns the functional form for $\pi(t) - \pi^*$ we assume the following Phillips-curve equation:

$$\pi(t) - \pi^* = \alpha u(t) + \beta(x(t) - x_n), \qquad \alpha, \beta \geq 0. \quad (7.2)$$

The higher[12] the $u$ the higher the inflation rate and its deviation from the core value $\pi^*$. This implies that an expansionary monetary policy raises actual inflation.[13] Further, the more the aggregate

---

[10] Note that we could define a moving core inflation rate as, for example, the German Bundesbank had proposed during the high inflationary period of the 1970s or the disinflation period of the 1980s and 1990s. This would not change our results developed below. For empirical estimates on the inflation target of the Bundesbank for the period 1980–1994, see Clarida et al. (1998). A moving target rate could be viewed as corresponding to a moving rate consistent with the stable branch of the saddle path.

[11] Sargent (1999) uses an adaptive learning scheme in a two agents' model—private agents and the central bank—in which the private agents update their believes about future inflation rates through adaptive learning.

[12] In the following we suppress the time argument $t$.

[13] In order to avoid an additional state variable we model the expected inflation rate here by using the core inflation. Yet, in place of the core inflation $\pi^*$, an expected inflation rate, adaptively obtained, can be used, see Semmler and Zhang (2004).

output level exceeds the natural output the greater is the inflationary pressure.[14]

The objective of the monetary authority is composed of two parts: first, as usual, it wants to keep the inflation rate $\pi$ as close to the exogenously given core rate $\pi^*$. This is achieved by assuming a quadratic penalty function $h_1(\pi)$ which attains its minimum at $\pi = \pi^*$.

Second, the monetary authority wants to stabilize aggregate output around the natural output. Deviation from the natural output are penalized by a quadratic penalty function $h_2(x)$ with the minimum given at $x = x_n$. Assuming an intertemporal perspective, the objective functional of the monetary authority is described as

$$\min_{u} \int_0^{\infty} e^{-\delta t}(h_1(\pi) + h_2(x))dt, \qquad (7.3)$$

subject to Equations 7.1 and 7.2, with $\delta$ denoting the discount rate.

The solution to this intertemporal optimization problem is unique, if the objective function is a quadratic function in $x$. However, if the objective function of the central bank is non-quadratic, a more complex dynamic outcome can be observed as we will demonstrate in detail in section 3. Let us first elaborate on some economic reasons which motivate the introduction of a non-quadratic objective function.

One possible justification for departing from a quadratic objective function is to assume a weighting function. As pointed out in a number of empirical studies, to be discussed below, we can assume that the goal of output stabilization should obtain a weight determining its significance relative to the goal of keeping inflation close to the core $\pi^*$. However, in contrast to what is frequently

---

[14] The fact that the control $u$ appears here in the Phillips-curve can be derived from the assumption that lags of output, as in Svensson (1997), are relevant for wage bargaining or price setting by firms. It can also stand for some exchange rate effect on inflation by presuming that the control $u$ is proxied by an interest rate, that in turn, moves exchange rate, see Ball (1999) and Semmler and Zhang (2004).

assumed, we posit that the weight on output stabilization is not a constant but a function depending on the level of actual output, see the results of Chapter 4. For high values of aggregate output the goal of raising output is less important compared to a situation when aggregate output is low. On the other hand, the weight for the inflation rate becomes more important when output rises and the inflation rate is high. We model this idea in a simple way by fixing the weight for the inflation rate equal to 1 and assume a weighting function $w(x)$ of the form

$$
w(x) = \begin{cases} a_1, & \text{for } x \in [0, x_1) \\ a(x), & \text{for } x \in [x_1, x_2) \\ a_0, & \text{for } x \geq x_2, \end{cases}
$$

with $da(x)/dx < 0$, $x_j$, $j = 1, 2$. This function implies that output stabilization is always less important than inflation control because the weight on output stabilization is always lower than the weight on inflation control (which is equal to 1). This is what many empirically specified Taylor rules assume. We set the maximum weight for output control equal to $a_1$. In order to model a simple situation we assume that the weight for the output stabilization decreases (the relative weight for inflation stabilization increases) as output increases. Once a certain threshold level, $x_2$, is reached the relative weight of output stabilization remains constant and equal to $a_0$.[15] Overall, we have formulated the change of the relative weight for output and inflation by solely making it depending on output.[16]

In Chapter 4 we have already presented results that indicate the state-dependent reaction functions of monetary authorities.

---

[15] In the numerical example below we set $a_0 = 0.1$ and $a_2 = 0.5$.

[16] In order to obtain an analytical tractable model we have refrained from assuming more complicated weighted functions, for example, we might have considered weighting functions depending on both the output as well as inflation gap. Although this appears to be more realistic than our empirical estimates in Chapter 4 suggest, we have refrained from modeling this more complicated case.

Inference on the size and change of the weights for inflation and output in the objective function can also be made from numerous recent empirical studies on central banks interest rate reaction functions.[17] Further stylized facts and empirical research on the central bank's interest rate reaction function, the Taylor rule, for the US and some European countries are obtained.

In line with our considerations above, the empirical studies, overwhelmingly reveal (with some minor exception) a higher weight for inflation than for output (or employment) gap for both the studies with one regime change (pre- and post-Volcker periods), Table 7.1, and with two regime changes, Table 7.2. The studies with one regime change show that in the second period (the post-Volcker time period) the weight on inflation has increased. This, however, as Table 7.2 shows, has mainly occurred during the 1980s when most central banks have engineered a process of disinflation. On the other hand, as Table 7.1 also shows, when there was a secular rise in unemployment in Europe, the weight on the employment gap increased again (absolute and relative to the inflation gap). Note, that even in the US the weight on the employment gap has increased again in the third period.

The study by Boivin (2001) undertaken for US time series data estimates time-varying weights on inflation and employment gap (with alternative measures for the NAIRU). Also here there are roughly three regimes visible. In a first regime, from 1973 to 1979 the weight on the employment gap is roughly 0.65 and on inflation 0.25. From 1979 to 1989 the weight switches for the employment gap from 0.65 to 0.2 and for the inflation gap from 0.25 to 0.5.

---

[17] As Chapter 6 for the LQ control problem shows, such an intertemporal central bank objective function can be transformed into an optimal central bank interest rate reaction function. There then the weight affects inversely the reaction coefficient of inflation gap. Thus, the relative increase in the weight of the inflation gap in the interest rate reaction function is equivalent to the decreasing weight for output in the intertemporal objective function.

Table 7.1:    Studies with one regime change.

| Study | Time period | $w_\pi$ | $w_x$ | $w_r$ |
|-------|-------------|---------|-------|-------|
| US[a] | 1960.1–1979.4 | 0.81 | 0.25 | – |
| US[a] | 1987.1–1997.3 | 1.53 | 0.76 | – |
| US[b] | 1961.1–1979.2 | 0.83 | 0.27 | 0.68 |
| US[b] | 1979.3–1996.4 | 2.15 | 0.93 | 0.79 |
| US[c] | 1960.1–1979.2 | 0.13 | 0.02 | −0.17 |
| US[c] | 1979.3–1995.1 | 0.44 | 0.01 | −0.28 |

Estimates are given here for two sub-periods. Some of the estimates included also a term for interest rates smoothing, denoted by $w_r$. The study by Flaschel et al. (1999c) refers to unemployment gap instead of the output gap where the natural rate is measured solely as average unemployment over the time period considered. The coefficient for interest rate smoothing is negative, since the estimate is undertaken with a first differenced interest rate. Both features of the estimate may explain the low coefficients for $w_x$.
[a]See Taylor (1999c).
[b]See Clarida et al. (1998).
[c]See Flaschel et al. (2001).

In the last period, from 1988 to 1993 the weight for employment remains roughly unchanged and for inflation it increases to 0.6. We want to note that the Boivin study captures also indirectly the influence of a possible change in the slope of the Phillips-curve on the coefficients of the inflation gap and employment gap.

Overall, in summarizing the above results we can say that, first, in most of the studies, for the US as well Europe, inflation stabilization has, most of the time, a higher weight than output stabilization. Second, the weights for the inflation and output (employment) gaps have undergone significant changes over time. Third, the weight for the output gap does not appear to solely depend on the output but also the inflation gap.[18] Altogether, as shown in Chapter 4, both the weight for output as well as price gap change over time.

---

[18] Further evidence of state-dependent weights in central banks' interest rate feedback rule is given in Chapter 4 where the Kalman filter is used to empirically estimate state-dependent reaction functions of central banks in some OECD countries.

Table 7.2:    Studies with two regime changes.

| Study | Time period | $w_\pi$ | $w_x$ | $w_r$ |
|-------|-------------|---------|-------|-------|
| US | 1970.1–1979.1 | 0.74 | 0.12 | – |
| US | 1979.1–1989.1 | 0.74 | −0.66 | – |
| US | 1989.2–1989.10 | 1.05 | 1.12 | – |
| Germany | 1970.1–1979.12 | 0.88 | 0.81 | – |
| Germany | 1979.12–1989.12 | 0.91 | 0.32 | – |
| Germany | 1989.12–1989.12 | 0.36 | 0.87 | – |
| France | 1970.1–1979.12 | 0.66 | 0.55 | – |
| France | 1979.12–1989.12 | 0.82 | −0.80 | – |
| France | 1989.12–1998.12 | 0.99 | 1.26 | – |

Estimates are given here for three subperiods. Estimates (for a study on the central bank's interest rate reaction function in other OECD countries, see Clarida et al., 1998) are undertaken by the authors with monthly data; data are from Eurostat (2000). The weight $w_x$ represents the coefficient on an employment gap. The negative sign for $w_x$ indicates interest rate increases in spite of the negative employment gap. Even if a term of interest rate smoothing was included in the regressions the relative weight of the coefficients for inflation and employment approximately remained the same. For Germany: $r$ is 3-month LIBOR; $\pi$ is the consumer price change. For USA: $r$ is "Federal Funds Rate" which is used as in the article by Clarida et al. (1998); $\pi$ is consumer price change. For France: $r$ is the call money rate (since some data for labor are not available); $\pi$ is consumer price change.

The latter empirical fact might complicate our model. Yet, for our purpose it suffices to consider a simple model where the weights on output and price stabilization solely depend on the output gap. Employing this presumption on the central bank's interest rate reaction function permits us to construct a welfare function with changing relative weight for inflation and output stabilization in the central bank's loss function. The exact relationship between the weights in the central bank's loss function and the central bank's interest rate reaction function is derived by Greiner and Semmler (2003).

Figure 7.1A–C shows a numerical example, with the function $h_2(x)$ displayed in Figure 7.1A given by the following assumed functional form $h_2(x) = -100 - 10(x - 50) + 3(x - 50)^2$. Note that we here assume certain functional forms in order to undertake numerical computations. The weighting function is shown in

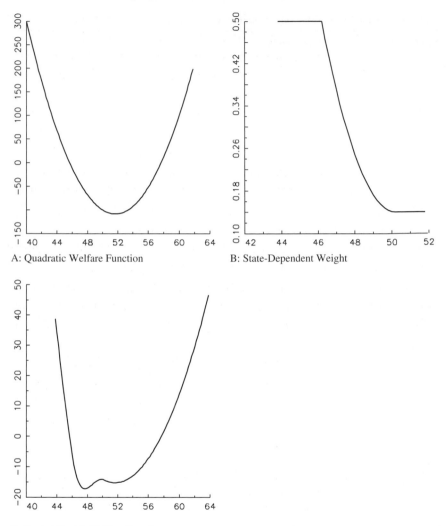

A: Quadratic Welfare Function

B: State-Dependent Weight

C: Central Bank's Welfare Function
   with State-Dependent Weights

Fig. 7.1:   Central bank's welfare function and state-dependent weight.

Figure 7.1B. Figure 7.1C, finally, gives the function $w(x)h_2(x)$, with $a_1$ set to $a_1 = 0.5$. This function displays two minima. The function $w(x)h_2(x)$ can be approximated by a polynomial of a higher degree which displays the same qualitative features[19] as the function[20] $w(x)h_2(x)$.

Thus, in order to obtain continuous function we choose an approximation given by a function such as $g(\cdot) = -10 - (x - 50) - 0.3(x - 50)^2 + 0.33(x - 50)^3 + 0.1(x - 50)^4$. This function is shown in Figure 7.2.[21] These considerations demonstrate that our assumption of an endogenous weighting function—here solely depending on the output gap—may give rise to an objective function which can simply be described by a convex–concave–convex function.

We would also like to point out that a less conservative central bank, i.e. a central bank which puts an even higher weight on output stabilization, would not change the basic message described above. One could even take a situation where output stabilization and inflation control are equivalent goals if output levels exceed a certain threshold, but output stabilization becomes more important when output is lower than this threshold. One could also fix the weight on output stabilization equal to 1 and make the weight on inflation stabilization state dependent (dependent on the inflation rate).[22] All of these options would not change our basic results.

---

[19] Note that this approximation is undertaken solely for computational reasons.

[20] Note if we start from a representative household's preference as in Rotemberg and Woodford (1999) the change of the weight $w(\cdot)$ would be determined by a change of the structural parameters.

[21] We do not need to attempt to find parameter values which give a more exact approximation of the function $w(x)h_2(x)$ since the basic message would remain unchanged.

[22] A non-linear central bank interest rate feedback rule, with, however, the weight to output stabilization set to zero, can be found in Benhabib et al. (1998, 2001). By adding the assumption of $\bar{\pi} > -r$, with $\bar{\pi}$ the steady state inflation rate and $r$ the real interest rate, they also obtain multiple steady state equilibria.

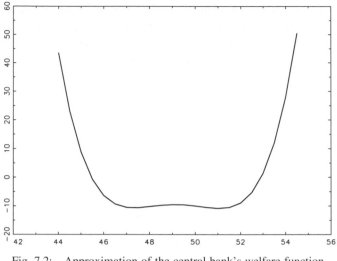

Fig. 7.2:   Approximation of the central bank's welfare function.

## 7.3. HYSTERESIS EFFECTS

Summarizing our discussions above and assuming an intertemporal perspective, the optimization problem of the monetary authority can be written as

$$\min_{u} \int_{0}^{\infty} e^{-\delta t}(h_{1}(\pi) + g(x))\mathrm{d}t, \qquad (7.4)$$

subject to

$$\dot{x} = u, \qquad (7.5)$$

with $\delta > 0$ the discount rate and $g(\cdot)$ a continuous function with continuous first and second derivatives. In particular, we assume that, in accordance with our considerations in section 2, $g(\cdot)$ is convex–concave–convex and satisfies in addition $\lim_{x\to-\infty} g(\cdot) = \lim_{x\to\infty} g(\cdot) = \infty$. As concerns the function $h_{1}(\pi)$ we take $h_{1}(\pi) = (\pi - \pi^{*})^{2}$, with $\pi - \pi^{*}$ given by Equation 7.2.

Candidates for optimal steady states and local solutions can be found either through the Hamiltonian or the HJB equation. Here we derive some results using the Hamiltonian. Details on the use of the HJB equation are given in Appendix A7.

We apply the current-value Hamiltonian $H(\cdot)$

$$H(\cdot) = (g(x) + (\pi - \pi^*)^2) + \lambda u, \tag{7.6}$$

with $\lambda$ the costate variable and $\pi - \pi^*$ determined by Equation 7.2, respectively. The Maximum principle gives

$$u = -\frac{\lambda}{2\alpha^2} - \frac{\beta}{\alpha}(x - x_n) \tag{7.7}$$

and the costate variable evolves according to

$$\dot{\lambda} = \delta\lambda - g'(x) - 2\beta(\alpha u + \beta(x - x_n)). \tag{7.8}$$

Further, the limiting transversality condition

$$\lim_{t \to \infty} e^{-\delta t} \lambda x = 0 \tag{7.9}$$

must hold. Using the Maximum principle 7.7 the dynamics is completely described by the two-dimensional autonomous differential equation system

$$\dot{u} = \delta u + \frac{\beta}{\alpha}\left(\frac{\beta}{\alpha} + \delta\right)(x - x_n) + \frac{g'(x)}{2\alpha^2} \tag{7.10}$$

$$\dot{x} = u. \tag{7.11}$$

Rest points of this differential equation system yield equilibrium candidates for our economy. At equilibrium candidates, we have $\dot{x} = \dot{u} = 0$, implying $u = 0$ and $x$ such that

$$\frac{\beta}{\alpha}\left(\frac{\beta}{\alpha} + \delta\right)(x - x_n) + \frac{g'(x)}{2\alpha^2} = 0 \tag{7.12}$$

holds. If $g(x)$ has a convex–concave–convex shape,[23] as argued in section 2, there may be three candidates for an equilibrium, which we denote as $\hat{x}_1, \hat{x}_2$ and $\hat{x}_3$ with $\hat{x}_1 < \hat{x}_2 < \hat{x}_3$. More concretely, since $g(x)$ is convex–concave–convex $g'(x)$ is concave–convex and the number of equilibria will depend on the linear term $(\beta/\alpha) \times ((\beta/\alpha) + \delta)(x - x_n)$. If this term is not too large so that Equation 7.12 is also concave–convex, multiple equilibria will exist. Below we will present a numerical example that illustrates this case. For now we will assume that this holds and derive results for our general model.

The local dynamics is described by the eigenvalues of the Jacobian matrix. The Jacobian matrix corresponding to this system is given by

$$J = \begin{pmatrix} \delta & (\beta/\alpha)(\delta + \beta/\alpha) + g''(x)/2\alpha^2 \\ 1 & 0 \end{pmatrix}.$$

The eigenvalues are obtained as

$$\mu_{1,2} = \frac{\delta}{2} \pm \sqrt{\left(\frac{\delta}{2}\right)^2 - \det J}. \tag{7.13}$$

The eigenvalues are symmetric around $\delta/2$ implying that the system always has at least one eigenvalue with a positive real part. For $\det J < 0$ the eigenvalues are real with one being positive and one negative. In case of $\det J > 0$ the eigenvalues are either real and both positive or complex conjugate with positive real parts. That is in the latter case the system is unstable.

Since Equation 7.12 is concave–convex, the $\dot{u} = 0$ isocline, given by $u = -[(\beta/\alpha)(\delta + \beta/\alpha)(x - x_n) + g'(x))/2\alpha^2]/\delta$, is convex–concave in $x$. Consequently, $(\beta/\alpha)(\delta + \beta/\alpha) + g''(x)/2\alpha^2$, which is equal to $-\delta \times$ the slope of the $\dot{u} = 0$ isocline, is positive for

---

[23] The additional assumption $\lim_{x \to -\infty} g(\cdot) = \lim_{x \to \infty} g(\cdot) = \infty$ is sufficient for the existence of a solution to Equation 7.12 with respect to $x$.

$x = \hat{x}_1$ and $x = \hat{x}_3$ while it is negative for $x = \hat{x}_2$. This implies that $\hat{x}_1$ and $\hat{x}_3$ are saddle point stable while $\hat{x}_2$ is unstable. This outcome shows that there exists, in between $\hat{x}_1$ and $\hat{x}_3$, a so-called Skiba point $x_s$ (see Brock and Malliaris, 1989; Dechert, 1984).

From an economic point of view the existence of a Skiba point has the following implication. If the initial level of production $x(0)$ is smaller than the Skiba point $x_s$, the monetary authority has to choose $u(0)$ such that the economy converges to $\hat{x}_1$ in order to minimize Equation 7.4. If $x(0)$ is larger than $x_s$ the optimal $u(0)$ is the one which makes the economy converging to $\hat{x}_3$. If $x_0$ is equal to $x_s$ the optimal long-run aggregate output level is indeterminate, that is convergence to $\hat{x}_1$ yields the same value for Equation 7.4 as convergence to $\hat{x}_3$.

Given this property of our model, history dependence and hysteresis effects on the labor market can arise in the following way. Assume that the economy originally is in the high-output equilibrium $\hat{x}_3$. If the economy is struck by a shock reducing output below the Skiba point, it is optimal for the central bank to steer the economy towards the low-output equilibrium $\hat{x}_1$, which is accompanied by a lower inflation rate. It should be noted that this monetary policy is optimal and the hysteresis effect arises given complete information and the central bank's knowledge of the Skiba point. So, it must also be pointed out that in reality the central bank does probably not dispose of the necessary information to achieve a minimum. In this case, however, the emergence of hysteresis is not less likely. For example, the central bank could conduct a sub-optimal monetary policy and steer the economy to the low-output equilibrium although convergence to the high-output equilibrium would be optimal. The emergence of hysteresis effects is independent of the assumption that the central bank conducts an optimal policy. What is crucial for hysteresis is the shape of the function $g(x)$.

To illustrate these theoretical considerations and in order to gain additional insight, we resort to the function of our numerical example in section 2, that is $g(\cdot) = -10 - (x - 50) - 0.3(x - 50)^2 + 0.33(x - 50)^3 + 0.1(x - 50)^4$. $\alpha$, $\beta$ and $\delta$ are set to $\alpha = 0.09$, $\beta = 0.01$ and $\delta = 0.05$. $x_n$ is assumed to be given by $x_n = 50$. With these parameters, candidates for optimal equilibria are $\hat{x}_1 = 47.3133$, $\hat{x}_2 = 49.1354$ and $\hat{x}_3 = 51.0763$. The eigenvalues are $\mu_1 = 1.687$ and $\mu_2 = -1.637$ corresponding to $\hat{x}_1$, $\mu_{1,2} = 0.025 \pm 1.182\sqrt{-1}$ for $\hat{x}_2$ and $\mu_1 = 1.74$ and $\mu_2 = -1.69$ for $\hat{x}_3$. Thus, $\hat{x}_1$ and $\hat{x}_3$ are saddle point stable while $\hat{x}_2$ is an unstable focus.

Figure 7.3 shows a qualitative picture of the phase diagram in the $x-u$ phase diagram where saddle points and the unstable focus are drawn.

To show that a Skiba-point exists we need two additional results. First, the minimum of Equation 7.4 is given by $H^0(x(0), u(0))/\delta$, with $H^0(\cdot)$ denoting the minimized Hamiltonian. Second, the minimized Hamiltonian, $H^0(\cdot)$, is strictly concave in $u$ and reaches its maximum along the $\dot{x} = 0 = u$ isocline. These results imply that for any $x(0)$ the minimizing $u(0)$ must lie on either the highest or lowest branch of the spirals converging to $\hat{x}_1 = 47.3133$ or to $\hat{x}_3 = 51.0763$ (because of the strict concavity of $H^0$ in $u$). For $x(0) = x_1$, we may set either $u(0) = 0$, leading to $\hat{x}_3 = 51.0763$, or $u(0) = u_1$, which implies convergence to $\hat{x}_1 = 47.3133$. Since the minimized

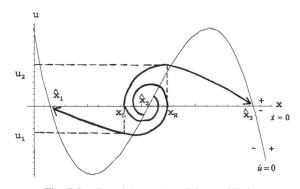

Fig. 7.3:   Local dynamics of the equilibria.

Hamiltonian takes its maximum along the $\dot{x} = 0$ isocline, $u(0) = 0$ yields a maximum and cannot be optimal. Instead, $u(0) = u_1$ yields the minimum for Equation 7.4.

If $x(0) = x_2$ the same argument shows that setting $u(0) = 0$, leading to $\hat{x}_1 = 47.3133$, is not optimal. In this case, $u(0) = u_2$ yields the minimum. Therefore, if $x(0) \leq (\geq) x_1 (x_2)$ convergence to $\hat{x}_1 = 47.3133$ ($\hat{x} = 51.0763$) yields the minimum for Equation 7.4. Consequently, the Skiba-point lies between $x_1$ and $x_2$. To find the exact location for the Skiba-point we would have to calculate the value function on the stable branch of the saddle point, what, however, we will not undertake here.[24]

It should be mentioned that the high equilibrium point $\hat{x}_3$ is expected to be lower than potential output which is about 51.7 in our example. This is due to the inclusion of the term $(\pi - \pi^*)^2$ in the central bank's objective function. Since the central bank wants to control inflation besides output it will not steer the economy towards potential aggregate output. Note, however, that in our example $\hat{x}_3$ is almost equal to potential output since we have chosen small values for $\alpha$ and $\beta$, implying that deviations from the potential output do not bring about strong inflationary pressure. Supposing that the core inflation $\pi^*$ equals 3%, the actual inflation rate is about 4.1% for the high-output equilibrium $\hat{x}_3$. The low equilibrium output $\hat{x}_1$ is

---

[24] If, as in our example, two saddle points, $\hat{x}_1$, $\hat{x}_3$ and one unstable point $\hat{x}_2$ for the state and co-state variables arise, one can numerically compute the threshold (Skiba point) by approximating the stable manifolds leading into the candidates for equilibria $\hat{x}_1$, $\hat{x}_3$. This is done by solving boundary value problems for differential equations (for details, see Beyn et al., 2001). In addition for each initial condition on the line $x$ one computes—by staying approximately on the stable manifold—the integral which represents the value of the objective function corresponding to the initial conditions. The connection of the integral points gives two value functions. The intersection of the two-value functions represents the threshold (a Skiba point) where the dynamics separate to the low- and high-level equilibria ($\hat{x}_1, \hat{x}_3$). For the details of procedure as well as the functions and parameters used, see Semmler and Greiner (1999).

accompanied by an inflation rate of about 0.3%. The capacity utilization in this equilibrium is about 92.6%.

We should also point out that it is not optimal to steer the economy to the NAIRU corresponding to $x_n$. This outcome results from our assumption that deviations from the NAIRU are explicitly considered in the objective function. Therefore, a higher level of aggregate output, which gives an inflation rate above the desired level $\pi^*$, may be optimal. This holds because the negative effect of a higher inflation rate is compensated by the benefits of a higher level of aggregate output. A lower level of aggregate output, in our example $\hat{x}_1$, is an optimal solution because it implies a lower inflation rate. If the NAIRU corresponding to the natural rate of output, $x_n$, coincides with a solution of $g(\cdot) = 0$, a steady state level of aggregate output can be achieved for which $\pi = \pi^*$ is optimal.

## 7.4. CONCLUSION

In this chapter we have attempted to show that monetary policy may contribute to hysteresis effects on the labor market. Yet, we do not want to neglect the hysteresis effects that stem from the labor market itself. The studies of hysteresis effects in labor markets originate in the work by Blanchard and Summers (1986, 1988) and have recently revived in Blanchard and Katz (1997) and Stiglitz (1997). This research agenda attempts to explain the time variation of the natural rate due to large shocks.[25] The hysteresis hypothesis

---

[25] The hysteresis hypothesis has been applied to compare the time variation of the natural rate in the US and Europe. Empirically it has been shown (Stiglitz, 1997; Gordon, 1997) that in the US the natural rate has moved from a high to a low level and, on the other hand, in Europe it has moved from a low to a high level. Each of those economies has experienced different levels of the natural rate over the last 40 years. Yet, whether econometrically the persistence of unemployment is described best by a unit root process (hysteresis process) or by a mean reverting process, with changing mean, is still controversial, see Phelps and Zoega (1998).

has been given some further foundation by labor market search theory (Mortensen, 1989; Howitt and McAffee, 1992). The hysteresis theory states that with a large negative economic shock the unemployment rate becomes history dependent. With large unemployment the improvement in unemployment benefits may generate less competition on the supply side for labor, a wage aspiration effect (Stiglitz, 1997) from previous periods of higher employment keeps real wage increasing (possibly higher than productivity), long-term unemployment may arise without pressure on the labor market and there may be loss of human capital, shortage of physical capital and a bias toward labor saving technologies (Blanchard, 1998). Thus, the natural rate of unemployment may tend to move up or the natural rate of employment may tend to move down with large shocks.[26] This process has been assumed to have occurred in Europe.[27]

In this chapter we have demonstrated that under reasonable assumptions central banks may add to the hysteresis effect on the labor market if the central bank's objective function is non-quadratic. The objective function of the central bank will be non-quadratic if it exhibits state-dependent weights for output or inflation stabilization. This may give rise to a convex−concave−convex shape of the function resulting in multiple optimal

---

[26] For the opposite view, namely that the currently higher European unemployment is a result of a moving natural rate, see Phelps and Zoega (1998). They associate the rise of the European natural rate with rising and high interest rates in Europe. Moreover, they argue that the hysteresis theory still lacks state variables such as wealth, capital stock or customer stock.

[27] On the other hand, with a positive shock to employment and rising employment the hysteresis effect may work in the opposite direction. The long term unemployed come back to the labor market, increase competition, wage aspiration is low (compared to productivity), there is reskilling of human capital due to higher employment and product market competition keeps prices down (Stiglitz, 1997; Rotemberg and Woodford, 1996). This case, is usually associated with the recent US experience, where the natural rate of unemployment has moved down or the natural rate of employment has moved up.

steady-state equilibria. In such a model there can be three candidates for steady-state equilibria but only two are optimal. There is history dependence since, the initial conditions crucially determine which equilibrium should be selected. "Optimal" hysteresis effects on the labor market arise if an exogenous shock leads to a decrease in production such that convergence to the low-level equilibrium becomes optimal whereas convergence to the high-level equilibrium may have been optimal before the shock. It must be underlined that, in this case, it is indeed optimal to realize the low-level equilibrium so that we may speak of "optimal" hysteresis effects.[28]

However, we should also point out that the central bank must be able to find out which equilibrium yields the optimum, a task which is definitely non-trivial in practice. Therefore, it is conceivable that the central bank chooses a non-optimal equilibrium and hysteresis effects may occur which turn out to be non-optimal. Again, imagine that an exogenous shock reduces output. If it is optimal to return to the high-level equilibrium after the shock, but the central bank conducts a monetary policy implying convergence to the low-level equilibrium, welfare losses will result. In this situation, the higher output equilibrium, if achievable, would yield an increase in welfare.

Finally, we want to note that the pursuit of a proper policy will be made feasible by computing, as we have suggested here, the welfare function (the value of the objective function) outside the steady-state equilibria which will reveal the thresholds at which a change of the policy should occur.

---

[28] This may be a scenario describing the situation in Europe with protracted period of high unemployment rate, see for example, Phelps and Zoega (1998) who have pointed to the high interest rate policy in Europe in the 1980s and 1990s as cause for protracted period of unemployment. Of course, as discussed above, labor market conditions presumably also have contributed to hysteresis effects.

**APPENDIX A7. NON-QUADRATIC WELFARE FUNCTION AND THE USE OF THE HJB EQUATION**

Our problem is

$$\max_u \int_0^\infty e^{-\delta t}(h, (\pi) + g(x))dt \qquad (7.14)$$

s.t.

$$\dot{x} = u \qquad (7.15)$$

where

$$h_1(\pi) = (\pi - \pi^*)^2 = (\alpha u + \beta(x - x_n))^2 = j(x, u)$$

HJB equation

$$\delta V(x) = \max_u [j(x, u) + g(x) + V'(x)u] \qquad (7.16)$$

$$\delta V(e) = j(e, 0) + g(e) = \beta^2(e - x_n)^2 + g(e) \qquad (7.17)$$

$$\delta V'(e) = j_x(e, 0) + g'(e) + V''(e) \times 0 = 2\beta^2(e - x_n) + g'(e) \qquad (7.18)$$

$$j_x(x, u) = 2\beta(\alpha u + \beta(x - x_n))$$

$e$ also satisfies Equation 7.16, thus

$$\delta V(e) = \max_u [j(e, u) + g(e) + V'(e)u]. \qquad (7.19)$$

Substituting Equations 7.17 and 7.18 into Equation 7.19, we have

$$\beta^2(e - x_n)^2 + g(e) = \max_u \left[ (\alpha u + \beta(e - x_n))^2 + g(e) \right.$$
$$\left. + \frac{1}{\delta}(2\beta^2(e - x_n) + g'(e))u \right], \qquad (7.20)$$

computing $\partial[\cdot]/\partial u = 0$ gives

$$\frac{\partial[\cdot]}{\partial u} = 2\alpha(\alpha u + \beta(e - x_n)) + \frac{1}{\delta}(2\beta^2(e - x_n) + g'(e)) = 0$$

or

$$2\delta\alpha^2 u + 2\delta\alpha\beta(e - x_n) + 2\beta^2(e - x_n) + g'(e) = 0. \qquad (7.21)$$

From Equations 7.15 and 7.21 equilibrium satisfies

$$u = \frac{-(2\delta\alpha\beta(e - x_n) + 2\beta^2(e - x_n) + g'(e))}{2\delta\alpha^2} \qquad (7.22)$$

($\dot{u} = 0$) and

$$\dot{x} = u = 0 \qquad (7.23)$$

or equivalently

$$\frac{-(2\delta\alpha\beta(e - x_n) + 2\beta^2(e - x_n) + g'(e))}{2\delta\alpha^2} = 0, \qquad (7.24)$$

which is the same equation for the equilibria as derived from the Hamiltonian, see Equation 7.12. From HJB equation

$$\delta V(e) = \max_u \left[ j(e, u) + g(e) + V'(e)u \right]$$

$$= \max_u \left[ (\alpha u + \beta(e - x_n))^2 + g(e) + V'(e)u \right], \qquad (7.25)$$

computing $\partial[\cdot]/\partial u = 0$ gives

$$\frac{d[\cdot]}{du} = 2\alpha(\alpha u + \beta(e - x_n)) + V'(e) = 0$$

or

$$u = \frac{-(2\alpha\beta(e - x_n) + V'(e))}{2\alpha^2}. \qquad (7.26)$$

Substituting Equation 7.26 into Equation 7.25,

$$\delta V(e) = \left( \frac{-(2\alpha\beta(e - x_n) + V'(e))}{2\alpha} + \beta(e - x_n) \right)^2 + g(e)$$

$$- V'(e) \frac{2\alpha\beta(e - x_n) + V'(e)}{2\alpha^2}$$

$$= \left( -\beta(e - x_n) - \frac{V'(e)}{2\alpha} + \beta(e - x_n) \right)^2 + g(e) \qquad (7.27)$$

$$- \frac{\beta}{\alpha}(e - x_n)V'(e) - \frac{1}{2\alpha^2}V'(e)^2$$

$$= \frac{1}{4\alpha^2}V'(e)^2 - \frac{1}{2\alpha^2}V'(e)^2 - \frac{\beta}{\alpha}(e - x_n)V'(e) + g(e)$$

$$0 = \frac{1}{4\alpha^2}V'(e)^2 + \frac{\beta}{\alpha}(e - x_n)V'(e) + \delta V(e) - g(e)$$

$$0 = V'(e)^2 + 4\alpha\beta(e - x_n)V'(e) + 4\alpha^2(\delta V(e) - g(e))$$

$$V'(e) = \frac{-4\alpha\beta(e - x_n) \pm \sqrt{16\alpha^2\beta^2(e - x_n)^2 - 16\alpha^2(\delta V(e) - g(e))}}{2}$$

$$= -2\alpha\beta(e - x_n) \pm \sqrt{4\alpha^2\beta^2(e \quad x_n)^2 - 4\alpha^2(\delta V(e) - g(e))}.$$

$$(7.28)$$

Furthermore, we solve the differential Equation 7.28 forward and backward with the initial condition

$$V(\hat{x}_i) = \frac{1}{\delta}h(\hat{x}_i). \qquad (7.29)$$

Finally, we compute

$$V(x) = \underset{i}{\text{Min}} \, V_i \qquad (7.30)$$

where $V(x)$, the value function, is the lower envelop of all our piecewise solutions generated by Equation 7.28 with initial conditions 7.29. Details of the numerical computations of Equations 7.28 and 7.30 and thus the Skiba point can be found in Semmler and Sieveking (1999).

# CHAPTER 8

# Asset Price Volatility and Monetary Policy

## 8.1. INTRODUCTION

Recently, it has been observed that the inflation rates in the industrial countries in the 1990s remained relatively stable and low, while the prices of equities, bonds and foreign exchanges experienced a strong volatility with the liberalization of financial markets. Some central banks, therefore, have become concerned with such volatility and doubt whether it is justifiable on the basis of economic fundamentals. The question has arisen whether a monetary policy should be pursued that takes into account financial markets and asset price stabilization. In order to answer this question, it is necessary to model the relationship between asset prices and the real economy. An early study of this type can be found in Blanchard (1981) who has analyzed the relation between the stock value, interest rate and output and hereby considered the effects of monetary and fiscal policies. Recent work that emphasizes the relationship between asset prices and monetary policy includes Bernanke and Gertler (1999), Smets (1997), Kent and Lowe (1997), Chiarella et al. (2001), Mehra (1998), Vickers (1999), Filardo (2000) and Dupor (2001).

Among these papers, the research by Bernanke and Gertler (1999) has attracted much attention. They employ a macroeconomic model and explore how the macroeconomy may be affected by alternative monetary policy rules, which may or may not take into account the asset-price bubble. There they conclude that it is desirable for central banks to focus on underlying inflationary pressures and "it is neither necessary nor desirable for monetary policy to respond to changes in asset price, except to the extent that they help to forecast inflationary or deflationary pressures" (Bernanke and Gertler, 1999, p. 43).

The shortcomings of the position by Bernanke and Gertler (1999) may, however, be expressed as follows. First, they do not derive monetary policy rules from certain estimated models, but instead design artificially alternative monetary policy rules, which may or may not consider asset-price bubbles and then explore the effects of these rules on the economy. Second, Bernanke and Gertler (1999) assume that the asset-price bubble always grows at a certain rate before breaking. However, the asset-price bubble in reality might not break suddenly, but may instead increase or decrease at a certain rate before becoming zero. Third, they assume that the bubble can exist for a few periods and will not occur again after breaking. Therefore, they explore the effects of the asset-price bubble on the real economy in the short-run. Fourth, they do not endogenize the probability that the asset-price bubble will break in the next period because little is known about the market psychology. Monetary policy with endogenized probability for bubbles to break may be different from that with an exogenous probability.

The difference between our model below and that of Bernanke and Gertler (1999) consists in the following. First, we employ an intertemporal framework to explore what the optimal monetary policy should be with and without the financial markets taken into account. Second, we assume that the bubble does not break suddenly and does not have to always grow at a certain rate; on the contrary, it may increase or decrease at a certain rate with some probability. The bubble does not have to break in certain periods and moreover, it can occur again even after breaking. Third, we assume that the probability that the asset-price bubble will increase or decrease in the next period can be endogenized. This assumption has also been made by Kent and Lowe (1997). They assume that the probability for an asset-price bubble to break is a function of the current asset-price bubble and the monetary policy. The drawback of Kent and Lowe (1997), however, is that they explore only positive bubbles and assume a linear probability function, which is not bounded between 0 and 1. Following Bernanke and Gertler (1999), we consider both positive and negative bubbles and employ a non-linear probability function which lies between 0 and 1.

What, however, complicates the response of monetary policy to asset price volatility is the relationship of asset prices and product prices, the latter being mainly the concern of the central banks. Low asset prices may be accompanied by low or negative inflation rates. Yet, there is a zero bound on the nominal interest rate. The danger of deflation and the so-called "liquidity trap" has recently attracted much attention because there exists, for example, a severe deflation and recession in Japan and monetary policy seems to be of little help since the nominal rate is almost zero and can hardly be lowered further. On the other hand, the financial market of Japan has also been in a depression for a long time. Although some researchers have discussed the zero interest-rate bound and liquidity trap in Japan, little attention has been paid to the asset price depression in the presence of a zero bound on the nominal rate. We will explore this problem with some simulations of a simple model.

The remainder of this chapter is organized as follows. In section 8.2, we set up the basic model under the assumption that central banks pursue monetary policy to minimize a quadratic loss function. We will derive a monetary policy rule from the basic model by assuming that the output can be affected by asset-price bubbles. The probability for the asset-price bubble to increase or decrease in the next period is assumed to be a constant. Section 8.3 explores evidence of the monetary policy with asset price in the Euro-area with a model set up by Clarida et al. (1998). Section 8.4 extends the model by assuming that the probability that the asset-price bubble will increase or decrease in the next period is influenced by the size of the bubble and the current interest rate. Section 8.5 explores how the asset price may affect the real economy in the presence of the danger of deflation and a zero bound on the nominal rate. The last section concludes this chapter.

## 8.2. THE BASIC MODEL

### 8.2.1. Monetary policy rule from a traditional model

Let us rewrite the simple model explored in Chapter 6:

$$\underset{\{r_t\}_0^\infty}{\text{Min}} \sum_{t=0}^{\infty} \rho^t L_t$$

with

$$L_t = (\pi_t - \pi^*)^2 + \lambda y_t^2, \qquad \lambda > 0,$$

subject to

$$\pi_{t+1} = \alpha_1 \pi_t + \alpha_2 y_t, \qquad \alpha_i > 0 \tag{8.1}$$

$$y_{t+1} = \beta_1 y_t - \beta_2 (r_t - \pi_t), \qquad \beta_i > 0, \tag{8.2}$$

where $\pi_t$ denotes the deviation of the inflation rate from its target $\pi^*$ (assumed to be zero here), $y_t$ is output gap and $r_t$ denotes the gap between the short-term nominal rate $R_t$ and the long-run level of the short-term rate $\bar{R}$ (i.e. $r_t = R_t - \bar{R}$). $\rho$ is the discount factor bounded between 0 and 1. In order for consistent expectations to exist, $\alpha_1$ is usually assumed to be 1.

From Chapter 6 one knows that the optimal policy rule reads

$$r_t = f_1 \pi_t + f_2 y_t, \tag{8.3}$$

with

$$f_1 = 1 + \frac{\rho\alpha_1^2\alpha_2\Omega_1}{(\lambda + \rho\alpha_2^2\Omega_1)\beta_2}, \tag{8.4}$$

$$f_2 = \frac{\beta_1}{\beta_2} + \frac{\rho\alpha_2^2\alpha_1\Omega_1}{(\lambda + \rho\alpha_2^2\Omega_1)\beta_2}, \tag{8.5}$$

and

$$\Omega_1 = \frac{1}{2}\left(1 - \frac{\lambda(1 - \rho\alpha_1^2)}{\rho\alpha_2^2} + \sqrt{\left(1 - \frac{\lambda(1 - \rho\alpha_1^2)}{\rho\alpha_2^2}\right)^2 + \frac{4\lambda}{\rho\alpha_2^2}}\right). \tag{8.6}$$

Equation 8.3 shows that the optimal short-term interest rate is a linear function of the inflation rate and output gap. It is similar to the Taylor rule (Taylor, 1993). The simulations undertaken in Chapter 6 show that the state and control variables converge to zero over time.

### 8.2.2. Monetary policy rule with asset-price bubbles

The model explored above does not take account of asset prices. Recently, however, some researchers argue that the financial markets can probably influence inflation and output. Filardo (2000), for example, surveys some research, which argues that the stock price may influence inflation. Bernanke and Gertler (1999) explore how asset-price bubbles can affect the real economy with alternative monetary policy rules. Smets (1997) derives an optimal monetary policy rule from an intertemporal model under the assumption that the stock price can affect output. In the research below, we also take into account the effects of the financial markets on output and explore what the monetary policy rule should be. Before setting up the model we will explain some basic concepts.

In the research below, we assume that the stock price $s_t$ consists of the fundamental value $\tilde{s}_t$ and the asset-price bubble $b_t$. We will not discuss how to compute the asset-price bubble or the fundamental value here, because this requires much work which is out of the scope of this chapter.[1] The stock price reads

$$s_t = \tilde{s}_t + b_t.$$

We further assume that if the stock price equals its fundamental value, the financial market exacts no effects on output gap, that is, the financial market affects output gap only through asset-price bubbles. The asset-price bubble can either be positive or negative. The difference between the bubble in our research and those of Blanchard and Watson (1982), Bernanke and Gertler (1999) and Kent and Lowe (1997) is briefly stated below.

The so-called "rational bubble" defined by Blanchard and Watson (1982) cannot be negative because a negative bubble can lead to negative expected stock prices. Another difference between the bubble in this chapter and a rational bubble is that the latter always increases before breaking. Therefore, a rational bubble is non-stationary. Bernanke and Gertler (1999) also define the bubble as the gap between the stock price and its fundamental value. It can be positive or negative. The reason that they do not assume a rational bubble is that the non-stationarity of a rational bubble leads to technical problems in their framework. Kent and Lowe (1997) explore only positive bubbles.

Bernanke and Gertler (1999) and Kent and Lowe (1997), however, have something in common: they all assume that the bubble will break in a few periods (four or five periods) from a certain value to zero *suddenly* rather than *gradually*. Moreover, if the bubble is broken, it will not occur again. This is, in fact, not true in practice, because in reality the bubble does not necessarily break suddenly from a large or low value, but may decrease or increase step by step before becoming zero rapidly or slowly. Especially, if the bubble is negative, it is implausible that the stock price will

---

[1] Alternative approaches have been proposed to compute the fundamental value and bubbles of the asset price. One example can be found in Shiller (1984).

return to its fundamental value suddenly. A common assumption of the rational bubble and those definitions of Bernanke and Gertler (1999) and Kent and Lowe (1997) is that they all assume that the bubble will grow at a certain rate before it bursts.

Although we also define the asset-price bubble as the deviation of the asset price from its fundamental value, the differences between the bubble in this chapter and those mentioned above are obvious. To be precise, the bubble in our research below has the following properties: (a) it can be positive or negative, (b) it can increase or decrease before becoming zero or may even change from a positive (negative) one to a negative (positive) one and does not have to burst suddenly, (c) nobody knows when it will burst and (d) it can occur again in the next period even if it becomes zero in the current period. Therefore, we assume the asset-price bubble evolves in the following way

$$b_{t+1} = \begin{cases} b_t(1 + g_1) + \varepsilon_{t+1}, & \text{with probability } p \\ b_t(1 - g_2) + \varepsilon_{t+1}, & \text{with probability } 1 - p \end{cases} \tag{8.7}$$

where $g_1, g_2(\geq 0)$ are the growth rate or decrease rate of the bubble; $g_1$ can, of course, equal $g_2$. $\varepsilon_t$ is an iid noise with zero mean and a constant variance. Equation 8.7 indicates that if the asset-price bubble $b_t$ is positive, it may increase at rate $g_1$ with probability $p$ and decrease at rate $g_2$ with probability $1 - p$ in the next period. If the bubble is negative, however, it may decrease at rate $g_1$ with probability $p$ and increase at rate $g_2$ with probability $1 - p$ in the next period. The probability $p$ is assumed to be a constant in this section, but state-dependent in the fourth section. From this equation one finds that even if the bubble is zero in the current period, it might not be zero in the next period.

Before exploring the monetary policy with asset-price bubbles theoretically, we explore some empirical evidence of the effects of the share bubbles on output gap. To be precise, we estimate the following equation by way of the OLS with the quarterly data of several OECD countries:

$$y_t = c_0 + c_1 y_{t-1} + c_2 b_{t-1} + \varepsilon_t, \qquad \varepsilon_t \sim N(0, \sigma_\varepsilon^2) \quad (8.8)$$

with $y_t$ denoting output gap. Following Clarida et al. (1998), we use the industrial production index (IPI) to measure output. The output gap is measured by the percentage deviation of the IPI (base year: 1995) from its Band-Pass filtered trend.[2] Similarly the asset-price bubble is measured by the percentage deviation of the share price index (base year: 1995) from its Band-Pass filtered trend just for simplicity. The estimation of Equation 8.8 is shown in Table 8.1 with $T$-statistics in parentheses. The estimate of $c_0$ is not shown just for simplicity. The estimation is undertaken for two samples: (a) 1980–1999 and (b) 1990–1999.

From Table 8.1 one finds that $c_2$ is significant enough in most cases. For the sample of 1990–1999 it is significant enough in the cases of all countries except the US, but for the sample of 1980–1999 it is significant enough in the case of the US. For the sample of 1980–1999 it is insignificant in the cases of France and Italy, but significant enough in the cases of both countries in the period of 1990–1999. It is significant enough in both samples of Japan. In short, the evidence in Table 8.1 does show some positive relation between the share bubbles and output gap.

In the estimation above, we have considered only the effect of the lagged asset-price bubble on output for simplicity, but in reality the expectation of financial markets may also influence output. As regards how financial variables may influence output, the basic argument is that the changes of the asset price may influence consumption (see Ludvigson and Steindel, 1999, for example) and

---

[2] The reader is referred to Baxter and King (1995) for the Band-Pass filter. As surveyed by Orphanides and van Norden (2002), there are many methods to measure the output gap. We find that filtering the IPI using the Band-Pass filter leaves the measure of the output gap essentially unchanged from the measure with the HP-filter. The Band-Pass filter has also been used by Sargent (1999).

Table 8.1: Estimation of Equation 8.8.

| Parameter | Sample | US | UK[a] | France | Germany | Italy | Japan |
|-----------|--------|-----|-------|--------|---------|-------|-------|
| $c_1$ | 1980.1 – 1999.1 | 0.902 (22.218) | 0.827 (16.821) | 0.879 (19.170) | 0.855 (19.313) | 0.912 (22.024) | 0.865 (18.038) |
|  | 1990.1 – 1999.1 | 0.925 (15.790) | 0.918 (22.362) | 0.836 (12.153) | 0.808 (16.267) | 0.843 (11.666) | 0.864 (12.889) |
| $c_2$ | 1980.1 – 1999.1 | 0.064 (5.158) | 0.050 (2.898) | 0.005 (0.713) | 0.021 (2.506) | 0.002 (0.385) | 0.045 (3.505) |
|  | 1990.1 – 1999.1 | 0.0005 (0.035) | 0.099 (5.517) | 0.032 (2.328) | 0.075 (6.085) | 0.020 (1.921) | 0.063 (3.220) |
| $R^2$ | 1980.1 – 1999.1 | 0.875 | 0.824 | 0.845 | 0.864 | 0.869 | 0.835 |
|  | 1990.1 – 1999.1 | 0.886 | 0.953 | 0.849 | 0.928 | 0.819 | 0.858 |

[a]The estimation of the UK is undertaken for 1980.1 – 1997.1 and 1990.1 – 1997.1 because the share price index after 1997 is not available. Data sources: OECD and IMF.

investment, which may in turn affect inflation and output. The investment, however, can be affected by both current and forward-looking behavior.

Therefore, in the model below we assume that output gap can be influenced not only by the lagged asset-price bubble but also by expectations of asset-price bubbles formed in the previous period, that is

$$y_{t+1} = \beta_1 y_t - \beta_2(r_t - \pi_t) + \beta_3 b_t + (1 - \beta_3)Eb_{t+1|t},$$
$$1 > \beta_3 > 0, \qquad (8.9)$$

where $Eb_{t+1|t}$ denotes the expectation of $b_{t+1}$ formed at time $t$. From Equation 8.7 and $E\varepsilon_{t+1|t} = 0$ one knows

$$Eb_{t+1|t} = [1 - g_2 + p(g_1 + g_2)]b_t. \qquad (8.10)$$

As a result, Equation 8.9 turns out to be

$$y_{t+1} = \beta_1 y_t - \beta_2(r_t - \pi_t) + \{1 + (1 - \beta_3)[p(g_1 + g_2) - g_2]\}b_t. $$
$$(8.11)$$

One can follow the same procedure as in Chapter 6 to solve the optimal control problem, since the bubble is taken as an exogenous variable. After replacing Equation 8.2 with Equation 8.11 one obtains the following monetary policy rule for the central bank

$$r_t = f_1 \pi_t + f_2 y_t + f_3 b_t, \qquad (8.12)$$

with $f_1$ and $f_2$ given by Equations 8.4 and 8.5 and

$$f_3 = \frac{1}{\beta_2} \{1 + (1 - \beta_3)[p(g_1 + g_2) - g_2]\}. \qquad (8.13)$$

This rule is similar to the one obtained before except that there is an additional term of the bubble. The effect of $p$ on the monetary policy rule can be explored from the following derivative

$$\frac{df_3}{dp} = \frac{1}{\beta_2}[(1 - \beta_3)(g_1 + g_2)] \geq 0. \qquad (8.14)$$

The interpretation of Equation 8.14 depends on whether the bubble is positive or negative. If the bubble is positive, a larger $p$ leads to a higher $f_3$ and as a result, a higher $r_t$. This is consistent with intuition, because in order to eliminate a positive bubble which is likely to continue to increase, it is necessary to raise the interest rate, since it is usually argued that there exists a negative relation between the interest rate and stock price.

  If the bubble is negative, however, a larger $p$ also leads to a higher $f_3$ but a lower $r_t$, since $b_t$ is negative. That is, in order to eliminate a negative bubble which is likely to continue to decrease further, the interest rate should be decreased because of the negative relation between the interest rate and asset price. As stated before, although $p$ may be state-dependent, we do not consider this possibility in this section.

## 8.3. MONETARY POLICY RULE IN PRACTICE: THE CASE OF THE EURO-AREA

So far we have explored theoretically the monetary policy rule with the asset price volatility considered. The question is then whether asset-price bubbles have been taken into account in practice. This section presents some empirical evidence on this problem.

Following Clarida et al. (1998) (CGG98 for short), Smets (1997) estimates the monetary reaction function of Canada and Australia by adding three financial variables into the CGG98 model, namely, the nominal trade-weighted exchange rate, 10-year nominal bond yield and a broad stock market index. His conclusion is that an appreciation of the exchange rate induces a significant change in the interest rates of the Bank of Canada. Moreover, he finds that changes in the stock market index also induces significant changes in the policy reaction function. The response coefficients in the case of Australia are, however, insignificant.

Bernanke and Gertler (1999) also follow CGG98 by adding stock returns into the model to test whether interest rates respond to stock returns in the US and Japan. Their conclusion is that the federal funds rate did not show a significant response to stock returns from 1979 to 1997. For Japan, however, they find different results. To be precise, for the whole period of 1979–1997, there is little evidence that the stock market played a role in the interest-rate setting, but for the two subperiods, 1979–1989 and 1989–1997, the coefficients of stock returns have enough significant $T$-statistics, but with different signs. Rigobon and Sack (2001), however, claim that the US monetary policy has reacted significantly to stock market movements.

In this section, we also follow CGG98 to test whether the Euro-area monetary policy shows a significant response to the stock market.[3] The model of CGG98 has been presented in Chapter 4.

---

[3] The aggregation of data is the same as in Chapter 2.

After adding the stock market into Equation 4.7, one obtains

$$R_t^* = \bar{R} + \beta(E[\pi_{t+n}|\Omega_t] - \pi^*) + \gamma(E[Y_t|\Omega_t] - Y_t^*)$$
$$+ \theta(E[s_{t+n}|\Omega_t] - \tilde{s}_{t+n}), \tag{8.15}$$

where $s_{t+n}$ is the asset price in period $t + n$ and $\tilde{s}_t$ denotes the fundamental value of the asset price. $\theta$ is expected to be positive, since we assume that central banks try to stabilize the stock market with the interest rate as the instrument. Define $\alpha = \bar{R} - \beta\pi^*$, $y_t = Y_t - Y_t^*$ and $b_{t+n} = s_{t+n} - \tilde{s}_{t+n}$ (namely the asset-price bubble), Equation 8.15 can be rewritten as

$$R_t^* = \alpha + \beta E[\pi_{t+n}|\Omega_t] + \gamma E[y_t|\Omega_t] + \theta E[b_{t+n}|\Omega_t], \tag{8.16}$$

after substituting Equation 8.16 into Equation (4.6), one has the following path for $R_t$:

$$R_t = (1 - \kappa)\alpha + (1 - \kappa)\beta E[\pi_{t+n}|\Omega_t] + (1 - \kappa)\gamma E[y_t|\Omega_t]$$
$$+ (1 - \kappa)\theta E[b_{t+n}|\Omega_t] + \kappa R_{t-1} + v_t. \tag{8.17}$$

One can rewrite the above equation as

$$R_t = (1 - \kappa)\alpha + (1 - \kappa)\beta\pi_{t+n} + (1 - \kappa)\gamma y_t$$
$$+ (1 - \kappa)\theta b_{t+n} + \kappa R_{t-1} + \eta_t, \tag{8.18}$$

where $\eta_t = -(1 - \kappa)\{\beta(\pi_{t+n} - E[\pi_{t+n}|\Omega_t]) + \gamma(y_t - E[y_t|\Omega_t]) + \theta(b_{t+n} - E[b_{t+n}|\Omega_t])\} + v_t$. Let $\mu_t$ ($\in \Omega_t$) be a vector of variables within the central bank's information set when it sets the interest rate that are orthogonal to $\eta_t$, one has

$$E[R_t - (1 - \kappa)\alpha - (1 - \kappa)\beta\pi_{t+n} - (1 - \kappa)\gamma y_t$$
$$- (1 - \kappa)\theta b_{t+n} - \kappa R_{t-1}|\mu_t] = 0. \tag{8.19}$$

Following CGG98 and the estimation in Chapter 4 we use the GMM to estimate this equation with the EU3 quarterly data.

Table 8.2: GMM estimation of Equation 8.19 with different $n$.

| Parameter | Estimates | | | | |
|---|---|---|---|---|---|
| | $n = 0$ | $n = 1$ | $n = 2$ | $n = 3$ | $n = 4$ |
| $\kappa$ | 0.813 (19.792) | 0.811 (18.561) | 0.894 (30.224) | 0.833 (15.870) | 0.832 (17.089) |
| $\alpha$ | 0.030 (4.581) | 0.028 (3.920) | 0.007 (0.466) | 0.020 (1.918) | 0.021 (2.074) |
| $\beta$ | 0.748 (5.446) | 0.777 (5.343) | 1.522 (3.921) | 0.940 (4.410) | 0.890 (4.567) |
| $\gamma$ | 2.046 (5.679) | 2.011 (5.300) | 1.626 (3.234) | 2.345 (3.990) | 2.363 (4.203) |
| $\theta$ | 0.014 (0.509) | 0.030 (0.927) | 0.240 (2.328) | 0.081 (1.264) | 0.082 (1.100) |
| $R^2$ | 0.914 | 0.913 | 0.930 | 0.904 | 0.904 |
| $J$-statistic | 0.088 | 0.087 | 0.111 | 0.069 | 0.074 |

Let $\pi_{t+n} = \pi_{t+4}$, as for $b_{t+n}$ we will try the estimation with different $n$ (0, 1, ...4).[4] The estimates with different $n$ of $b_{t+n}$ are presented in Table 8.2, with $T$-statistics in parentheses.

As shown in Table 8.2, $\beta$ and $\gamma$ always have the correct signs and significant $T$-statistics, indicating that the inflation and output always play important roles in the interest-rate setting. As for $\theta$, one finds that it always has the correct sign, but the $T$-statistics are not always significant enough. When $n = 0$ and 1, it is insignificant, when $n = 3$ and 4, it is not enough significant, but when $n = 2$ it is significant enough. Therefore, one may say that the asset price may have played a role (although not necessarily an important one) in the interest-rate setting in the Euro-area. The simulated interest rate with $b_{t+n} = b_{t+2}$ is presented together with the actual interest rate in Figure 8.1. It is clear that the two rates are close to each other, especially after the second half of the 1980s.

---

[4] Correction for MA(4) autocorrelation is undertaken, and $J$-statistics are presented to illustrate the validity of the overidentifying restrictions. A brief explanation of the $J$-statistic is given in footnote 7 in Chapter 2.

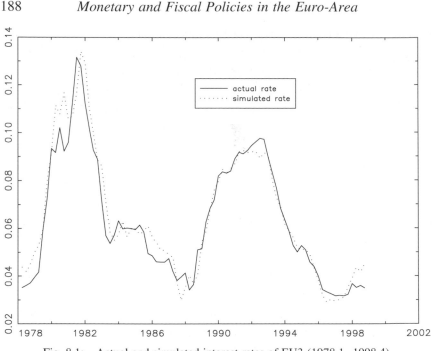

Fig. 8.1:   Actual and simulated interest rates of EU3 (1978.1 – 1998.4).

## 8.4.  ENDOGENIZING PROBABILITIES AND A NON-LINEAR MONETARY POLICY RULE

Up to now we have explored monetary policy with a constant probability for the asset-price bubble to increase or decrease in the next period. This is, in fact, a simplified assumption. Monetary policy and other economic variables can probably influence the path of $p$. Bernanke and Gertler (1999) take it as an exogenous variable because so little is known about the effects of policy actions on $p$ that it is hard to endogenize $p$. Kent and Lowe (1997), however, endogenize the probability for the bubble to break as follows:

$$p_{t+1} = \phi_0 + \phi_1 b_t + \phi_2 r_t, \qquad \phi_i > 0. \qquad (8.20)$$

This function implies that the probability for the asset-price bubble to break in the next period depends on three factors: (a) an exogenous probability $\phi_0$, (b) the size of the current bubble and (c) the level of the current interest rate. The larger the size of the current bubble and the higher the current interest rate, the larger the probability for the bubble to break in the next period. Note that, as mentioned before, Kent and Lowe (1997) analyze only positive asset-price bubbles. As mentioned by Kent and Lowe (1997), as the bubble becomes larger and larger, more and more people recognize it and become reluctant to buy the asset and this, in turn, makes it more likely for a bubble to break. The effect of the current interest rate level on $p$ is clear. That is, as the interest rate increases, the economic agents may expect the asset price to decrease, which raises the probability that the bubble will break in the next period.

In this section, we will endogenize the $p$. Although the function given by Equation 8.20 seems to be a reasonable choice, we will not employ it below for the following reasons: (a) as stated above, Kent and Lowe (1997) explore only positive bubbles, while we consider both positive and negative ones. When the asset-price bubble is positive, Equation 8.20 is a reasonable choice. If the bubble is negative, however, this function has problems. (b) A probability function should be bounded between 0 and 1, but Equation 8.20 is an increasing function without bounds. (c) Equation 8.20 is a linear function, indicating that $p$ changes proportionally to the changes of the bubble size and the interest rate. This may not be true in reality. (d) The $p$ in our model describes the probability that the bubble will increase (if the bubble is positive) or decrease (if the bubble is negative) in the next period, while it in the model of Kent and Lowe (1997) describes the probability that the positive bubble will break in the next period.

Before designing the probability function, we introduce a function $h(x)$ that will be used below. To be precise, define

$$h(x) = \tfrac{1}{2}[1 - \tanh(x)]. \tag{8.21}$$

It is clear that

$$\frac{dh(x)}{dx} = -\frac{1}{2\cosh^2(x)} < 0,$$

with $\lim_{x \to \infty} h(x) = 0$ and $\lim_{x \to -\infty} h(x) = 1$. The function $h(x)$ is shown in Figure 8.2.

Next, we define the probability function $p_{t+1}$ as

$$p_{t+1} = \tfrac{1}{2}\{1 - \tanh[\vartheta(b_t, r_t)]\}, \tag{8.22}$$

with

$$\vartheta(b_t, r_t) = \phi_1 f(b_t) + \phi_2 \operatorname{sign}(b_t) r_t, \qquad \phi_i > 0,$$

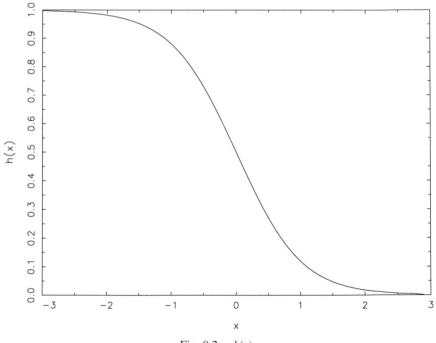

Fig. 8.2: $h(x)$.

where sign($b_t$) is the sign function which reads

$$\text{sign}(b_t) = \begin{cases} 1, & \text{if } b_t > 0, \\ 0, & \text{if } b_t = 0, \\ -1, & \text{if } b_t < 0, \end{cases} \tag{8.23}$$

and $f(b_t)$ is the so-called LINEX function which is non-negative and asymmetric around 0. The LINEX function, which can be found in Varian (1975) and Nobay and Peel (2003), reads

$$f(x) = \kappa[e^{\varphi x} - \varphi x - 1], \qquad \kappa > 0, \quad \varphi \neq 0. \tag{8.24}$$

$\kappa$ scales the function and $\varphi$ determines the asymmetry of the function. An example of $f(x)$ with $\kappa = 0.1$ and $\varphi = \pm 1.2$ is shown in Figure 8.3. In the work below we take $\kappa = 1$ and $\varphi > 0$.

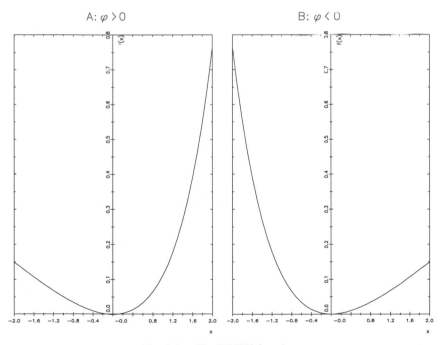

Fig. 8.3: The LINEX function.

The function $f(x)$ with a positive $\varphi$ is flatter when $x$ is negative than when $x$ is positive.

It is clear that

$$\frac{\partial p_{t+1}}{\partial b_t} = -\frac{\phi_1 \varphi (e^{\varphi b_t} - 1)}{2 \cosh^2[\vartheta(b_t, r_t)]} \begin{cases} < 0, & \text{if } b_t > 0, \\ > 0, & \text{if } b_t < 0. \end{cases} \qquad (8.25)$$

Therefore, the probability function given by Equation 8.22 indicates that the effects of the current asset-price bubble $b_t$ on $p_{t+1}$ depends on whether the bubble is positive or negative. In fact, the probability function defined above is asymmetric around $b_t = 0$. If it is positive, a larger bubble in the current period implies a lower probability that it will increase in the next period. This is consistent with the implication of the model of Kent and Lowe (1997): as more and more economic agents realize the bubble, they will become reluctant to buy the asset as the stock price becomes higher and higher. This in turn prevents the stock price from increasing further. Note that if the bubble is negative, $p$ represents the probability that $b_t$ will decrease in the next period. In the case of a negative bubble, Equation 8.25 indicates that the lower the stock price (but the larger the absolute value of the bubble in this case), the lower the probability that the (negative) bubble will continue to decrease in the next period. The justification is the same as for the positive bubble. As the stock price becomes lower and lower, it is also closer and closer to its lowest point (stock price does not decrease without end!) and may, therefore, be more and more likely to increase in the future. But we assume that the negative bubble does not influence $p_{t+1}$ as strongly as a positive one, because in reality economic agents are usually more pessimistic in a bear market than optimistic in a bull market.

Moreover, it seems more difficult to activate a financial market when it is in recession than to hold it down when it is booming. This is what the function $f(b_t)$ implies. It is flatter when $b_t < 0$ than when $b_t$ is positive. An example of $p_{t+1}$ with $\phi_1 = 0.4$, $\varphi = 10$ and $r_t = 0$

is shown in Figure 8.4, it is flatter when $b_t$ is negative than when it is positive. Note that in Figure 8.4 one finds if $b_t = 0$, then $p_{t+1} = 0.5$. From the process of the bubble one knows if $b_t = 0$ and $r_t = 0$, $b_{t+1}$ is $\varepsilon_{t+1}$ which can either be positive or negative. Because little is known about the sign of the noise $\varepsilon_{t+1}$, the economic agents then expect it to be positive or negative with an equal probability of 0.5.

The effect of $r_t$ on $p_{t+1}$ can be seen from below:

$$\frac{\partial p_{t+1}}{\partial r_t} = -\frac{\phi_2 \ \text{sign}(b_t)}{2 \cosh^2[\vartheta(b_t, r_t)]} \begin{cases} < 0, & \text{if } b_t > 0, \\ > 0, & \text{if } b_t < 0. \end{cases} \tag{8.26}$$

This indicates that if the asset-price bubble is positive, an increase in the interest rate will lower the probability that the bubble will increase in the next period. If the bubble is negative, however, an increase in $r_t$ will increase the probability that the bubble will decrease in the next period. The probability function with $\phi_1 = 0.4$, $\phi_2 = 0.8$ and $\varphi = 10$ is shown in Figure 8.5.

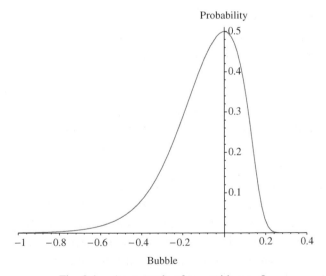

Fig. 8.4:   An example of $p_{t+1}$ with $r_t = 0$.

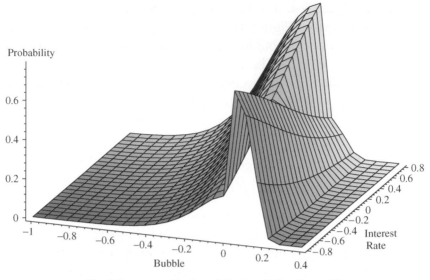

Fig. 8.5:    $p_{t+1}$ with $\phi_1 = 0.4$, $\phi_2 = 0.8$ and $\varphi = 10$.

With the probability function defined by Equation 8.22 one knows that

$$Eb_{t+1|t} = [1 - g_2 + \tfrac{1}{2}\{1 - \tanh[\vartheta(b_t, r_t)]\}(g_1 + g_2)]b_t. \quad (8.27)$$

Following the same procedure as in section 8.2, one finds that the optimal monetary policy rule must satisfy the following equation:

$$r_t = f_1 \pi_t + f_2 y_t$$
$$+ \frac{1}{2\beta_2} \{2 + (1 - \beta_3)\langle g_1 - g_2 - (g_1 + g_2)\tanh[\vartheta(b_t, r_t)]\rangle\}b_t,$$

$$(8.28)$$

with $f_1$ and $f_2$ given by Equations 8.4 and 8.5. Different from the monetary policy rule given by Equation 8.12, in which the optimal interest-rate rule is a linear function of the inflation rate, output gap and asset-price bubble, $r_t$ is now a non-linear function of $\pi_t$, $y_t$ and $b_t$. Moreover, the effects of $\pi_t$, $y_t$ and $b_t$ on $r_t$ are much more complicated than in the previous section. $r_t$ can be affected not only by parameters such as $g_1$ and $g_2$, but also by the parameters, $\phi_1$, $\phi_2$ and $\varphi$ which measure the effects of the size of the bubble and the interest rate on the probability function. Because $r_t$ is non-linear in $\pi_t$, $y_t$ and $b_t$, there might exist multiple equilibria in such a model. It is difficult to obtain an analytical solution of the optimal interest-rate rule from Equation 8.28, we will, therefore, undertake some numerical computation.

Assuming $\pi_t = y_t = 0$ just for simplicity, Figure 8.6 presents Equation 8.28 with alternative values of the parameters with the horizontal axis denoting the asset-price bubble and the vertical axis denoting the interest rate. It is clear that the response of $r_t$ to $b_t$ changes with the parameters. $r_t$ is a monotonic function of $b_t$ when the parameters are assigned some values (see Figure 8.6(5) and (6)). When the parameters are assigned some other values, however, $r_t$ can be a non-monotonic function of $b_t$. In Figure 8.6(1) and (4) the curve cuts the horizontal axis three times, indicating that there may exist multiple equilibria in the model. The parameters for Figure 8.6 are set as follows: $\beta_2 = 0.30$, $\phi_1 = 1.0$, $\phi_2 = 0.80$ and $\varphi = 10$. The other parameters of $\beta_3$, $g_1$ and $g_2$ are assigned different values in different figures as follows: (1) $\beta_3 = 0.005$, $g_1 = 0.001$ and $g_2 = 1.05$; (2) $\beta_3 = 0.10$, $g_1 = 0.01$ and $g_2 = 0.90$; (3) $\beta_3 = 0.005$, $g_1 = 0.001$ and $g_2 = 0.95$; (4) $\beta_3 = 0.005$, $g_1 = 0.001$ and $g_2 = 1.50$; (5) $\beta_3 = 0.25$, $g_1 = 0.10$ and $g_2 = 6.50$; (6) $\beta_3 = 0.25$, $g_1 = 0.01$ and $g_2 = 0.70$. The effects of $g_1$ and $g_2$ on $r_t$ can be seen from Figure 8.6(3) and (4). With other parameters unchanged, the values of $g_1$ and $g_2$ may determine the direction of how $r_t$ moves. In fact, one can compute the derivative of $r_t$ with respect to $b_t$ from Equation 8.28 and find that it is a non-linear function of $r_t$ and $b_t$, with an indeterminate sign.

This section endogenizes the probability that the asset-price bubble will increase or decrease in the next period. Defining $p$ as a function of the asset-price bubble and the current interest rate, one finds that the monetary policy turns out to be a non-linear function of the inflation rate, output gap and asset-price bubble, and there might exist multiple equilibria in the economy.

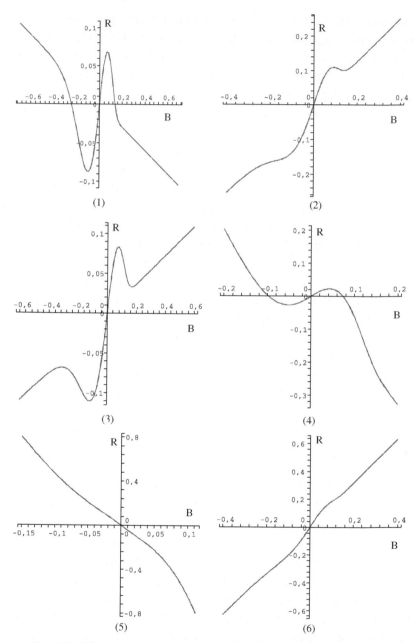

Fig. 8.6:   The response of $r_t$ to $b_t$ with alternative values of parameters.

Recently, some researchers argue that the linear interest-rate rules may not have captured the truth of monetary policy. Meyer (2000), for example, claims that non-linear monetary policy rules are likely to arise under uncertainty. He argues that "...a nonlinear rule could be justified by nonlinearities in the economy or by a non-normal distribution of policymakers' prior beliefs about the NAIRU." Meyer et al. (2001) provide a theoretical justification for this argument and show some empirical evidence on the relative performance of linear and non-linear rules. Non-linear monetary policy rules can also be induced by a non-linear Phillips curve and a non-quadratic loss function of central banks. Monetary policy with non-linear Phillips curves has been studied by Semmler and Zhang (2004) and Dolado et al. (2002), for example. Dolado et al. (2002) find that the US monetary policy can be characterized by a non-linear policy rule after 1983, but not before 1979. Kim et al. (2002), however, find that the US monetary policy rule has been non-linear before 1979, and little evidence of non-linearity has been found for the period after 1979. Our research above shows that a non-linear monetary policy rule can also arise in a model with financial markets, assuming an endogenous probability for the asset-price bubble to increase or decrease in the next period.

## 8.5. THE ZERO BOUND ON THE NOMINAL INTEREST RATE

Above we have discussed the relationship of monetary policy rule and asset prices. In the case of a constant probability ($p$) for the asset-price bubble to increase or decrease in the next period, the optimal monetary policy turns out to be a linear function of the inflation, output gap and asset-price bubbles, similar to the simple Taylor rule except that the asset-price bubble is added as an additional term. However, if $p$ is assumed to be an endogenous variable depending on the monetary policy and the asset-price bubble size, the monetary policy rule turns out to be a non-linear function of the inflation rate, output gap and asset-price bubble.

A drawback of the Taylor rule, and also of the monetary policy discussed above, is that the monetary policy instrument—the short-term interest rate—is assumed to be able to move without bounds. This is, however, not true in practice. One example is the so-called liquidity trap in which a monetary policy cannot be of much help because the short-term nominal interest rate is almost zero and cannot be lowered further. This problem has recently become important because of the liquidity trap in Japan and the low interest rate in the US. If, furthermore, there is deflation, the real interest rate will rise. Considering the zero bound on the short-term interest rate and the possibility of deflation at very low interest rates, the monetary policy can be very different from that without bounds on the interest rate.

Benhabbib and Schmitt-Grohé (2001), for example, argue that once the zero bound on nominal interest rates is taken into account, the active Taylor rule can easily lead to unexpected consequences. To be precise, they find that there may exist an infinite number of trajectories converging to a liquidity trap even if there exists a unique equilibrium.

Kato and Nishiyama (2005) analytically prove and numerically show that the optimal monetary policy in the presence of the zero bound is highly non-linear even in a linear-quadratic model. Eggertsson and Woodford (2003) simulate an economy with zero bound on the interest rate and argue that monetary policy will be effective only if interest rates can be expected to persistently stay low in the future. Coenen and Wieland (2003) explore the effect of a zero-interest-rate bound on the inflation and output in Japan in the context of an open economy. Ullersma (2003) surveys several researchers' views on the zero lower bound.

Most of the recent research on the liquidity trap has been concerned with deflation, namely the decrease of the price level in the product markets. Yet most literature has ignored the depression in the financial markets. The depression of the financial markets can also be a problem in practice, if the financial markets can influence the output and, as a result, affect the inflation rate. Take Japan as an example, the share price index was about 200 in 1990 and decreased to something below 80 in 2001. The IPI was about 108 in 1990 and fluctuated between 107 and 92 afterwards. The inflation rate (changes in the CPI), IPI and share price index of Japan are shown in Figure 8.7(A)–(C) (Data sources: OECD and IMF). The depression in the share market seems to be as serious as the deflation. One finds that the correlation coefficient between the IPI and share price index is as high as 0.72 from 1980 to 2001 and the correlation coefficient between the IPI and the two-quarter lagged share price index is even as high as 0.80. Moreover, the estimates of $c_2$ in Equation 8.8 have enough significant $T$-statistics (3.505 for the sample from 1980.1 to 1999.1 and 3.220 for the sample from 1990.1 to 1999.1). This seems to suggest that the influence of the financial markets on the output should not be overlooked.

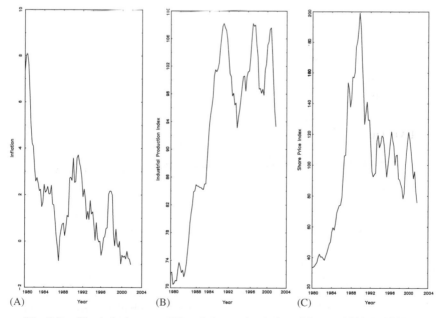

Fig. 8.7: The inflation rate, IPI and share price index of Japan, 1980.1–2001.4.

Let us now return to the liquidity trap problem. The main difference of our research from that of others is that we will explore the zero bound on the nominal interest rate with depression in the financial markets as well as in the product markets (namely deflation).

Let us define $r_t = R_t - \bar{R}$, with $R_t$ being the nominal rate and $\bar{R}$ the long-run level of $R_t$. In the research below we assume $\bar{R} = 0$ for simplicity. In the presence of the zero bound on the nominal rate, we then assume[5]

$$
r_t = \begin{cases} r_o, & \text{if } r_o \geq 0, \\ 0, & \text{if } r_o < 0, \end{cases} \tag{8.29}
$$

where $r_o$ denotes the optimal monetary policy rule derived from the models in the previous sections. The equation above implies that if the optimal monetary policy rule is non-negative, the central bank will adopt the optimal rule, if the optimal rule is negative, however, the nominal rate is set to zero, since it cannot be negative.[6]

We will first undertake some simulations without asset prices considered, as the simple model Equations 8.1 and 8.2. The parameters are set as follows:[7] $\alpha_1 = 0.8$, $\alpha_2 = 0.3$, $\beta_1 = 0.9$, $\beta_2 = 0.3$, $\lambda = 0.5$ and $\rho = 0.97$. In order to explore the effect of the zero bound of the nominal rate on the economy, we assume there exists deflation. The starting values of $\pi_t$ and $y_t$ are set as $-0.08$ and $0.1$, respectively. The optimal monetary policy rule from the basic model is given by Equation 8.3. The simulations with and without the zero-interest-rate bound are shown in Figure 8.8.

---

[5] This is similar to the assumption of Coenen and Wieland (2003) who analyze the effect of a zero-interest-rate bound on inflation and output in Japan in the context of an open economy.

[6] There are some exceptional cases with negative nominal rates, see Cecchetti (1988), for example, but we will ignore these exceptional cases here.

[7] In order for consistent expectations to exist, $\alpha_1$ is usually assumed to be 1. The simulations with $\alpha_1 = 1$ are found essentially unchanged from those with $\alpha_1 = 0.8$.

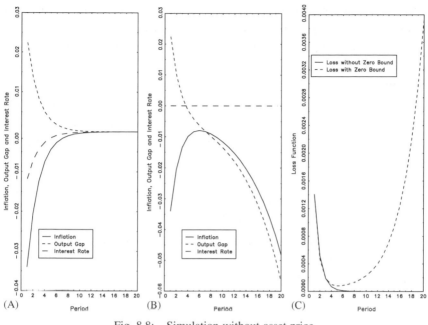

Fig. 8.8:   Simulation without asset price.

In Figure 8.8(A) we show the simulation of the inflation, output gap and $r_t$ without the zero bound on the nominal rate. Therefore $r_t$ is always set in line with Equation 8.3. It is clear that all three variables converge to zero over time. The loss function can, as a result, be minimized to zero. Figure 8.8(B) shows the simulation with a zero-interest-rate bound. One finds that the optimal nominal rate, which is negative as shown in Figure 8.8(A), cannot be reached and has to be set to zero. The inflation and output gaps, as a result, do not converge to zero, but instead evolve into a recession. The deflation becomes more and more severe and the output gap changes from positive to negative and continues to go down over time.

Figure 8.8(C) shows the loss function $\pi^2 + \lambda y^2$ with and without a zero-interest-rate bound. One observes that in the case of no zero-interest-rate bound the loss function converges to zero as $\pi_t$ and $y_t$

goes to zero. In the presence of a zero-interest-rate bound, however, the loss function increases rapidly over time because of the recession.

The simulation undertaken above does not consider the effects of asset prices on the inflation and output. The simulation below assumes that the asset prices can influence the output as Equation 8.9 and the asset-price bubble has the path 8.7. In order to simplify the simulation we just take $b_{t+1} = Eb_{t+1|t}$, therefore, with an initial value of the bubble one can obtain a series of $b_t$. With other parameters assigned the same values as above, the remainder of the parameters are assigned the following values: $g_1 = 0.1$, $g_2 = 0.2$, $p = 0.5$ and $\beta_3 = 0.5$. The initial values of $\pi_t$ and $y_t$ are the same as above. The initial value of $b_t$ is $-0.02$, indicating a depression in the financial markets. The optimal rate $r_0$ is given by Equation 8.12. The simulations with and without a zero-interest-rate bound are shown in Figure 8.9(A)–(C).

In Figure 8.9(A), we show the simulation without a zero bound on $r_t$, this is similar to the case in Figure 8.8(A) where all three variables converge to zero except that $r_t$ in Figure 8.9(A) is lower and converges more slowly than in Figure 8.8(A). Figure 8.9(B) shows the simulation with a zero bound on $r_t$. Again one finds that the optimal rate cannot be reached and $r_t$ has to be set to zero. The economy experiences a recession. This is similar to the case in Figure 8.8(B), but the recession in Figure 8.9(B) is more severe than that in Figure 8.8(B). In Figure 8.8(B), $\pi_t$ and $y_t$ decrease to about $-0.06$ with $t = 20$, but in Figure 8.9(B), however, $\pi_t$ and $y_t$ experience larger and faster decreases and go down to about $-0.8$ in the same period. This is because the output is affected by the depression in the financial markets (negative $b_t$), which also accelerates the deflation through the output. In Figure 8.9(C), we show the loss function with and without a zero bound on $r_t$. The loss function when no zero-interest-rate bound exists converges to zero over time but increases rapidly when there exists a zero-interest-rate bound. But the loss function with a zero-interest-rate bound in Figure 8.9(C) is higher

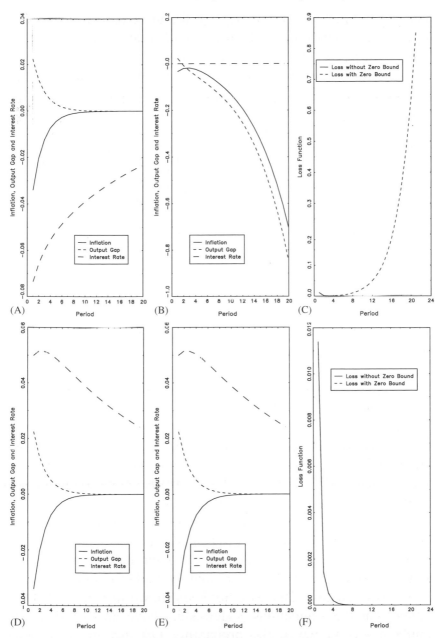

Fig. 8.9: Simulation with asset price.

than that in Figure 8.8(C) because of the more severe recession in Figure 8.9(B) caused by the financial market depression.

Next, we assume that the financial market is not in depression but instead in a boom, that is, the asset-price bubble is positive. We set $b_0 = 0.02$ and obtain a series of positive bubbles. The simulation with the same parameters as above is shown in Figure 8.9(D)–(F). In Figure 8.9(D), all three variables converge to zero when no zero bound on $r_t$ is implemented. In Figure 8.9(E), however, all three variables also converge to zero over time even if there exists a zero bound on the nominal rate. This is different from the cases in Figures 8.8(B) and 8.9(B) where a severe recession occurs. The reason is that in Figure 8.9(E), the asset-price bubble is positive and the optimal interest rate turns out to be positive. The zero-interest-rate bound is, therefore, not binding. As a result, Figure 8.9(E) is exactly the same as Figure 8.9(D). The two loss functions with and without a zero-interest-rate bound are, therefore, also the same, as shown in Figure 8.9(F).

The simulations in this section indicate that in the presence of a zero-interest-rate bound, a deflation can become more severe and the economy may go into a severe recession. Moreover, the recession can be worse if the financial market is also in a depression, because the asset price depression can then decrease the output and as a result makes the deflation more severe. Facing the zero-interest-rate bound and a liquidity trap, some researchers have proposed some policy actions, see Clouse et al. (2003), for example. The simulations above indicate that policy actions that aim at escaping a liquidity trap should not ignore the asset prices, since the financial market depression can make the real-economy recession worse.

On the other hand, a positive asset-price bubble can make the zero-interest-rate bound non-binding, since the optimal rate which takes the financial markets into account may be higher than zero even if there exists deflation. This case has been shown in Figure 8.9(E).

Note that the simulations undertaken above are based on the simple model in which the probability ($p$) that the asset-price bubbles will increase or decrease in the next period is assumed to be exogenous. If $p$ is taken as an endogenous variable, however, the analysis can be more complicated. In the basic model one finds that the optimal monetary policy rule turns out to be a linear function of $b_t$, but in the model with an endogenous $p$, the monetary policy rule turns out to be non-linear in the inflation rate, output gap and asset-price bubble. This has been shown in the simulations in Figure 8.6. In the case of a linear rule it is clear that a negative asset-price bubble lowers the optimal policy rule and may, therefore, increase the likelihood of the zero-interest-rate bound being binding, while a positive bubble increases the optimal nominal rate and may, as a result, reduce the likelihood for the zero-interest-rate bound to be binding. When the optimal policy rule is a non-linear function of the asset price, however, a positive bubble may increase the likelihood for the zero-interest-rate bound to be binding, since the optimal rule can be lowered by the positive bubble. On the other hand, a negative bubble may reduce the likelihood of the zero-interest-rate bound being binding because a negative bubble can raise the optimal rule. An example of the linear and non-linear policy rules in the presence of a zero-interest-rate bound is shown in Figure 8.10(A) and (B).

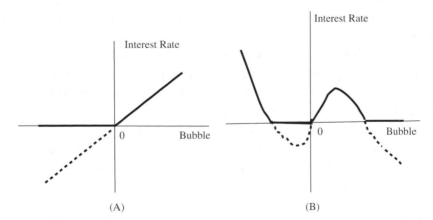

Fig. 8.10:   An example of linear and non-linear policy rules in the presence of the zero-interest-rate bound.

Figure 8.10(B) looks similar to Figure 8.6(1). In Figure 8.10, we set the optimal rule to be zero if it is negative. In some cases, an endogenous $p$ can make the optimal policy rule very different from that with a constant $p$. Figure 8.6(5) is a good example: unlike the linear rule which is an increasing function of the asset-price bubble, $r_t$ in Figure 8.6(5) is a decreasing function of $b_t$ and the effect of the zero-interest-rate bound on the economy through the channel of financial markets can, therefore, be greatly changed.

## 8.6. CONCLUSION

In this chapter, a dynamic model has been set up to explore monetary policy with asset prices. If the probability for the asset-price bubble to increase or decrease in the next period is assumed to be a constant, the monetary policy turns out to be a linear function of the state variables. However, if such a probability is endogenized as a function of the asset-price bubble and interest rate, the policy reaction function becomes non-linear in the inflation rate, output gap and asset-price bubble. Some empirical evidence has shown that the monetary policy rule in the Euro-area has, to some extent, taken into account the financial markets in the past two decades. We have also explored the effect of a zero-interest-rate bound on the real economy with financial markets considered. The simulations indicate that a depression of the financial markets can make a recession economy worse in the presence of a lower bound on the nominal rate. Therefore, policy actions, which aim at escaping a liquidity trap, should not ignore the financial markets. We have also shown that the effect of the zero-interest-rate bound on the economy can be greatly changed if the probability for the asset price to increase or decrease in the next period is an endogenous variable rather than an exogenous one.

PART II

# *Fiscal Policy*

In this part of the book, we consider fiscal policy from both the long-run as well as short-run perspective. We first introduce, in Chapter 9, specific fiscal regimes that result in different macroeconomic growth performances in the long-run. After this, in Chapter 10, we will study the sustainability of fiscal policy in Euro-area countries. In Chapter 11, we explore the efforts to stabilize public debt and bring about sustainability of fiscal policy and study what impact this might have on the macroeconomic performance. In this part again the proposed models will be estimated by employing time series data of the Euro-area member states and contrasting the results, to some extent, with the US estimates.

CHAPTER 9

# *Fiscal Policy and Economic Growth*

## 9.1. INTRODUCTION

In the Euro-area programs have been discussed and initiated many times to set incentives and to promote economic growth. We first deal with fiscal policy from the long-run perspective and then concentrate on the impact of the fiscal policy on economic growth. We use modern growth theories as starting point, but we want to note that recently there have emerged a variety of growth models that attempt to explain the relation of fiscal policy and economic growth which may be relevant for our considerations.[1]

Along the line of the work by Barro (1990) and Barro and Sala-i-Martin (1992) and Turnovsky (1995, Chapter 13) in the present chapter we want to study the contribution of public services and more generally fiscal policy to economic growth. Yet, instead

---

[1] A first variant, referring back to Arrow (1962), as, for example, Romer (1986), assumes externalities of technological knowledge and perpetual growth results from learning by doing effects (see also Greiner and Semmler, 1996). In the Lucas (1988) version the creation of human capital is emphasized as a source of perpetual growth. The Romer (1990) version stresses the intentional build up of knowledge capital. Lastly, a variant has been suggested where public services are included in growth models (Barro, 1990; Barro and Sala-i-Martin, 1992) allowing for endogenous growth. A more detailed survey and empirical evaluation of recent growth models is given in Greiner et al. (2005).

of considering the flow of public infrastructure and public services we will refer to the stock of public capital when studying the growth effects. In contrast to the above literature we also admit deficit spending and thus capital market borrowing by the government. This has often been disregarded in previous work when the effect of public spending (public consumption, infrastructure investment) is analyzed. Productive inputs in the production function of firms have been considered in Aschauer (1989) who has estimated strong effects of public capital on economic growth.[2] In our model there will be one decision variable, private consumption, and three state variables, private and public capital stock and public debt.

Since the tax rate and the components of public expenditure are not choice variables we need to define budgetary regimes (rules) which define the tax rates, spending and borrowing behavior of the government.[3] In order to undertake a comparative static analysis of expenditure effects we define two fiscal regimes and the associated rules for borrowing and spending by the government. In the strict fiscal regime public sector borrowing is used only for public investment. In the less strict regime it can be used for debt service and public investment. In both regimes capital market borrowing by the government does not necessarily entail a declining growth rate of the economy but the growth effects will be different according to which fiscal rule is adopted. We also show that the results of our model are relevant for the optimal tax literature. The growth maximizing income tax rate will not be zero.

---

[2] Models with government expenditure have also been discussed in the context of RBC models (see Baxter and King, 1995, for a model with a balanced budget and Chari et al., 1994, for a model with public deficit).

[3] This has been implicitly or explicitly undertaken in a variety of macroeconomic studies on public debt, see for example, Domar (1957), Blinder and Solow (1973), Barro (1979); see also the survey on this matter by van Ewijk (1991).

The major endeavor in this chapter is to test whether the proposed model is compatible with time series data. Intertemporal macro-economic models have already been estimated by a variety of techniques. There are now a considerable number of studies that estimate stochastic growth models, which have become the basis of the RBC model. The maximum likelihood method has been employed by Altug (1989), Chow (1993) and Semmler and Gong (1996). The Generalized Method of Moments (GMM) has been used by Christiano and Eichenbaum (1992). In intertemporal versions the econometric models to be estimated are non-linear in parameters and may often exhibit multiple optima. To circumvent this problem global optimization algorithms are employed, for example, the simulated annealing. To our knowledge, although empirical predictions of endogenous growth models have been tested through cross section regressions or co-integration techniques (Pedroni, 1992), endogenous growth models, there is not much work to estimate endogenous growth models employing time series techniques.[4] In the subsequent study we employ a similar estimation strategy as has been employed for RBC models. On the basis of our results the contribution of public capital to economic growth and the different growth experiences of the US and German economies in the post-war period can be interpreted.

The remainder of this chapter is organized as follows. In section 9.2 we outline the endogenous growth model with private and public capital and government capital market borrowing and study the steady-state properties of the model. Section 9.3 focuses on the estimation strategy and the actual estimation of different model variants for the US and Germany. Section 9.4 compares our results with the literature and section 9.5, concludes the chapter. In Appendix A9 some derivations are collected. A sketch of our computer algorithm used for the estimation is given in Greiner et al. (2005).

---

[4] See, however, Greiner et al. (2005).

## 9.2. THE GROWTH MODEL AND STEADY-STATE RESULTS

We consider a closed economy which is composed of three sectors: the household sector, a representative firm and the government. The household is supposed to maximize the discounted stream of utilities arising from consumption subject to its budget constraint:

$$\max_{C(t)} \int_0^\infty e^{-\rho t} u(C(t)) dt, \qquad (9.1)$$

subject to

$$C(t) + \dot{S}(t) = (w(t) + r(t)S(t))(1 - \tau) + T_{\mathrm{p}}(t). \qquad (9.2)$$

$C(t)$ gives private consumption at time $t$, $S(t) = K(t) + B(t)$ denotes assets which comprise physical capital $K(t)$ plus government bond or public debt $B(t)$. $T_{\mathrm{p}}(t)$ stands for lump-sum transfer payments, the household takes as given in solving its optimization problem, $\tau$ gives the income tax rate and $w(t)$ and $r(t)$ denote the wage rate and the interest rate, respectively. $\rho$ gives the constant rate of time preference and the labor supply is assumed to be constant and normalized to one so that all variables give per capita quantities. The depreciation rate of physical capital is set equal to zero.

As to the utility function we assume a function of the form $(C(t)^{1-\sigma})/(1 - \sigma)$, with $-\sigma$ denoting the elasticity of marginal utility with respect to consumption or the negative of the inverse of the instantaneous elasticity of substitution between consumption at two points in time, which is assumed to be constant. For $\sigma = 1$ the utility function is the logarithmic function $\ln C(t)$. If the utility function is used to describe attitudes towards risk $\sigma$ has an alternative interpretation. In this case $\sigma$ is the coefficient of relative risk aversion. A number of empirical studies have been undertaken aiming at estimating this coefficient under the assumption that it is constant, by looking at the consumers' willingness to shift consumption across time in response to changes in interest rates. The estimates of $\sigma$ vary to a great degree but are usually at or above unity (see Blanchard and Fischer, 1989, p. 44; Lucas, 1990; Hall, 1988).

To find this solution we formulate the current value Hamiltonian which is given by[5] $H(\cdot) = u(c) + \gamma((w + rS)(1 - \tau) + T_p - C)$. The necessary optimality conditions are then obtained as

$$\gamma = C^{-\sigma}, \tag{9.3}$$

$$\dot{\gamma} = \gamma(\rho - (1 - \tau)r), \tag{9.4}$$

$$\dot{S} = -C + (rS + w)(1 - \tau) + T_p. \tag{9.5}$$

These conditions are also sufficient if the limiting transversality condition $\lim_{t \to \infty} e^{-\rho t} \gamma(t)(K(t) + B(t)) = 0$ is fulfilled.[6] Differentiating $\gamma = C^{-\sigma}$ with respect to time and using $\dot{\gamma} = \gamma(\rho - (1 - \tau)r)$, this system can be reduced to a two-dimensional differential equation system:

$$\frac{\dot{C}}{C} = -\frac{\rho}{\sigma} + \frac{(1 - \tau)r}{\sigma}, \tag{9.6}$$

$$\frac{\dot{S}}{S} = -\frac{C}{S} + (r + w/S)(1 - \tau) + \frac{T_p}{S}. \tag{9.7}$$

The productive sector is assumed to be represented by one firm, which behaves competitively exhibiting a production function of the form,

$$f(K, G) = K^{1-\alpha}G^{\alpha}. \tag{9.8}$$

$G$ gives the stock of productive public capital which is a non-rival and non-excludable good[7] and $1 - \alpha$, $\alpha \in (0, 1)$, denotes the share

---

[5] In the following we omit the time argument if no ambiguity arises.
[6] This condition is automatically fulfilled if $g < \rho$ holds, with $g$ the long run balanced growth rate. This also guarantees the boundedness of the utility functional.
[7] For an analysis where the public good is non-excludable but rival or subject to congestion, see Barro and Sala-i-Martin (1992). In another version of this model we take account of congestion effects and population growth, see Greiner and Semmler (1999a).

of private capital in the production function. Since $K$ denotes per capita capital, the wage rate and the interest rate are determined as $w = \alpha K^{1-\alpha} G^{\alpha}$ and $r = (1 - \alpha)K^{-\alpha}G^{\alpha}$.

The budget constraint of the government, finally, is given by $\dot{B} + T = rB + C_p + T_p + \dot{G}$. $C_p$ stands for public consumption and $T$ is the tax revenue, which is given by $T = r(w + rS)$. As to public consumption we suppose that it is a pure drain on resources and provides no benefits to the economy as it is often assumed in the optimal tax literature. An alternative specification, which would not change our results, would be to assume that public consumption enters the utility function in an additively separable way (for a discussion and an economic justification of that assumption see Judge et al., 1985, p. 301; Turnovsky, 1995, p. 405). We suppose that public consumption and transfer payments to the household constitutes a certain part of the tax revenue, i.e. $C_p = \varphi_2 T$ and $T_p = \varphi_1 T$, $\varphi_1, \varphi_2 < 1$. Moreover, the government is not allowed to play a Ponzi game, i.e. $\lim_{t \to \infty} B(t)\exp(-\int_0^t r(s)ds) = 0$ must hold, and we define three alternative budgetary regimes to which the government must stick.[8]

The first states that government expenditures for public consumption, transfer payments and interest payments must be smaller than the tax revenue, $C_p + T_p + rB = \varphi_0 T$, with $\varphi_0 < 1$. We will refer to this regime as regime (A). This regime is called the "Golden Rule of Public Finance" and postulates that it is not justified to run a deficit in order to finance non-productive expenditures which do not yield returns in the future. Public deficit then are only feasible in order to finance productive public investment which increases a public capital stock and raise aggregate production.[9]

---

[8] It should also be mentioned that increases in government expenditure would lead to proportional decreases in consumption if the first did not influence production possibilities and if we had non-distortionary taxes. This follows from the Ricardian equivalence theorem, see Blanchard and Fischer (1989, Chapter 2).

[9] Regime (A) can be found in the German constitution and is binding for the government.

Table 9.1: Regime, target and deficit.

| Regime | Target | Deficit due to |
|---|---|---|
| (A) | $C_p + T_p + rB < T$ | Public investment |
| (B) | $C_p + T_p + \varphi_4 rB < T$ | Public investment $+ (1 - \varphi_4)rB$ |
| (C) | $C_p + T_p + \dot{G} > T,$ | $(C_p + T_p + \dot{G}) + rB$ |
| | $C_p + T_p + < T$ | |

A slight modification of this regime, and in a way natural extension, is obtained when allowing that only a certain part of the interest payments on public debt must be financed out of the tax revenue and the remaining part may be paid by issuing new bonds. In this case, the budgetary regime is described by $C_p + T_p + \varphi_4 rB = \varphi_0 T$, with $\varphi_4 \in (0, 1)$. We refer to this regime as regime (B). The third regime, regime (C), states that public consumption plus transfers to individuals must not exceed the tax revenue, but the government runs into debt in order to finance public investment and interest payments, $C_p + T_p + \varphi_0 T$, $\varphi_0 < 1$.

Further, in all regimes investment in infrastructure is supposed to constitute a certain part of the remaining tax revenue, $\dot{G} = \varphi_3(1 - \varphi_0)T$, $\varphi_3 \geq 0$. In regime (A) for example this implies that government debt only increases if $\varphi_3 > 1$. Table 9.1 gives a survey of the regimes.

Let us in the next section take a closer look at our economy described by this basic model and derive some implications of those different regimes for the growth rate of economies.

## 9.3. ANALYTICAL RESULTS

Before we analyze our economy we first state that regimes (A), (B) and (C) can be derived from regime (B) for appropriate values of $\varphi_4$ and $\varphi_3$. To see that more clearly we write down the budgetary regime for regime (B) which is given by

$$C_p + T_p + \varphi_4 rB = \varphi_0 T.$$ (9.9)

Further, the debt accumulation equation for regime (B) is given by

$$\dot{B} = rB + C_p + T_p + \dot{G} - T$$

$$= (\varphi_0 - 1)(1 - \varphi_3)T + (1 - \varphi_4)rB.$$ (9.10)

Setting $\varphi_4 = 1$ in Equations 9.9 and 9.10 and $\varphi_3 > 1$, it is immediately seen that we obtain regime (A). In that case the whole interest payments on outstanding public debt must be financed by the tax revenue. If $\varphi_4 \in (0, 1)$ only $\varphi_4$ of the interest payments is financed by the tax revenue and the rest, $(1 - \varphi_4)rB$, is paid by raising public debt, giving regime (B). In the extreme, i.e. for $\varphi_4 = 0$, all interest payments on outstanding debt are financed by issuing new debt and we now have regime (C), for $\varphi_3 > 1$. In that case we get $C_p + T_p + \dot{G} - T = (\varphi_0 - 1) \times (1 - \varphi_3)T > 0$.

To find the differential equation describing the evolution of physical capital, i.e. the economy wide resource constraint, we first note that the budget constraint of the individual gives $\dot{K} + \dot{B} = -C + (w + rK + rB)(1 - \tau) + T_p$. Using the definition of $\dot{B}$ the term $\dot{K} + \dot{B}$ can be written as $\dot{K} + \dot{B} = \dot{K} + rB + \varphi_2 T + T_p + \varphi_3(1 - \varphi_0)T - T$. Combining those two expressions then yields $\dot{K} = -C + (w + rK) - (\varphi_2 + \varphi_3(1 - \varphi_0))\tau(w + rK + rB)$. Using the equilibrium conditions $w + rK = K^{1-\alpha}G^\alpha$ and $r = (1 - \alpha) \times G^\alpha K^{-\alpha}$ then gives the economy wide resource constraint as

$$\frac{\dot{K}}{K} = -\frac{C}{K} + \left(\frac{G}{K}\right)^\alpha - \tau(\varphi_2 + \varphi_3(1 - \varphi_0))$$

$$\times \left(\frac{G}{K}\right)^\alpha \left(1 + (1 - \alpha)\frac{B}{K}\right).$$ (9.11)

The description of our economy is completed by Equation 9.6 giving the evolution of consumption and by the differential equation describing the path of the stock of public capital $\dot{G}$. Thus, we get the following four-dimensional differential equation system with appropriate initial conditions and the limiting transversality condition:

$$
\frac{\dot{K}}{K} = -\frac{C}{K} + \left(\frac{G}{K}\right)^{\alpha} - \tau(\varphi_2 + \varphi_3(1 - \varphi_0))\left(\frac{G}{K}\right)^{\alpha}
$$
$$
\times \left(1 + (1 - \alpha)\frac{B}{K}\right),
\tag{9.12}
$$

$$
\frac{\dot{B}}{B} = (\varphi_0 - 1)(1 - \varphi_3)\tau\left((1 - \alpha) + \frac{K}{B}\right)\left(\frac{G}{K}\right)^{\alpha}
$$
$$
+ (1 - \varphi_4)(1 - \alpha)\left(\frac{G}{K}\right)^{\alpha},
\tag{9.13}
$$

$$
\frac{\dot{C}}{C} = -\frac{\rho}{\sigma} + \frac{(1 - \tau)(1 - \alpha)K^{-\alpha}G^{\alpha}}{\sigma},
\tag{9.14}
$$

$$
\frac{\dot{G}}{G} = \varphi_3(1 - \varphi_0)\tau\left(\left(\frac{G}{K}\right)^{\alpha-1} + (1 - \alpha)\left(\frac{G}{K}\right)^{\alpha}\frac{B}{G}\right).
\tag{9.15}
$$

We write that system in the rates of growth, which tend to zero if the decline in the marginal product of physical capital, caused by a rising capital stock, is not made up for by an increase in public capital. However, if the stock of public capital is sufficiently large so that the marginal product of private capital does not converge to zero in the long run we can observe endogenous growth. In this case the RHS of our system is always positive and we first have to perform a change of the system in order to be able to continue our analysis.

Defining $c = C/K$, $b = B/K$ and $x = G/K$ the new system of differential equations is given by $\dot{c}/c = \dot{C}/C - \dot{K}/K$, $\dot{b}/b = \dot{B}/B - \dot{K}/K$, and $\dot{x}/x = \dot{G}/G - \dot{K}/K$ leading to

$$\frac{\dot{c}}{c} = -\frac{\rho}{\sigma} + x^\alpha \left( \frac{(1-\tau)(1-\alpha)}{\sigma} + \tau(\varphi_2 + \varphi_3(1-\varphi_0))(1+(1-\alpha)b) \right)$$
$$+ c - x^\alpha, \tag{9.16}$$

$$\frac{\dot{b}}{b} = x^\alpha \tau \left( \left[ (1-\alpha) + b^{-1} \right](\varphi_0 - 1)(1 - \varphi_3) \right.$$
$$\left. + [\varphi_2 + \varphi_3(1-\varphi_0)][1+(1-\alpha)b] \right)$$
$$+ x^\alpha(1-\alpha)(1-\varphi_4) + c - x^\alpha, \tag{9.17}$$

$$\frac{\dot{x}}{x} = x^{\alpha-1}(1+(1-\alpha)b)\varphi_3(1-\varphi_0)\tau$$
$$+ x^\alpha \tau(\varphi_2 + \varphi_3(1-\varphi_0))(1+(1-\alpha)b) + c - x^\alpha. \tag{9.18}$$

A stationary point of this system then corresponds to a balanced growth path of the original system where all variables grow at the same rate. In the following we will confine our analytical analysis to this path and examine how fiscal policy financed through additional debt affects the growth rate on that path.[8] Moreover, we will exclude the economically meaningless stationary point $c = x = b = 0$ so that we can consider system 9.16–9.18 in the rates of growth and confine our analysis to an interior stationary point.

Doing so we get for $c$ from $\dot{c}/c = 0$,

$$c = \frac{\rho}{\sigma} - x^\alpha \left( \tau(\varphi_2 + \varphi_3(1-\varphi_0))(1+(1-\alpha)b) - 1 + \frac{(1-\tau)(1-\alpha)}{\sigma} \right). \tag{9.19}$$

Further, we know that the constraint $C_p + T_p + \varphi_4 rB = \varphi_0 T$ must be fulfilled on the balanced growth path. This condition makes $\varphi_0$ an endogenous variable which depends on $b$, $\varphi_1$, $\varphi_2$, $\varphi_4$, $\tau$ and $\alpha$.

Using $T = \tau(K^{1-\alpha}G^\alpha + rB)$, it is easily seen that in the steady-state $\varphi_0$ is determined as

$$\varphi_0 = (\varphi_1 + \varphi_2) + \frac{\varphi_4(1-\alpha)}{\tau((1-\alpha)+b^{-1})}. \tag{9.20}$$

But it must be noted that $\varphi_0 < 1$ is imposed as an additional constraint, which must always be fulfilled.

Inserting $c$ from $\dot{c}/c = 0$ and $\varphi_0 = \varphi_0(b, \varphi_1, \varphi_2, \varphi_4, \tau, \alpha)$ in $\dot{b}/b$ and $\dot{x}/x$ and setting the LHS equal to zero completely describes the balanced growth path of our economy. The equations are obtained as

$$0 = q(\cdot) \equiv \frac{\dot{b}}{b}$$
$$= x^\alpha \left[ \tau((1-\alpha)+b^{-1})(\varphi_0(\cdots) - 1)(1-\varphi_3) - \frac{(1-\tau)(1-\alpha)}{\sigma} \right]$$
$$+ \frac{\rho}{\sigma} + (1-\varphi_4)(1-\alpha)x^\alpha, \tag{9.21}$$

$$0 = q_1(\cdot) \equiv \frac{\dot{x}}{x}$$
$$= x^{\alpha-1}(1+(1-\alpha)b)\varphi_3(1-\varphi_0(\cdots))\tau - x^\alpha \frac{(1-\tau)(1-\alpha)}{\sigma} + \frac{\rho}{\sigma}. \tag{9.22}$$

Solving for $b$ and $x$ then determines the balanced growth path for our economy, on which all variables grow at the same constant rate. The ratio $G/K = x$ denotes the ratio of public capital to private capital which determines the marginal product of private capital and, as a consequence, the balanced growth rate. The balanced growth rate is obtained from Equation 9.14, which merely depends on $x$ at the steady state and on the exogenously given parameters.

In the following, we intend to investigate the impact of fiscal policy on the balanced growth rate of our economy. To do so we implicitly differentiate system 9.21 and 9.22 with respect to the parameter under consideration. This shows how the ratio $G/K$ changes and, together with Equation 9.14, gives the impact on the growth rate of our economy.

Using $\dot{b}/b \equiv q(x, b, \varphi_0; \ldots)$ and $\dot{x}/x \equiv q_1(x, b, \varphi_0; \ldots)$, and implicitly differentiating Equations 9.21 and 9.22 with respect to the parameters leads to

$$\begin{bmatrix} \partial b/\partial z \\ \partial x/\partial z \end{bmatrix} = -M^{-1} \begin{bmatrix} \partial q(\cdot)/\partial z \\ \partial q_1(\cdot)/\partial z \end{bmatrix}.$$

$z$ stands for the parameters and the matrix $M$ is given by

$$M = \begin{bmatrix} \partial q(\cdot)/\partial b & \partial q(\cdot)/\partial x \\ \partial q_1(\cdot)/\partial b & \partial q_1(\cdot)/\partial x \end{bmatrix}$$

The negative of its inverse is calculated as

$$-M^{-1} = -\frac{1}{\det M} \begin{bmatrix} \partial q_1(\cdot)/\partial x & -\partial q(\cdot)/\partial x \\ -\partial q_1(\cdot)/\partial b & \partial q(\cdot)/\partial b \end{bmatrix},$$

with det $M$ denoting the determinant of $M$. Now, we can analyze how the growth rate in our economy reacts to fiscal policy.

A result which holds independent of the budgetary regime under consideration is that an increase in public consumption and transfer payments reduces the balanced growth rate. From an economic point of view this result is due to the fact that more non-productive public spending imply that there are less resources left for growth stimulating public investment. Here we may speak of internal crowding out (as in van Ewijk and van de Klundert, 1993, p. 123). More formally, that outcome is seen from Equation 9.20 which shows that an increase in $\varphi_1$ and $\varphi_2$ reduce $\varphi_0$.[10] This result is not too surprising. Therefore, we only mention the outcome but do not go into the details. A more interesting topic is the question of how

---

[10] The proof is contained in Appendix A9.

a deficit financed increase in public investment and how the choice of the budgetary regime affects economic growth. To begin with, we consider regimes (A) and (B).

### 9.3.1. Regimes (A) and (B)

First, we study regime (A) which is obtained from Equations 9.21 and 9.22 by setting $\varphi_4 = 1$ and $\varphi_3 > 1$. The question we want to answer is whether a rise in public investment financed through additional government debt increases economic growth if we take into account feedback effects of the higher level of public debt. To investigate this case we note that it can be represented by an increase in the parameter $\varphi_3$. On the one hand, a higher $\varphi_3$ means more direct investment in public capital but, on the other hand, it also changes the ratio of $b$ which determines $\dot{G}/G$ both directly and indirectly through $\varphi_0$.

Analyzing our model it turns out that a deficit financed increase of investment in public capital raises (reduces) the balanced growth rate in regime (A) if $Z \equiv \tau(1 - \varphi_0)(1 + (1 - \alpha)b)[\varphi_3 + (\varphi_3 - 1)/(b(1 - \alpha))] > (<)1$ holds. To derive that result we first note that under a slight additional technical assumption it can be shown that in regime (A) $\det M > 0$ holds.[11] Further, to prove this outcome we derive from Equation 9.11,

$$\frac{\partial g}{\partial \varphi_3} = \frac{(1 - \tau)(1 - \alpha)}{\sigma} \alpha x^{\alpha - 1} \frac{\partial x}{\partial \varphi_3}.$$

Implicitly differentiating Equations 9.21 and 9.22 again gives an expression for the change in $x$ at the steady state. Since $-\det M < 0$, $x$, and thus the balanced growth rate, rises if $-(\partial q_1(\cdot)/\partial b) \times (\partial q(\cdot)/\partial \varphi_3) + (\partial q(\cdot)/\partial b)(\partial q_1(\cdot)/\partial \varphi_3) < 0$ and vice versa. The sign of that expression is negative (positive) if $1 - \tau(1 - \varphi_0) \times (1 + (1 - \alpha)b)[\varphi_3 + (\varphi_3 - 1)/(b(1 - \alpha))] \equiv -Z + 1 < (>)0$.

---

[11] Since the calculations are rather long we do not include them in the book. They are available from the authors upon request.

It should be noted that it is the feedback effect of government debt that exerts a negative influence on the growth rate if investment in infrastructure is financed through additional debt. This is seen by setting $\partial\varphi_0/\partial b = 0$. The expression $(\partial q(\cdot)/\partial b)(\partial q_1(\cdot)/\partial\varphi_3) - (\partial q_1(\cdot)/\partial b)(\partial q(\cdot)/\partial\varphi_3)$ then is always negative and a deficit financed rise in investment in infrastructure raises $x$ and the balanced growth rate. In that case our result would be equivalent to the one derived by Turnovsky (1995, p. 418). The introduction of budgetary regimes, however, implies that a deficit financed increase in public investment shows a feedback effect which acts through two channels: first, an increase in public debt raises interest payments which must be financed by the tax revenue and consequently reduces the resources available for public investment. Again, we may call this effect internal crowding out. But that effect only holds for regimes (A) and (B). Second, the introduction of the budgetary regimes implies that the interest payments on public debt appear in the economy wide resource constraint Equation 9.11 and lead to a (external) crowding out of private investment. That effect holds for all three regimes.

Since governments are not allowed to increase public debt arbitrarily because public debt does have effects (see, e.g. Easterly and Rebelo, 1993; Fischer, 1993), it is apparent that the introduction of budgetary regimes to model negative feedback effects of higher government debt is justified. That is also the reason why budgetary regimes have frequently been introduced in the economics literature (for a detailed survey of budgetary regimes see van Ewijk, 1991).

As to the effect concerning the ratio of public debt to private capital, $b$, no unambiguous result can be derived, that is this ratio may rise or fall. Therefore, we will present a numerical example below in order to gain further insight into that problem.

It can also be shown that in economies with a high share of non-productive government spending, like high interest payments, public consumption and/or transfer payments, i.e. a large value for $\varphi_0$, a deficit financed rise in public investment is more likely to produce negative growth effects. This is immediately seen by differentiating $Z$ with respect to $\varphi_0$ which is negative.

Another point which we would like to treat is how the tax rate must be chosen in order to maximize economic growth. Since a certain part of the tax revenue is used for investment in public capital, which raises the balanced growth rate, it becomes immediately clear that the growth maximizing income tax rate does not equal zero. Thus, our result is consistent with the one derived by Barro (1990) and similar to the outcome observed by Jones et al. (1993), who demonstrate that the optimal income tax rate does not equal zero if government spending has a direct positive effect on private investment. But this outcome clearly is in contrast to the result of the standard Ramsey type growth model and also to endogenous growth models with physical and human capital (see, e.g. Lucas, 1990, or Milesi-Ferretti and Roubini, 1994). The growth maximizing income tax rate is computed by differentiating Equation 9.11 with respect to $\tau$. This leads to

$$\frac{\partial g}{\partial \tau} = \frac{1 - \alpha}{\sigma} x^\alpha \left[ -1 + \alpha \frac{1 - \tau}{\tau} \frac{\partial x}{\partial \tau} \frac{\tau}{x} \right].$$

This shows that the increase in the income tax rate raises or lowers the balanced growth rate if the elasticity of $G/K$ with respect to $\tau$ is larger or smaller than the expression $\tau/(1 - \tau)\alpha$. The economic mechanism behind this result becomes immediately clear. For given parameter values an economy with a high elasticity of $G/K$ with respect to $\tau$ is more likely to experience growth if the income tax rate is increased because the higher investment in public capital, caused by more tax revenue, leads to a relatively strong increase in the ratio $G/K$ and, thus, in the marginal product of private physical capital. This positive effect then dominates the negative direct one of higher income taxes leading to a reallocation of private resources from investment to consumption. However, it is not possible to calculate the term $\partial x/\partial \tau$ for our analytical model in detail, because this expression becomes extremely complicated. This also motivates the use of numerical examples in order to gain further insight in our model.

Another point of interest is the question what happens if a less strict budgetary regime is assumed in which only a certain part of the government's interest payments must be financed by the tax revenue. Formally, that is obtained by setting $\varphi_4 \in (0, 1)$ which gives regime (B). Now, the negative feedback effect of public investment financed by public debt is expected to be lower in magnitude since only $\varphi_4 rB$ of the interest payments must be financed by the current tax revenue.

To find growth effects we proceed as above, i.e. we derive the balanced growth rate with respect to $\varphi_3$. This shows that $x$ and, thus the balanced growth rate rises if $Z_1 \equiv \tau(1 - \varphi_0)(1 + (1 - \alpha)b) \times [\varphi_3 + (\varphi_3 - 1)/(b(1 - \alpha))] > \varphi_4$. Since $\varphi_4 \in (0, 1)$ and $\varphi_0$ positively varies with $\varphi_4$ one realizes that for a given value of the national debt/private capital ratio, $b$, a positive growth effect of a deficit financed rise in public investment is more likely, compared to regime (A).

With that result one could be tempted to come to the conclusion that governments only have to follow less restrictive budgetary policies and can thus generate positive growth effects of a deficit financed public investment on the balanced growth rate. But two points must be taken into account. First, that proposition is only valid for a given debt/capital ratio, which is an endogenous variable. That is, if a less strict budgetary regime is in use this regime may cause a higher debt/capital ratio which probably compensates the positive direct effect of less interest payments to be financed out of the tax revenue so that the economy ends up with less economic growth.[12] The second point we have not yet addressed is the question of whether such a balanced growth path exists at all, on which

---

[12] This is indeed the case in the numerical examples we present below.

economic per capita variables grow at a constant rate. Above we mentioned that such a path is only feasible if the decline in the marginal product of private capital is compensated by investment in public capital. However, in our analytical model we unfortunately cannot answer that question more precisely because the resulting expression becomes too complicated. Therefore, we will conduct some numerical simulations in order to highlight the problem of the existence of a steady-state growth path and try to find whether a less strict budgetary regime probably makes endogenous growth impossible.

Further our simulations we present below show that the balanced growth rate of the economy does not rise if a less strict budgetary regime is imposed. A higher value for $\varphi_4$ may well be compatible with a higher steady-state growth rate. This ambiguity results from the fact that $\varphi_4$ in this regime shows two different effects. On the one side, a lower value for $\varphi_4$ implies that less interest payments on public debt must be financed through the tax revenue, leaving more resources for investment in public capital. In our model that direct effect tends to decrease $\varphi_0$, what can be seen by differentiating $\varphi_0$ with respect to $\varphi_4$. On the other hand, there is an indirect effect of $\varphi_4$ by influencing the steady-state value for $b$. If less interest payments must be financed out of the tax revenue, the level of public debt will probably be higher and thus the steady-state value of public debt per private capital, $b$. That indirect effect tends to increase the amount of tax revenue used for the debt service, increasing $\varphi_0$ in our economy and, thus, tends to lower investment in public capital what will show negative repercussions for economic growth. Whether the direct effect dominates the indirect one, implying that a less strict budgetary regime is accompanied by higher economic growth, or vice versa cannot be determined for the analytical model and depends on the specific conditions of the economy under consideration.

Before we present some simulations we derive analytical results for our model assuming the budgetary regime (C).

### 9.3.2. Regime (C)

In regime (C) the government does not have to finance any part of its interest payments and investment out of the tax revenue. But the latter must be sufficiently high to meet public consumption and transfer payments. The constraint is then written as $C_p + T_p = \varphi_0 T$, $\varphi_0 < 1$, which is obtained from Equation 9.9 by setting $\varphi_4 = 0$. It should be noted that for $\varphi_4 = 0$, $\varphi_0$ is given by $\varphi_0 = \varphi_1 + \varphi_2$. The evolution of the government debt in that regime is $\dot{B} = rB + C_p + T_p + \dot{G} - T = rB + (1 - \varphi_0)(\varphi_3 - 1)T$, where $\dot{G} = \varphi_3(1 - \varphi_0)T$ and $\varphi_3 > 1$. Formally, regime (C) is obtained from Equations 9.21 and 9.22 by setting $\varphi_4 = 0$ and $\varphi_3 > 1$.

Let us now consider regime (C) and try to find some analytical results. To gain further insight, we explicitly compute $b$ at the steady state from $q(\cdot) = 0$ as

$$b = \frac{-\sigma\tau(\varphi_0 - 1)(1 - \varphi_3)}{x^{-\alpha}\rho - (1 - \tau)(1 - \alpha) + \sigma(1 - \alpha)(1 - \varphi_4 + (\varphi_0 - 1)(1 - \varphi_3)\tau)}. \tag{9.23}$$

It is immediately seen that for $\varphi_3 > 1$, $(1 - \tau) > \sigma(1 - \varphi_4 + (\varphi_0 - 1)(1 - \varphi_3)\tau)$ must hold if $b$ is to be positive. This demonstrates that for $\varphi_4 = 0$, i.e. for regime (C), $\sigma$ must be smaller than $1 - \tau$, and thus smaller than 1, for a balanced growth path with a positive level of government debt to exist. Since $\sigma$ is the inverse of the instantaneous elasticity of substitution, the economic interpretation of this result is that the representative individual in this economy must have a utility function with a high instantaneous elasticity of substitution for a balanced growth path with government debt to exist. That is, the household must be very willing to forgo current consumption and shift it into the future. Most empirical studies suggest that $\sigma$ takes on a value around 1. In this case a balanced growth path can only exist in regime (C) if the government has a negative level of debt, that is if it is a creditor.

Since the balanced growth rate which is given by Equation 9.14 does not directly depend on $\varphi_3$ the variation in $x$, induced by a change in this parameter, shows whether the growth rate increases or declines. The growth effect of a deficit financed rise in public investment is again derived as for regimes (A) and (B). Again $\det M > 0$ holds. Then, the sign of $(\partial q_1(\cdot)/\partial b)(\partial q(\cdot)/\partial \varphi_3) - (\partial q(\cdot)/\partial b)(\partial q_1(\cdot)/\partial \varphi_3)$ determines the effect on $x$ and on the balanced growth rate. If it is positive the growth rate rises and vice versa. In Appendix A9 we show that this expression is unambiguously positive. Thus, we can state that in regime (C) a deficit financed increase in public investment raises the balanced growth rate.

This result states that a rise in public investment raises the balanced growth rate. This outcome is probably due to the fact that there is no internal crowding out in this regime. But we should like to point out that this regime (C) is of less relevance for real world economies. That holds because one always has to be aware of the existence problem concerning the balanced growth path. For $\sigma \geq 1 - \tau$, which seems to be quite realistic, this proposition can only be applied if the government is a creditor. In the more realistic case of a positive government debt, the instantaneous elasticity of substitution has to be very high for this proposition to be relevant.

As to the growth maximizing income tax rate we immediately see that it is given by the same expression as in regimes (A) and (B) and cannot be precisely determined in the analytical model. Therefore, we present some numerical simulations in order to find its magnitude.

Before we continue the presentation let us briefly summarize what we have achieved. We have analyzed how a government may influence the balanced growth rate by increasing productive investment in public capital. As to the financing of this spending we have assumed that the government issues new bonds. It turned out that the results crucially depend on the budgetary regime under consideration. For regime (A) we saw that a deficit financed increase of investment in infrastructure raises balanced growth if a certain condition is met. In particular, a positive effect is more likely the lower the share of non-productive government spending, other things equal. Further, we could show that applying this regime less strictly, that is by requiring that only a certain part of debt payments be financed out of the tax revenue, what gave regime (B), a positive effect of deficit financed increases in public investment is more likely, but only for a given debt/capital ratio which, however, is an endogenous variable that is expected to be higher when the budgetary regime is less restrictive. As to the growth rate itself no concrete results could be derived, implying that both cases could occur. So, a less strict budgetary regime could be accompanied either by a higher or a lower balanced growth rate.

In regime (C), where only public consumption and transfer payments are financed by the current tax revenue, we found that only for very high values of the instantaneous elasticity of substitution a balanced growth path with a positive government debt can exist. For $\sigma \geq 1$, what most empirical studies consider as realistic, the government must be a creditor if endogenous growth is to hold. Moreover, we could show that in this regime a deficit financed increase in public investment always raises economic growth.

In the next section we present some numerical examples in order to illustrate our analytical results and in order to shed some light on the question of whether the existence of a balanced growth path is influenced by the choice of the budgetary regime as well as to find the growth maximizing income tax rate, because these questions could not be answered within our analytical framework.

### 9.4. NUMERICAL EXAMPLES

To start with we fix some of our parameter values. As to the elasticity of output with respect to public capital we take the same value as in Barro (1990) and set $\alpha = 0.25$. The utility function is supposed to be logarithmic giving $\sigma = 1$. The discount rate is taken

Table 9.2: Results with $\varphi_3 = 1.5$.

| $\tau$ | $x$ | $b$ | $g$ | $\varphi_0$ | $\tau$ | $x$ | $b$ | $g$ | $\varphi_0$ |
|---|---|---|---|---|---|---|---|---|---|
| 0.15 | 0.153 | 0.0511 | 0.0990 | 0.896 | 0.23 | 0.244 | 0.0813 | 0.1058 | 0.900 |
| 0.20 | 0.208 | 0.0694 | 0.1052 | 0.897 | 0.25 | 0.269 | 0.0896 | 0.1051 | 0.902 |
| 0.22 | 0.232 | 0.0772 | 0.1058 | 0.899 | 0.30 | 0.337 | 0.1124 | 0.1001 | 0.909 |

to be $\rho = 0.3$. Interpreting one time period as 5 years then implies that the annual discount rate is 6%. These values are kept constant throughout all simulations.

First, let us present an example to illustrate regime (A). In this regime all expenditures with the exception of public investment had to be financed out of the tax revenue. The parameter values for $\varphi_1$ and $\varphi_2$, giving that part of the tax revenue which is used for transfer payments and public consumption, are set to $\varphi_1 = 0.3$ and $\varphi_2 = 0.35$. These are about the ratios of transfers to individuals per total government revenue and of public consumption per total government revenue for West Germany for the mid-1980s (see Sachverständigenrat, 1993, Table 38). The parameter $\varphi_3$ is set to $\varphi_3 = 1.5$. For these parameters, Table 9.2 reports the steady-state values[13] for $x$, $b$ and $\varphi_0$ as well as the growth rate for different income tax rates.[14] The values are rounded to the third and fourth decimal point, respectively.

This table shows that the maximum growth occurs for income tax rates of about 22–23%, which are a little smaller than the elasticity of output with respect to public capital $\alpha$. It must be noted that we took one time period to comprise 5 years so that the annual growth rate is about 2%. If we raise the parameter $\varphi_3$, i.e. if we increase public investment financed by additional debt and set $\varphi_3 = 1.65$, we obtain the results in Table 9.3.

---

[13] In all sim ulations, the dynamic behavior of the system is characterized by saddle point stability. The eigenvalues of the Jacobian are given in Appendix A9.
[14] There exist two steady states with these parameters. But the second yields $\varphi_0 = 1$ and a zero growth rate.

Table 9.3:   Results with $\varphi_3 = 1.65$.

| $\tau$ | $x$ | $b$ | $g$ | $\varphi_0$ | $\tau$ | $x$ | $b$ | $g$ | $\varphi_0$ |
|---|---|---|---|---|---|---|---|---|---|
| 0.15 | 0.142 | 0.0559 | 0.0912 | 0.918 | 0.23 | 0.225 | 0.0887 | 0.0978 | 0.921 |
| 0.20 | 0.192 | 0.0758 | 0.0974 | 0.919 | 0.25 | 0.248 | 0.0977 | 0.0969 | 0.923 |
| 0.22 | 0.214 | 0.0843 | 0.0979 | 0.920 | 0.30 | 0.310 | 0.1220 | 0.0917 | 0.930 |

This demonstrates that the feedback effect in regime (A) is so high that the positive effect of higher investment in public capital is more than compensated by the additional interest payments generated through deficit financing. In this case, increasing $\varphi_3$ leads to less public investment because the additional interest payments caused by this fiscal policy increase $\varphi_0$ in a way so that in the end less resources are available for public investment. In this situation reducing the government debt or public consumption or transfer payments sets free resources, which can then be used for public investment and may raise economic growth. We also see that the ratio of public debt to private capital, $b$, rises. That was to be expected because a higher $\varphi_3$ means a higher public deficit, other things equal.

It should be mentioned that a deficit financed increase in public investment is to be seen as a crowding out of private investment if this policy reduces the ratio $x = G/K$. This holds because a lower value for $x$ reduces the return to private investment, i.e. lowers the marginal product of private capital $r - (1 - \alpha)x^\alpha$. With the parameter values in Table 9.2 a rise in $\varphi_3$ leads to

$$\frac{\partial r}{\partial \varphi_3} = -0.0189 \qquad \text{for } \tau = 0.15$$

$$\frac{\partial r}{\partial \varphi_3} = -0.0743 \qquad \text{for } \tau = 0.2$$

$$\frac{\partial r}{\partial \varphi_3} = -0.0818 \qquad \text{for } \tau = 0.25$$

$$\frac{\partial r}{\partial \varphi_3} = -0.0910 \qquad \text{for } \tau = 0.3$$

Table 9.4:   Results with $\varphi_4 = 0.95$.

| $\tau$ | $x$ | $b$ | $g$ | $\varphi_0$ | $\tau$ | $x$ | $b$ | $g$ | $\varphi_0$ |
|------|------|------|------|------|------|------|------|------|------|
| 0.15 | 0.131 | 0.0599 | 0.0837 | 0.922 | 0.22 | 0.196 | 0.0908 | 0.0894 | 0.925 |
| 0.20 | 0.178 | 0.0813 | 0.0895 | 0.923 | 0.25 | 0.224 | 0.1061 | 0.0869 | 0.930 |
| 0.21 | 0.187 | 0.0860 | 0.0896 | 0.924 | 0.30 | 0.265 | 0.1360 | 0.0765 | 0.943 |

In Table 9.4 we present the results for $\varphi_4 = 0.95$, meaning that 95% of the interest payments must be met by the tax revenue, whereas the rest is financed by additional debt. All other parameters are as in the simulation for Table 9.2.

That table illustrates the discussion following the derivation of the analytical result. It shows that a less strict budgetary regime does not necessarily lead to a higher balanced growth rate. The reason for that outcome is that, in this case, the parameter $\varphi_0$ is larger than in the economy with regime (A) and, therefore, investment in public capital is lower. This result holds because the direct effect of less interest payments which must be financed out of the tax revenue, which would lead to a lower $\varphi_0$, is more than compensated by the higher level of government debt per private capital, $b$, which tends to increase $\varphi_0$, so that the economy ends up with a higher value for $\varphi_0$. But it must be emphasized that the reverse effect could probably be also observed and the outcome depends on the specification of the economy. This holds because for the analytical model no unambiguous result could be obtained.

In order to find how this economy reacts to increases in public investment financed by a higher debt, we calculate the derivative of $x$ with respect to $\varphi_3$ yielding

$$\frac{\partial x}{\partial \varphi_3} = \frac{-0.320537}{2.67813} = -0.119687 \qquad \text{for } \tau = 0.15$$

$$\frac{\partial x}{\partial \varphi_3} = \frac{-0.266592}{1.65434} = -0.161147 \qquad \text{for } \tau = 0.2$$

$$\frac{\partial x}{\partial \varphi_3} = \frac{-0.151911}{0.435745} = -0.348625 \qquad \text{for } \tau = 0.30.$$

These results show that $\partial x / \partial \varphi_3$ is still negative for $\varphi_4 = 0.95$. This effect is again due to the higher debt/capital ratio $b$ which causes an increase in $\varphi_0$ which offsets the positive effect of a lower $\varphi_4$. Therefore, this example underlines that Proposition 10.2 is only valid for a given debt/capital ratio.

If we further decrease $\varphi_4$ and set $\varphi_4 = 0.9$ the balanced growth path does not exist any longer, meaning that there is no sustained per capita growth for our economy. This demonstrates that a less strict budgetary regime does probably not allow sustained per capita growth at all. Reducing $\varphi_4$ further, we observe that sustained per capita growth is again possible for $\varphi_4$ around $\varphi_4 = 0.05$. But it must be emphasized that this regime is only feasible if the government is a creditor, that is for a negative level of public debt. For $\varphi_4 = 0$ ($\varphi_4 = 0.05$) the steady-state value for $b$ is $b = -0.0641$ ($-0.0718$). The balanced growth rate associated with this steady state is $0.187$ ($0.190$). Recalling that one time period comprises 5 years, this corresponds to an annual growth rate of about $3.74$ ($3.8$)%.

## 9.5. THE ESTIMATION OF THE MODEL

In this section we estimate the structural parameters of our theoretical model where we allow for population growth, $n$, and for depreciation of private and public capital, $\delta_1$ and $\delta_2$, respectively. We employ time series data on consumption, public debt and public capital stock to estimate our model for the US and German economies after World War II. All variables are defined relative to the private capital stock. That is we define the following new variables:

$$c \equiv \frac{C}{K}, \qquad b \equiv \frac{B}{K}, \qquad x \equiv \frac{G}{K}.$$

Deriving these new variables with respect to time gives

$$\frac{\dot{c}}{c} = \frac{\dot{C}}{C} - \frac{\dot{K}}{K}, \qquad \frac{\dot{b}}{x} = \frac{\dot{B}}{B} - \frac{\dot{K}}{K}, \qquad \frac{\dot{x}}{x} = \frac{\dot{G}}{G} - \frac{\dot{K}}{K} \quad (9.24)$$

We use the GMM estimation strategy to estimate the structural parameters, $\rho$, $\sigma$, and $\alpha$, of this system.[15]

Next, we need to discuss the data set for the US and German economies. Since some of the variables are real while others are nominal we have to detrend all nominal variables. This was done using the consumer price index. The time series are quarterly data for the US from 1960.4 to 1992.1. The consumption series is from OECD (1998). Total government debt, federal, state and local is taken from OECD (1999). The series for the private capital stock was obtained from quarterly investment by applying the perpetual inventory method with a quarterly discount rate of 0.075/4. The data for investment were taken from OECD (1998). For the public capital stock we take the gross non-military capital stock as reported in Musgrave (1992, Table 13), which includes federal, state and local public capital stock (equipment and structures). Since these data are only available annually we generated quarterly data by linear interpolation. For the computation of the income tax rate and budgetary regime parameters $\varphi_0$, $\varphi_1$, $\varphi_2$, $\varphi_3$, $\varphi_4$ we have computed average values using OECD (1999), the Economic Report of the President (1994) and Citibase (1992).

As regards to Germany we employ the same ratios as in the case of the US the data are again quarterly and cover the period from 1966.1–1995.1. Private consumption and public gross debt are from OECD (1998, 1999). The private capital stock is again obtained from quarterly investment data (from OECD, 1998) by using the perpetual inventory method with a quarterly depreciation rate of 0.075/4. The quarterly public capital stock was computed from annual data by linear interpolation. The data are from Statistisches

---

[15] The system is equal to Equations 9.16–9.18 with the additional parameters $n$, $\delta_1$ and $\delta_2$.

Table 9.5: Results of the GMM estimation for US Time Series, 1960.4–1992.1, with $(\tau, \varphi_0, \varphi_1, \varphi_2, \varphi_3, \varphi_4) = (0.32, 0.815, 0.4, 0.35, 1.3, 0.9)$ from empirical data.

| | $\rho$ | $\sigma$ | $1 - \alpha$ |
|---|---|---|---|
| Estimated parameters | 0.061 | 0.053 | 0.244 |
| (standard errors) | (75,096) | (614,621) | (0.0179) |

Bundesamt (1991, 1994, 1995a). The data to compute the parameters $\varphi_0$, $\varphi_1$, $\varphi_2$, $\varphi_3$ and $\varphi_4$ are from Statistisches Bundesamt (1984) and Sachverständigenrat (1995). The tax rate is the ratio of taxes and social contributions to GDP. The GDP is from the Statistisches Bundesamt (1974, 1995a,b).

The subsequent tables report the results of the GMM estimation employing the simulated annealing as optimization algorithm.[16] Table 9.5 shows the GMM estimation for the US economy assuming regime (B). For the US the deficit has been larger than public investment but smaller than the sum of public investment plus interest payments on public debt so that it can be described by our regime (B). The quarterly depreciation parameters are set as follows $\delta_1 = 0.075/4$ and $\delta_2 = 0.05/4$ and the population growth is $n = 0.015/4$.

The private capital share $1 - \alpha$ is statistically significant and about 25% which seems a bit low. Normally, one would expect a capital share of about 0.3. This low value implies that the share of the public capital stock is extremely high, namely about $\alpha = 0.75$. We think that this is an implausibly high value since it would imply that the elasticity of aggregate per capita output with respect to public capital is 75%. This may hold at most for underdeveloped countries with a low level of public infrastructure capital. However,

---

[16] We have also employed several local optimization algorithms as available in 'Gauss'; none of the algorithms could compute the global optimum properly. Various different initial conditions always lead to different local optima. Only when the parameter set reported below obtained by the simulated annealing, was used as initial condition for the local algorithms the proper parameters that globally minimize the distance function were recovered.

in developed economies, such as the US or Germany, with a relatively high infrastructural capital stock an additional unit of public capital is expected to have smaller output effect. Looking at empirical studies which try to evaluate the contribution of public capital to aggregate output one sees that the results vary to a great degree but are in general lower than 30%, which is also regarded as implausible by some economists (see Sturm et al., 1998).

The high public capital share is, of course, due to our specification of the aggregate production function which has constant returns to scale in private and public capital. Thus, all factors contributing to economic growth in the US are either summarized in private or public capital so that it is not possible to get reasonable values for both of these parameters. Therefore, our empirical estimation is certainly not suited to detect the share of public capital in the aggregate production function. Here, other procedures are more appropriate (for a detailed survey see also Sturm et al., 1998).

As concerns the two other structural parameters $\rho$ and $\sigma$, Table 9.5 shows that the standard errors are extremely high such that these estimates are not reliable. We assume that this is due to the fact that $\rho$ and $\sigma$ only appear in the equation $\dot{c}/c$ but not in the equations $\dot{x}/x$ and $\dot{b}/b$. Therefore, in order to get reliable values for $\rho$ and $\sigma$ we take the estimated value of the parameter $\alpha$ from Table 9.5 and insert it in the equation $\dot{c}/c$. Then, we estimate $\dot{c}/c$ with least squares (LS) to obtain $\rho$ and $\sigma$. The result is presented in Table 9.6.

Table 9.6 shows that we now get reliable estimates for both the rate of time preference, $\rho$ as well as for the inverse of the intertemporal elasticity of substitution, $\sigma$. The estimated value

Table 9.6: Results of the LS estimation of $\dot{c}/c$ for US Time Series, 1960.4–1992.1, with $\alpha$ set to the value in Table 9.5.

|  | $\rho$ | $\sigma$ |
| --- | --- | --- |
| Estimated parameters | 0.052 | 0.192 |
| (standard errors) | (0.0006) | (0.0066) |

Table 9.7:   Results of the GMM estimation for German Time Series, 1966.1–1995.1, with $(\tau, \varphi_0, \varphi_1, \varphi_2, \varphi_3, \varphi_4,) = (0.4, 0.945, 0.4, 0.42, 1.5, 1)$ from empirical data.

|  | $\rho$ | $\sigma$ | $1 - \alpha$ |
|---|---|---|---|
| Estimated parameters | 0.004 | 0.224 | 0.135 |
| (standard errors) | (230,566) | (8,425,716) | (0.0287) |

for $\rho$ implies that the annual rate of time preference is about 28% which seems a bit high but can still be considered as plausible we think. The intertemporal elasticity of substitution is about five, which also seems to be very high. Here, we should like to point out that our theoretical model which considers only public and private capital as affecting economic growth cannot yield the same structural parameters obtained in other studies.

Next, we estimate our model for Germany. Table 9.7 reports the estimation results for the German economy assuming that the fiscal Regime 1 prevailed in Germany with the same depreciation parameters as for the US but a zero population growth rate, i.e. $n = 0$.

As in the case of the US only the private capital share, $1 - \alpha$, is reliable while the standard errors of both $\rho$ and $\sigma$ are extremely high so that these cannot be relied upon. Again, we suppose that this is due to the fact that these parameters only appear in the equation $\dot{c}/c$ as in the case of the US. Therefore, we again take the estimated parameter for $\alpha$ from Table 9.7 and estimate equation $\dot{c}/c$ with LS to obtain values for $\rho$ and $\sigma$. The result is shown in Table 9.8.

Again, this procedure yields reliable estimates for $\rho$ and $\sigma$. However, the estimate for $\rho$ implies that the annual rate of time

Table 9.8:   Results of the LS estimation of $\dot{c}/c$ for German Time Series, 1966.1–1995.1, with $\alpha$ set to the value in Table 9.7.

|  | $\rho$ | $\sigma$ |
|---|---|---|
| Estimated parameters | 0.0015 | 0.151 |
| (standard errors) | (0.0004) | (0.0067) |

preference in Germany is only 0.6% which is very low. On the other hand, the intertemporal elasticity $1/\sigma$ is about 6.6 which is very high.

Given our estimated parameter set $\psi = (\rho, \sigma, \alpha)$ for the US and Germany we can compute the in-sample predictions of the time paths of our variables using system 9.24. The results are depicted in Figure 9.1 for the US and Figure 9.2 for Germany representing the actual and predicted time series for the variables $c$, $b$ and $x$ for the two countries.

As Figure 9.1 shows, the actual time paths for both countries are closely tracked by our growth model for the US and Germany using the estimated parameters from Tables 9.5–9.7. Thus, our model is able to replicate the time paths of economic variables in the US and Germany in the post-war period.

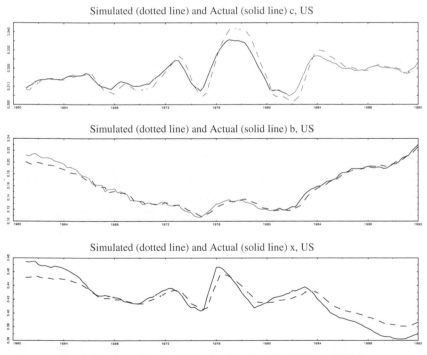

Fig. 9.1:  Actual and predicted $c$, $b$ and $x$, US 1960.4–1992.1.

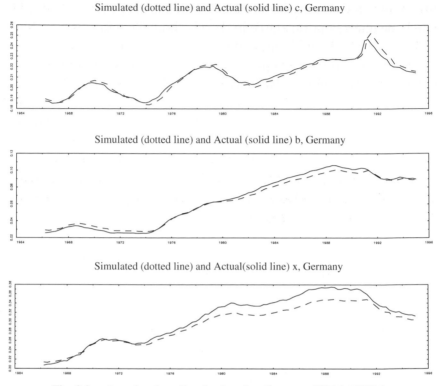

Fig. 9.2:   Actual and predicted $c, b$ and $x$, Germany 1996.1–1995.1.

In order to compare the time paths of the economic variables in both countries we consider the equations giving the growth rates of per capita GDP and of per capita consumption.

The growth rate of per capita GDP is given by

$$\frac{\dot{Y}}{Y} = (1 - \alpha)\frac{\dot{K}}{K} + \alpha\frac{\dot{G}}{G}.$$

The introduction of the budgetary regimes implies, as mentioned above, that the ratio of public capital to private capital, $B/K$, enters the economy wide resource constraint leading to a crowding-out of private capital. This, for its part, implies a lower investment share and, consequently, a lower growth rate of per capita GDP. Further, our model predicts that higher interest payments on public debt go along with less public resources available for public investment implying a lower growth rate of the public capital stock. Comparing the US and Germany, one realizes that the debt ratio was higher in the US than in Germany, while the growth rate of the public capital stock was lower over the time period we considered.[17] A lower growth rate of public capital also has a negative effect on GDP growth in our framework and, thus, contributes to the different growth experience of these two countries.

From the expression giving the growth rate of per capita consumption, Equation 9.14, we realize that a higher intertemporal elasticity of substitution, $1/\sigma$, for Germany tends to raise the growth rate of private consumption. Empirically, a high intertemporal elasticity of consumption implies that households are more willing to forego consumption today and shift it into future as the interest rate rises. Further, the smaller rate of time preference, $\rho$, in Germany also tends to raise the growth rate of consumption. That is, a high intertemporal elasticity of consumption and a low growth rate, respectively, have a stimulating effect on the investment share and, thus, on the growth rate of consumption. Consequently, the estimated values for the preference parameters in our model, $1/\sigma$ and $\rho$, tend to give a higher growth rate of consumption for Germany than for the US, which is compatible with the empirics. On the other hand, however, the higher tax rate, $\tau$, as well as the lower level of public capital to private capital, $x$, (see the last panels of Figure 9.1 and Figure 9.2) tend to lower the German growth rate of consumption.

---

[17] But it should be noted that the level of public capital relative to private capital was higher in the US than in Germany.

## 9.6. COMPARISON OF OUR RESULTS WITH
   THE LITERATURE

The literature on intertemporal models and fiscal policy has provided a number of predictions that are worth contrasting to the results of our study. One has, however, to distinguish between exogenous and endogenous growth models. In the first type of models only the stationary state values are affected by fiscal policies whereas in models with endogenous growth fiscal policies are likely to impact the growth rate.

In endogenous growth models with no public services only lump-sum taxes and, if labor supply is exogenous, consumption and labor taxes are non-distortionary having no effect on the growth rate. Capital income taxes have a detrimental effect on the long run growth rate. The optimal income or capital tax, when there are no government services affecting the utility or production functions, is thus shown to be zero (see Lucas, 1990). In our model variants with public investment the growth maximizing income tax is non-zero for all of our regimes. As our numerical study showed the growth rate may be hump-shaped. It may first rise with higher income tax and then fall giving us a growth maximizing income tax rate.

As regards to public expenditure most exogenous growth models show that an increase in public consumption or transfers should have no effect on long run per capita income, only the per capita private consumption declines (see Blanchard and Fischer, 1989, Chapter 2, for a detailed study with productive and non-productive government expenditures, see Turnovsky and Fisher, 1995). In our model with endogenous growth, for all of our regimes, a rise in transfers and public consumption reduces the long run growth rate (see also Barro, 1990). In models that include productive government investment one should expect a positive effect of public investment on growth since this type of activity is likely to enhance productivity of the private sector (Aschauer, 1989; Barro, 1990; Turnovsky, 1995, Chapter 13). This also occurs in our model variants.

Government deficit when later financed through lump-sum taxes to meet the government intertemporal budget constraint should have no effect on the per capita capital stock and thus on per capita income. This holds for both exogenous as well as endogenous growth models. This is frequently shown as a result of the Ricardian equivalence theorem. Government deficit eventually financed by income or capital taxes affects the long run per capita income negatively since the per capita capital stock will be lower. In an endogenous growth model like ours with budgetary regimes where we allow for both public deficit and infrastructure investment positive effects on economic growth may occur. There are, however, as we demonstrate two counterbalancing effects on the change of the growth rates. The growth rate may increase or decrease depending on the strength of the direct investment effect on the public capital, on the one hand, and the effect on the debt service, on the other.

Empirically, certain predictions of such models have been studied by regression techniques. Some of the empirical predictions of the standard models have been confirmed others not. In extensive cross section studies, undertaken by Easterly and Rebelo (1993) it has been found that "the evidence that the tax rates matter for growth is disturbingly fragile" (Easterly and Rebelo, 1993, p. 442). This seems to be in accordance with the result of our model variants with productive government expenditure. The growth maximizing tax rate (income tax in our case) should not be negatively correlated with the growth of the economy but hump-shaped which is not captured in linear regressions.

Public consumption expenditures and transfers are usually shown to have negative growth effects (see Barro, 1990; Easterly and Rebelo, 1993). On the other hand, public infrastructure investment seems to have positive effects.

Empirically high deficits appear to be associated with low growth rates (Easterly and Rebelo, 1993). This might, however, rather be the recession effect on the public deficit and does not necessarily show a negative effect of public sector borrowing on growth when the recession effect is eliminated. The fact that recessions cause the deficit to go up has been shown in a number of empirical studies.[18] In our long-run growth model where we have neglected the impact of underutilized capital and labor on public deficits we could find that deficits can have ambiguous effects on growth rates.

### 9.7. CONCLUSION

The chapter has presented and estimated an endogenous growth model with public capital and government capital market borrowing. Our study showed that a more strict budgetary regime, where public deficit is only allowed for public investment, appears to have a higher growth rate and a lower debt to private capital ratio. But as to the growth effects of a debt financed increase in public investment we saw that in the analytical model less strict budgetary regimes do not necessarily show a worse performance. Yet the numerical study revealed that less strict budgetary regimes are in general associated with higher debt to private capital ratios which again can offset the positive growth effect. Further, if too large a fraction of interest payment on public debt is paid by issuing new debt sustained per capita growth may not be feasible at all.

In the empirical part we used an estimation strategy similar to the one as employed for estimating the structural parameters of RBC models. Estimating the structural parameters of our endogenous growth model appears to be encouraging. So the model replicates

---

[18] The empirical trends in public deficits and debt (as well as the components of public expenditures contributing to the increase in public deficit and debt) are studied by Roubini and Sachs (1989a,b) who have started an important empirical work on the public debt in OECD countries. They argue that particularly in the 1970s the oil shock and the higher unemployment rate have increased deficits and debt. A related type of work although with a different methodology, is pursued by Petruzzello (1995).

well the time paths of the main economic variables in the US and Germany and suggests an explanation for the different growth performance of these two countries in the post-war period.

However, it must also be stated that the estimated parameters are partly implausible ($\alpha$) or plausible but different from the estimations obtained in other studies ($\rho$). But this is in part due to the theoretical model which postulates constant returns to scale of private and public capital in the aggregate per capita production function, which is necessary to generate endogenous growth. Further, it will be difficult or even impossible to construct an endogenous growth model with only private and public capital, which can replicate real time series with structural parameter values, which are commonly regarded as realistic. This holds because all factors generating economic growth are summarized in private and public capital while other important factors such as human capital, R&D or positive externalities of investment are not explicitly taken into account.[19]

Nevertheless, it is important to study the effects of fiscal policy on the growth rate of the euro-area economies assuming that public investment can have productive effects. This holds because there is sufficient evidence that public spending may have productivity stimulating effects (see the above mentioned paper by Sturm et al., 1998, and in particular the detailed survey by Pfähler et al., 1996). Therefore, theoretical endogenous growth models with productive government spending are worth being considered where the long run effects of fiscal policy in the Euro-area countries are studied. We also can conclude that our study of the composition of public spending, and in particular of the deficit, should have very important implications for the discussion on the 3% deficit rule in the Euro-area countries.

---

[19]For a more extensive account of other forces of economic growth, see Greiner et al. (2005).

**APPENDIX A9. GROWTH EFFECTS OF AN INCREASE IN PUBLIC CONSUMPTION, TRANSFER PAYMENTS AND AN INCREASE IN PUBLIC CONSUMPTION**

### A9.1. A rise in public consumption and transfer payments

To formally prove that a rise in public consumption and transfer payments reduces the balanced growth rate we derive from Equation 9.14

$$\frac{\partial g}{\partial \varphi_j} = \frac{(1-\tau)(1-\alpha)}{\sigma} \alpha x^{\alpha-1} \frac{\partial x}{\partial \varphi_j}, \qquad j = 1, 2.$$

To obtain $\partial x / \partial \varphi_j$ we implicitly differentiate $q_1$ and $q_2$.
   Knowing that $-\det M < 0$ (see below) the expression

$$-\frac{\partial q_1(\cdot)}{\partial b} \frac{\partial q(\cdot)}{\partial \varphi_j} + \frac{\partial q(\cdot)}{\partial b} \frac{\partial q_1(\cdot)}{\partial \varphi_j}, \qquad j = 1, 2,$$

determines the change of $x$.
   As $\partial \varphi_0 / \partial \varphi_1 = \partial \varphi_0 / \partial \varphi_2 = 1$ we get

$$-(\partial q_1(\cdot)/\partial b)(\partial q(\cdot)/\partial \varphi_j) + (\partial q(\cdot)/\partial b)(\partial q_1(\cdot)/\partial \varphi_j)$$

$$= -x^{\alpha-1}(1-\alpha)\varphi_3(1-\varphi_0)\tau$$

$$\quad - (1+(1-\alpha)b)^{-1})x^{\alpha}((1-\alpha)+b^{-1})(1-\varphi_3)\tau$$

$$\quad + x^{\alpha-1}(b(1-\alpha)+1)\varphi_3\tau(x^{\alpha}(\varphi_0-1)(1-\varphi_3)\tau b^{-2}$$

$$\quad - (1-\alpha)(1-\varphi_3)x^{\alpha}(b+(1-\alpha)b^2)^{-1}$$

$$= -x^{2\alpha-1}(1-\alpha)\varphi_3(\varphi_3-1)\tau b^{-1}$$

$$\quad - x^{2\alpha-1}(1-\alpha)\varphi_3(\varphi_0-1)(\varphi_3-1)\tau^2(1+(1-\alpha)b)b^{-1}$$

$$\quad \times x^{2\alpha-1}(1-\varphi_0)(\varphi_3-1)\tau^2 b^{-2}(1+(1-\alpha)b)\varphi_3$$

$$\quad + x^{2\alpha-1}(\varphi_3-1)(1-\alpha)\varphi_3\tau b^{-1} > 0, \quad j = 1, 2.$$

The first and the last term cancel out so that this expression is positive. This result together with $-\det M < 0$ demonstrates that $x$ at the steady-state declines and, thus, the balanced growth rate. This holds for all three regimes.

### A9.2. A rise in public investment in regime (A)

The sign of $-(\partial q_1(\cdot)/\partial b)(\partial q(\cdot)/\partial \varphi_3) + (\partial q(\cdot)/\partial b)(\partial q_1(\cdot)/\partial \varphi_3)$ determines whether a deficit financed increase in public consumption raises the balanced growth effects. It is calculated as

$$
\begin{aligned}
&- (\partial q_1(\cdot)/\partial b)(\partial q(\cdot)/\partial \varphi_3) + (\partial q(\cdot)/\partial b)(\partial q_1(\cdot)/\partial \varphi_3) \\
&= -x^{\alpha-1}\varphi_3(1-\alpha)((1-\varphi_0)\tau - (1+(1-\alpha)b)^{-1})x^\alpha \tau(1-\varphi_0) \\
&\quad \times((1-\alpha)+b^{-1}) + x^{\alpha-1}(1+(1-\alpha)b)(1-\varphi_0)\tau(-x^\alpha(1-\varphi_0) \\
&\quad \times(\varphi_3 - 1)b^{-2}\tau + (1-\alpha)(1-\varphi_3)x^\alpha(b+(1-\alpha)b^2)^{-1} \\
&= x^{2\alpha-1}(1-\alpha)(1-\varphi_0)\tau b^{-1} - x^{2\alpha-1}\varphi_3(1-\alpha)(1-\varphi_0)^2\tau^2 b^{-1} \\
&\quad \times(1+(1-\alpha)b) - x^{2\alpha-1}(1+(1-\alpha)b)(1-\varphi_0)^2(\varphi_3 - 1)\tau^2 b^{-2}
\end{aligned}
$$

Dividing by $x^{2\alpha-1}(1-\varphi_0)\tau b^{-1}(1-\alpha)$ the sign of this expression is equivalent to the sign of $1 - \tau(1-\varphi_0)(1+(1-\alpha)b)[\varphi_3 + (\varphi_3 - 1)/(b(1-\alpha))] \equiv -Z + 1$.

### A9.3. A rise in public investment in regime (B)

To study the effects of an increase in public investment we proceed as above. Doing the same steps as above with $\varphi_0$ now given by $\varphi_0 = (\varphi_1 + \varphi_2) + \varphi_4(1-\alpha)b\tau^{-1}(1+(1-\alpha)b)^{-1}$ and taking into account the derivatives of this term with respect to $\tau$ and $b$ we get

$$
-(\partial q_1(\cdot)/\partial b)(\partial q(\cdot)/\partial \varphi_3) + (\partial q(\cdot)/\partial b)(\partial q_1(\cdot)/\partial \varphi_3)
$$

$$
= \varphi_4 - \tau(1-\varphi_0)(1+(1-\alpha)b)[\varphi_3 + (\varphi_3 - 1)/(b(1-\alpha))].
$$

In analogy to regime A, the balanced growth rate rises if this expression is negative, i.e. if $Z_1 \equiv \tau(1 - \varphi_0)(1 + (1 - \alpha)b) \times [\varphi_3 + (\varphi_3 - 1)/(b(1 - \alpha))] > \varphi_4$. Since $\varphi_4 \in (0, 1)$ and $\varphi_0$ positively varies with $\varphi_4$ it is immediately seen that a positive growth effect is more likely for a fixed value of $b$.

### A9.4. A rise in public investment in regime (C)

The growth effect of a deficit financed rise in public investment is positive if and only if $(\partial q_1(\cdot)/\partial b)(\partial q(\cdot)/\partial \varphi_3) - (\partial q(\cdot)/\partial b) \times (\partial q_1(\cdot)/\partial \varphi_3) > 0$. $\partial q_1(\cdot)/\partial b$ and $\partial q(\cdot)/\partial b$ have already been calculated as

$$\frac{\partial q_1(\cdot)}{\partial b} = x^{\alpha-1}(1 - \alpha)\tau(1 - \varphi_0)\varphi_3 > 0,$$

$$\frac{\partial q(\cdot)}{\partial b} = -\left(\frac{1}{b}\right)^2 x^\alpha(\varphi_0 - 1)(1 - \varphi_3)\tau < 0, \qquad \text{for } \varphi_3 > 1.$$

$\partial q(\cdot)/\partial \varphi_3$ and $\partial q_1(\cdot)/\partial \varphi_3$ are computed as

$$\frac{\partial q(\cdot)}{\partial \varphi_3} = -x^\alpha((1 - \alpha) + b^{-1})\tau(\varphi_0 - 1) > 0,$$

$$\frac{\partial q_1(\cdot)}{\partial \varphi_3} = x^{\alpha-1}(1 + (1 - \alpha)b)(1 - \varphi_0)\tau > 0.$$

This demonstrates that $(\partial q_1(\cdot)/\partial b)(\partial q(\cdot)/\partial \varphi_3) - (\partial q(\cdot)/\partial b) \times (\partial q_1(\cdot)/\partial \varphi_3) > 0$.

Table 9.9:   Eigenvalues of the Jacobian for Table 9.2.

| $\tau$ | $\lambda_1$ | $\lambda_2$ | $\lambda_3$ | $\tau$ | $\lambda_1$ | $\lambda_2$ | $\lambda_3$ |
|------|-------|-------|-------|------|-------|-------|-------|
| 0.15 | $-7.45$ | 0.87 | $-0.77$ | 0.23 | $-5.26$ | 0.84 | $-0.51$ |
| 0.20 | $-5.95$ | 0.85 | $-0.60$ | 0.30 | $-4.04$ | 0.81 | $-0.35$ |
| 0.22 | $-5.48$ | 0.85 | $-0.54$ | 0.40 | $-2.85$ | 0.77 | $-0.18$ |

Table 9.10:  Eigenvalues of the Jacobian for Table 9.3.

| $\tau$ | $\lambda_1$ | $\lambda_2$ | $\lambda_3$ | $\tau$ | $\lambda_1$ | $\lambda_2$ | $\lambda_3$ |
|------|--------|--------|--------|------|--------|--------|--------|
| 0.15 | $-5.90$ | 0.88 | $-0.51$ | 0.21 | $-4.49$ | 0.85 | $-0.39$ |
| 0.20 | $-4.70$ | 0.86 | $-0.41$ | 0.30 | $-3.10$ | 0.81 | $-0.17$ |

## A9.5. The eigenvalues of the Jacobian

Tables 9.9 and 9.10 give the eigenvalues of the Jacobian for the numerical examples.

The eigenvalues of the Jacobian ($\lambda_{1,2,3}$) for the parameters and the corresponding steady-state values giving Table 9.2 are shown in Table 9.9.

Table 9.10 gives the eigenvalues of the Jacobian for the example of Table 9.3.

For $\varphi_4 = 0 \, (\varphi_4 = 0.05)$ the eigenvalues of the Jacobian are given by $\lambda_1 = -6.81$, $\lambda_2 = 0.94$, and $\lambda_3 = -0.65$ ($\lambda_1 = -5.49$, $\lambda_2 = 0.94$, and $\lambda_3 = -0.64$) for $\tau = 0.2$ and the corresponding parameter values.

# CHAPTER 10

# Testing Sustainability of Fiscal Policies

## 10.1. INTRODUCTION

A side effect of the involvement of the governments of the EU member states in economic growth and building and sustaining of a welfare state has been the rise of the public deficit and debt since the middle of the 1970s. Fiscal policy has been threatened to become unsustainable. This chapter is thus concerned with formal econometric procedures that allow one to test for the sustainability of fiscal policy. The issue of public debt has become a primary interest of both economists and politicians since the 1990s. Indeed most of the OECD countries have revealed a chronic government deficit since the middle of the 1970s, which has led to an increase in the debt to GDP ratio entering more or less a non-Ricardian regime. In Germany, it was in particular the unification of East and West Germany that has given rise to a debt to GDP ratio from about 44% in 1990 to roughly 58% in 1995.

From the theoretical point of view the question of how large a private agent's debt can be is usually answered as follows. Private households are subject to the borrowing constraint stating that, given no initial debt, the expected present value of expenditures (exclusive of interest payments) should not exceed the expected present value of receipts, known as the no-Ponzi game condition. This condition means that a private household cannot continually borrow money and pay the interest by borrowing more.

For government debt this question has somewhat been left unsettled from the theoretical point of view. If a government could borrow and pay the interest by borrowing more, any fiscal policy would be sustainable and in some model economies this is indeed possible. In overlapping generations models, for example, which are dynamically inefficient a government can borrow in order to pay interests on outstanding debt (see Diamond, 1965), i.e. it may run a Ponzi scheme. However, that possibility is not given any longer when the economy is dynamically efficient.[1] Then the government faces a present-value borrowing constraint staling that the current value of public debt must equal the discounted sum of future surpluses exclusive of interest payments. McCallum (1984) has studied a perfect foresight version of the competitive equilibrium model of Sidrauski (1967) and proved that permanent primary deficits are not possible if the deficit is defined exclusive of interest payments. Bohn (1995) has proved that in an exchange economy with infinitely lived agents the government must always satisfy the no-Ponzi game condition.

In any case, empirical studies which help to clarify whether governments follow the intertemporal budget constraint or not are desirable. For the US there exist numerous studies starting with the paper by Hamilton and Flavin (1986). In this chapter we propose a framework for analyzing whether governments run a Ponzi scheme or not and apply the test to US data. Other papers followed which also investigated this issue and partly reached different conclusions (see, e.g. Kremers, 1988; Wilcox, 1989; Trehan and Walsh, 1991). However, these tests have been criticized by Bohn (1995, 1998) because they make assumptions about future states of nature that are difficult to estimate from a single observed time series of data.

---

[1] For an empirical study analyzing whether the US economy is dynamically efficient, see Abel et al. (1989).

The new idea in this chapter is to pursue a new approach developed by Bohn (1998) that tests for a mean reversion of government debt.

   The remainder of this chapter is organized as follows. In section 2 we elaborate on some theoretical considerations dealing with the intertemporal budget constraint. Section 3 presents our estimation results and section 4 concludes.

## 10.2. THEORETICAL CONSIDERATIONS

The accounting identity describing the accumulation of public debt in continuous time is given by

$$\dot{B}(t) = B(t)r(t) - S(t), \tag{10.1}$$

where $B(t)$ stands for real public debt,[2] $r(t)$ is the real interest rate, and $S(t)$ is real government surplus exclusive of interest payments.

   Solving Equation 10.1 we get for the level of public debt at time $t$

$$B(t) = \exp\left(\int_0^t r(\tau)\mathrm{d}\tau\right)\left[B(0) - \int_0^t \exp\left(-\int_0^\tau r(\mu)\mathrm{d}\mu\right)S(\tau)\mathrm{d}\tau\right], \tag{10.2}$$

with $B(0)$, public debt at time $t$. Multiplying both sides of Equation 10.2 with $\exp(-\int_0^t r(\tau)\mathrm{d}\tau)$, to get the present value of the government debt at time $t$, yields

$$\exp\left(-\int_0^t r(\tau)\mathrm{d}\tau\right)B(t) + \int_0^t \exp\left(-\int_0^\tau r(\mu)\mathrm{d}\mu\right)S(\tau)\mathrm{d}\tau = B(0). \tag{10.3}$$

Assuming that the interest rate is constant[3] then Equation 10.3 becomes

$$e^{-rt}B(t) + \int_0^t e^{r\tau}S(\tau)\mathrm{d}\tau = B(0). \tag{10.4}$$

---

[2] Strictly speaking, $B(t)$ should be real public net debt.

[3] In the following we make this assumption since it simplifies the analysis. In Appendix A10 we discuss our main result (Proposition 10.2) for a time-varying interest rate and a time-varying GDP growth rate.

If the first term in Equation 10.4, $e^{-rt}B(t)$, goes to zero in the limit the current value of public debt equals the sum of the expected discounted future non-interest surpluses. Then we have

$$B(0) = E \int_0^t e^{-r\tau} S(\tau) \mathrm{d}\tau, \qquad (10.5)$$

with $E$ denoting expectations. Equation 10.5 is the present-value borrowing constraint and we can refer to a fiscal policy which satisfies this constraint as a sustainable policy. It states that public debt at time zero must equal the expected value of future present-value surpluses. Equivalent to requiring that Equation 10.5 must be fulfilled is that the following condition holds:

$$\lim_{t \to \infty} E e^{-rt} B(t) = 0. \qquad (10.6)$$

That equation is usually referred to as the no-Ponzi game condition (see, e.g. Blanchard and Fischer (1989), Chapter 2).

In the economics literature numerous studies exist which explore whether Equations 10.5 and 10.6 hold in real economies (see Hamilton and Flavin, 1986; Kremers, 1988; Wilcox, 1989; Trehan and Walsh, 1991; Greiner and Semmler, 1999b). As remarked in section 10.1 these tests, however, have been criticized by Bohn (1995, 1998). Bohn argues that they need strong assumptions because the transversality condition involves an expectation about states in the future that are difficult to obtain from a single set of time series data and because assumptions on the discount rate have to be made. As a consequence, the hypothesis that a given fiscal policy is sustainable has been rejected too easily.

Therefore, Bohn (1995, 1998) introduces a new sustainability test which analyzes whether a given time series of government debt is sustainable. The starting point of his new analysis is the observation that in a stochastic economy discounting future government spending and revenues by the interest rate on government bonds is not correct. Instead, the discount factor on future spending and revenues depends on the distributions of these variables across possible states of nature.

As an alternative test, Bohn proposes to test whether the primary deficit to GDP ratio is a positive linear function of the debt to GDP ratio. If this holds, a given fiscal policy is said to be sustainable. The reasoning behind this argument is that if a government raises the primary surplus, if public debt increases, it takes a corrective action, which stabilize the debt ratio. This implies that the debt to GDP ratio should display mean-reversion and thus the ratio should remain bounded. Before we undertake empirical tests we pursue some theoretical considerations about the relevance of this test for deterministic economies.

We assume a deterministic economy in continuous time in which the primary surplus of the government relative to GDP depends on the debt to GDP ratio and on a constant, i.e.

$$\frac{T(t) - G(t)}{Y(t)} = \alpha + \beta\left(\frac{B(t)}{Y(t)}\right), \tag{10.7}$$

with $T(t)$ tax revenue at time $t$, $G(t)$ public spending exclusive of interest payments at time $t$, $Y(t)$ GDP at time $t$, $B(t)$ public debt at time $t$ and $\alpha$, $\beta \in \mathbb{R}$ constants.[4] All variables are real variables.

Defining $b \equiv B/Y$ the public debt to GDP ratio evolves according to the following differential equation

$$\dot{b} = b\left(\frac{\dot{B}}{B} - \frac{\dot{Y}}{Y}\right) = b\left(r + \frac{G - T}{B} - \gamma\right), \tag{10.8}$$

with $r > 0$ the constant real interest rate and $\gamma > 0$ the constant growth rate of real GDP.

---

[4] In the following we leave aside the time argument $t$ if no ambiguity arises.

Using Equation 10.7 the differential equation describing the evolution of the debt–GDP ratio can be rewritten as

$$\dot{b} = b(r - \gamma - \beta) - \alpha. \tag{10.9}$$

Solving this differential equation we get the debt to GDP ratio $b$ as a function of time which is given by

$$b(t) = \frac{\alpha}{(r - \beta - \gamma)} + e^{(r-\beta-\gamma)t}C_1, \tag{10.10}$$

where $C_1$ is a constant given by $C_1 = b(0) - \alpha/(r - \beta - \gamma)$, with $b(0) \equiv B(0)/Y(0)$ the debt–GDP ratio at time $t = 0$. We assume that $b(0)$ is strictly positive, i.e. $b(0) > 0$ holds. With the debt–GDP ratio given by Equation 10.10 we can state our first result in Proposition 10.1 defining conditions for the boundedness of the debt–GDP ratio.

**Proposition 10.1.** *For our economy the following turns out to be true.*

(i) *$\beta > 0$ is a sufficient condition for the debt–GDP ratio to remain bounded if $r < \gamma$.*

(ii) *For $\beta > 0$ and $r > \gamma$ the debt–GDP ratio remains bounded if and only $r - \gamma < \beta$.*

(iii) *For $\beta < 0$ a necessary and sufficient condition for the debt–GDP ratio to remain bounded is $r - \beta < \gamma$.*

**Proof.** The proof follows from Equation 10.10. $\beta > 0$ and $r < \gamma$ gives $\lim_{t\to\infty} e^{(r-\beta-\gamma)t}C_1 = 0$. If $\beta > 0$ and $r > \gamma$, $\lim_{t\to\infty} \times e^{(r-\beta-\gamma)t}C_1 = 0$ holds if and only if $r - \beta - \gamma < 0$. This proves (i) and (ii). If $\beta < 0$ the second term in Equation 10.10 converges to zero if and only if $r - \beta - \gamma$ holds. This proves (iii). $\square$

This proposition demonstrates that a linear increase in the primary surplus to GDP ratio as a result of an increase in the debt to GDP ratio, i.e. $\beta > 0$, is neither a necessary nor a sufficient condition for the debt to GDP ratio to remain bounded for our deterministic economy with a constant real interest rate and a constant growth rate of real GDP unless additional conditions hold. Provided that the GDP growth rate exceeds the interest rate a positive $\beta$ is sufficient for the boundedness of the debt to GDP ratio. If the interest rate equals the marginal product of capital and if there are decreasing returns to capital the economy is dynamically inefficient if the growth rate of GDP exceeds the interest rate.

If the interest rate is larger than the growth rate the economy is dynamically efficient and the debt–GDP ratio remains bounded if $\beta$ exceeds the difference between the interest rate and the GDP growth rate. If the latter inequality does not hold the debt–GDP ratio does not converge. This shows that the response of the surplus ratio to a rise in the debt ratio must be sufficiently large, larger than $r - \gamma$, for the debt ratio to remain bounded.

On the other hand, a negative $\beta$ may imply a bounded debt to GDP ratio. A necessary and sufficient condition is that the growth rate of GDP must be sufficiently large, that is, it must exceed the interest rate plus the absolute value of $\beta$. But this can only hold for dynamically inefficient economies. So, in a dynamically efficient economy, where $r > \gamma$ holds, a negative $\beta$ is sufficient for the debt to GDP ratio to become unbounded.

Proposition 10.1 gives conditions which assure that the debt to GDP ratio remains bounded. However, the proper intertemporal budget constraint of the government requires that the discounted stream of government debt converges to zero. Therefore, we next study whether the intertemporal budget constraint of the government holds, which requires $\lim_{t \to \infty} e^{-rt} B(t) = 0$,[5] given our assumption that the primary deficit to GDP ratio is a linear function of

---

[5] Here, it should be noted that we exclude a strictly negative limit implying that the government would accumulate wealth since this is of less relevance for real economies.

the debt–GDP ratio as postulated in Equation 10.7. Using that equation the differential equation describing the evolution of public debt can be written as

$$\dot{B}(t) = rB(t) + G(t) - T(t) = (r - \beta)B(t) - \alpha Y(t). \quad (10.11)$$

Solving this differential equation gives public debt as an explicit function of time. Thus, $B(t)$ is given by

$$B(t) = \left( \frac{\alpha}{r - \gamma - \beta} \right) Y(0) e^{\gamma t} + e^{(r - \beta)t} C_2, \quad (10.12)$$

with $B(0) > 0$ debt at time $t = 0$ which is assumed to be strictly positive and with $C_2$ a constant given by $C_2 = B(0) - Y(0)\alpha/(r - \gamma - \beta)$. Given this expression we can state conditions which must be fulfilled so that the intertemporal budget constraint of the government can hold.

**Proposition 10.2.** *For our model economy the following turns out to hold true.*

(i) *For $\alpha \geq 0$, the intertemporal budget constraint of the government holds if $\beta > 0$.*

(ii) *For $\alpha < 0$, the intertemporal budget constraint of the government is fulfilled for $\beta > 0$ and $r > \gamma$.*

(iii) *For $\beta < 0$ the intertemporal budget constraint of the government is not fulfilled except for $B(0) = Y(0)\alpha/(r - \gamma - \beta)$ and $r > \gamma$.*

**Proof.** To prove this proposition we write the expression $e^{-rt}B(t)$ as

$$e^{-rt}B(t) = \left( \frac{\alpha}{r - \gamma - \beta} \right) Y(0) e^{(\gamma - r)t} + e^{-\beta t} C_2.$$

For $\beta > 0$ the term $e^{-\beta t} C_2$ converges to zero for $t \to \infty$. The first term of $e^{-rt}B(t)$ also converges to zero for $t \to \infty$ if $r > \gamma$ holds. If $r < \gamma$ holds the first term converges to $-\infty$ for $t \to \infty$ and $\alpha > 0$.

This case, however, is excluded by assumption. Thus, (i) is proven. For $\alpha < 0$ and $\beta > 0$ the first term of $e^{-rt}B(t)$ converges to zero for $t \to \infty$ if $r > \gamma$ holds. This proves (ii). For the sake of completeness we note that $r > \gamma$ implies $e^{-rt}B(t) \to \pm\infty$ depending on the sign of $r - \gamma - \beta$. Finally, for $\beta < 0$ the expression $e^{-rt}B(t)$ converges to zero if $C_2 = 0$, which is equivalent to $B(0) = Y(0)\alpha/(r - \gamma - \beta)$, and if $r > \gamma$ holds. If this does not hold $e^{-rt}B(t)$ diverges either to $+\infty$ or to $-\infty$. $\qquad\square$

Proposition 10.2 shows that the discounted value of public debt converges to zero if the surplus to GDP ratio positively reacts to increases in the debt ratio, i.e. if $\beta > 0$ holds, provided that there is no autonomous decrease in the primary surplus ratio, i.e. for $\alpha \geq 0$. This implies that the level of the primary surplus must not decline with an increase in GDP. If the reverse holds, i.e. if the level of the primary surplus declines with a rise in GDP ($\alpha < 0$), $\beta > 0$ guarantees that the intertemporal budget constraint of the government holds if the interest rate exceeds the growth rate of GDP, i.e. for dynamically efficient economies.

Thus, as long as economies are dynamically efficient, $\beta > 0$ guarantees that the discounted public debt converges to zero and, therefore, is a sufficient condition for sustainability of a given fiscal policy. It should also be noted that sustainability may be given even if the debt ratio is not constant, i.e. for $0 < \beta < r - \gamma$ (case (ii) in Proposition 10.1).

If the reverse holds, i.e. in dynamically inefficient economies where $r < \gamma$ holds, the present value of government debt explodes and the intertemporal budget constraint is not fulfilled. However, it must be pointed out that in such economies the intertemporal budget constraint is irrelevant. This holds because in dynamically inefficient economies the government can issue debt and roll it over indefinitely and cover interest payments by new debt issues, i.e. the government can indeed play a Ponzi game. Finally, the intertemporal budget constraint is not fulfilled if the government reduces its primary surplus as the debt ratio rises, i.e. for $\beta < 0$, except for the hairline case $B(0) = Y(0)\alpha/(r - \gamma - \beta)$.[6]

It must also be pointed out that in a stochastic economy dynamic efficiency does not necessarily imply that the interest rate on government debt exceeds the growth rate of the economy, i.e. $\gamma > r$ may occur. This holds because with risky assets the interest rate on safe government bonds can be lower than the marginal product of capital. If the stochastic economy is dynamically efficient and the growth rate exceeds the interest rate on government bonds, a positive $\beta$ is nevertheless also sufficient for the intertemporal budget constraint to be fulfilled if $\alpha = 0$ holds. A formal proof of this assertion can be found in the appendix to Bohn (1998) and in Canzonerie et al. (2001).

These theoretical considerations demonstrate that in a deterministic economy an increase in the primary surplus to GDP ratio as a consequence of a rise in the debt to GDP ratio guarantees that the intertemporal budget constraint of the government is fulfilled in dynamically efficient economies. So, looking at the relationship between the primary surplus ratio and the debt ratio allows to draw conclusions about the sustainability of a given fiscal policy so that empirically estimating Equation 10.7 seems to be a powerful test. Yet, we might also have to control other variables impacting the dynamics of Equation 10.7.

In section 10.3, we perform this test for some countries in the EMU which have been recently characterized by high deficits or by a high debt ratio.

## 10.3. EMPIRICAL ANALYSIS

Section 10.2 has highlighted two alternative estimation strategies to test for sustainability of fiscal policy. We here pursue the test where

---

[6] It should be recalled that we exclude the case where $e^{-rt}B(t)$ becomes strictly negative.

it is proposed to study how the primary surplus reacts to the debt–GDP ratio in order to see whether a given fiscal policy is sustainable. The main idea is to estimate the following equation:

$$s_t = \bar{\beta} b_t + \alpha^{\mathrm{T}} Z_t + \varepsilon_t \qquad (10.13)$$

where $s_t$ and $b_t$ is the primary surplus and debt ratio, respectively, $Z_t$ is a vector which consists of the number 1 and of other factors related to the primary surplus and $\varepsilon_t$ is an error term which is i.i.d. $N(0, \sigma^2)$.[7]

As concerns the other variables contained in $\mathbf{Z}_t$, which are assumed to affect the primary surplus, we include the net interest payments on public debt relative to GDP (Interest) and a variable reflecting the business cycle (YVAR). YVAR is calculated by applying the HP-Filter twice on the GDP-Series.[8]

Further, in the first two estimations the social surplus ratio (Social) is subtracted from the primary surplus ratio and is considered as exogenous in order to catch possible effects of transfers between the social insurance system and the government.[9] In the third equation to be estimated the social surplus ratio is included in the primary surplus ratio. The last equation, finally, is Equation 10.7 which only contains a constant and the debt ratio as explanatory variables. We do not expect this equation to yield good estimation results but we nevertheless estimate it because this equation was used to derive Propositions 10.1 and 10.2.

In addition, we decided that it is more reasonable to include the lagged debt ratio $b_{t-1}$ instead of the instantaneous $b_t$, although theory says that the response of the surplus on higher debt should be

---

[7] See Bohn (1998, p. 951).

[8] Arby (2001) suggested to first extract the long-run trend from the original series and then to filter out the cyclical component from the rest.

[9] $Social_t$ is computed by subtracting Social Benefits Paid By Government from the Social Security Contributions Received By Government.

immediate. We do this, because interest payments on debt and repayment of the debt occurs at later periods.[10]

Summarizing our discussion the equations to be estimated are as follows:

$$s_t = \alpha_0 + \bar{\beta} b_{t-1} + \alpha_1 \text{Social}_t + \alpha_2 \text{Interest}_t$$
$$+ \alpha_3 \text{YVAR}_t + \varepsilon_t, \tag{10.14}$$

$$s_t = \alpha_0 + \bar{\beta} b_{t-1} + \alpha_2 \text{Interest}_t + \alpha_3 \text{YVAR}_t + \varepsilon_t, \tag{10.15}$$

$$s_t^{\text{soc}} = \alpha_0 + \bar{\beta} b_{t-1} + \alpha_2 \text{Interest}_t + \alpha_3 \text{YVAR}_t + \varepsilon_t, \tag{10.16}$$

$$s_t^{\text{soc}} = \alpha_0 + \bar{\beta} b_{t-1} + \varepsilon_t \tag{10.17}$$

where $s_t$ is the primary surplus ratio exclusive of the social surplus and $s_t^{\text{soc}}$ denotes the primary surplus ratio including the social surplus.

Including interest payments as an independent variable on the right-hand side of Equation 10.13 implies that we have to correct the estimated coefficient $\bar{\beta}$ for the interest rate multiplied by the coefficient obtained for the interest payments ($\alpha_2$ in Equations 10.14–10.16). This holds because our estimations imply that Equation 10.7 is given by

$$\frac{T(t) - G(t)}{Y(t)} = \alpha + \bar{\beta} \left( \frac{B(t)}{Y(t)} \right) + \alpha_2 r \left( \frac{B(t)}{Y(t)} \right)$$
$$= \alpha + (\bar{\beta} + \alpha_2 r) \left( \frac{B(t)}{Y(t)} \right). \tag{10.18}$$

Thus, it is immediately seen that the coefficient $\beta$ in Equation 10.7 is given by $\beta = \bar{\beta} + \alpha_2 r$. Consequently, $\beta = \bar{\beta} + \alpha_2 r > 0$ must hold so that public debt is sustainable.

Estimating Equations 10.14–10.17 with ordinary least squares (OLS) may give biased standard errors and $T$-statistics because of

---

[10] We also made the estimations with $b_t$ instead of $b_{t-1}$. The result are basically the same but the standard errors of the coefficients are different. Details are available on request.

possible heteroskedasticity and autocorrelation in the residuals. In spite of this problem we use OLS estimation but calculate heteroskedasticity- and autocorrelation-consistent $T$-statistics to get robust estimates (see White, 1980; and Newey and West, 1987).

The estimations are undertaken for five countries: Germany, France, Italy, Portugal and US. The chosen Euro-area countries suffered from high debt and deficits having violated the Maastricht criteria recently, and so they motivate our choice for the tests whether their fiscal policies can be regarded as sustainable.

### 10.3.1. France

Figure 10.1 indicates that the debt ratio has been growing most of the time and increased very fast at the beginning of the 1990s. Until the mid-1990s France experienced deficits (net of the social surplus) which has led to a further deterioration of the high debt ratio.

The primary deficit displays a remarkably different trend. Relative low deficits, and in some cases primary surpluses, generated only a moderate growth of the debt ratio. The recession in the early 1990s caused higher deficits and reduced social surpluses created higher debt ratios. In face of the Maastricht criteria France strengthened its fiscal discipline and reduced the debt ratio. Since the last recession, at the beginning of 2001, the fiscal situation worsened and the debt ratio has been growing again.

Going back to the relationship between the primary surplus and debt ratio the next figure shows a slightly positive relationship between the surplus and debt. As Figure 10.2 shows, after the debt ratio reached the 50% limit, apparently corrective measures were taken and a positive slope can be observed.

Equation 10.14 is estimated for the entire sample period. We obtain the result in Table 10.1.

The parameter of interest $\bar{\beta}$ is positive and significant at the 10% level ($T$-statistic $= 1.812$). As one can observe corrective measures were taken if an increase in the debt ratio of the last period was

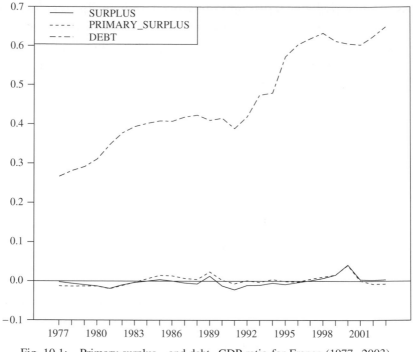

Fig. 10.1:   Primary surplus– and debt–GDP ratio for France (1977–2003).

observed. The coefficient $\alpha_2$ giving the influence of the interest payments is negative but not statistically significant. Nevertheless, computing $\beta = \bar{\beta} + \alpha_2 r$, with $r = 0.043$ the average long-term real interest rate for France from 1977 to 2003, shows that $\beta$ is strictly positive in each observation. Thus, our estimations indicate that French fiscal policy has followed a sustainable path.

The good fit of the model is displayed by a high $R^2$ of 0.749. The Durbin–Watson (DW) statistic is 1.063. The $\alpha_1$ parameter shows a negative response of the primary surplus ratio to the social surplus ratio. This might be interpreted that a high social surplus weakens the fiscal discipline and lowers the deficit. The positive sign of the $\alpha_2$ parameter indicates the efforts of the government to run surpluses to pay the debt service.

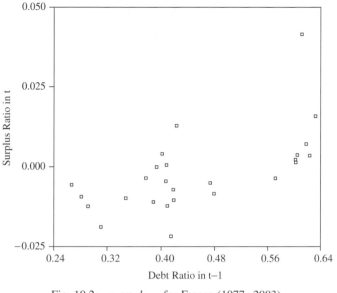

Fig. 10.2: $s_t$ vs. $b_{t-1}$ for France (1977–2003).

The cyclical variable is insignificant at all usual levels which might be caused by the fact that the French business cycle was following the German business cycle because of the fixed European exchange rate system and because of the Bundesbank interest rate policy.

Furthermore, we have estimated Equation 10.15 as well as Equations 10.16 and 10.17 where we replaced the primary surplus

Table 10.1: Estimates for Equation 10.14.

|  | Coefficient | Standard error (*T*-statistic) |
| --- | --- | --- |
| Constant | $-0.012$ | $0.019\ (-0.597)$ |
| $b_{t-1}$ | $0.077$ | $0.042\ (1.812)$ |
| Social$_t$ | $-0.913$ | $0.297\ (-3.078)$ |
| Int$_t$ | $-1.256$ | $0.753\ (-1.667)$ |
| YVAR$_t$ | $-0.048$ | $0.187\ (-0.257)$ |
| $R^2$DW | 0.749/1.063 | |

Table 10.2: Estimates for Equations 10.15–10.17, France.

| | Dependent variable, $s_t$ | | Dependent variable, $s_t^{soc}$ | | Dependent variable, $s_t^{soc}$ | |
|---|---|---|---|---|---|---|
| | Coefficient | T-statistic | Coefficient | T-statistic | Coefficient | T-statistic |
| Constant | −0.061 | −7.655 | −0.007 | −0.997 | −0.009 | −1.523 |
| $b_{t-1}$ | 0.140 | 4.830 | 0.071 | 2.206 | 0.012 | 0.928 |
| $Int_t$ | −0.993 | −1.447 | −1.281 | −1.706 | | |
| $YVAR_t$ | −0.321 | −1.834 | −0.022 | −0.114 | | |
| $R^2$ | 0.683 | | 0.294 | | 0.031 | |
| DW | 0.941 | | 1.076 | | 0.657 | |

($s_t$) by the primary surplus inclusive of the social surplus ($s_t^{soc}$). The results are presented in Table 10.2.

The estimate of $\bar{\beta}$ in Equation 10.15 and in Equation 10.16 is in both cases positive and significant at the 1% level. In both estimations the cyclical variable remains insignificant and the net interest variable becomes also insignificant at the 5% level. Further, a reduction in the $R^2$ value can be observed which leads to the conclusion that Equation 10.14 fits the data best. The estimation of Equation 10.17 yields the coefficients which have the same signs as in the other regressions. However, none of the coefficients is statistically significant.

Summarizing, one can reject the hypothesis that the primary surplus ratio does not increase as the debt ratio rises. So according to Proposition 10.2, sustainability of fiscal policy seems to be given although the constant $\alpha_0$ is negative. This holds because the interest rate in France has exceeded the growth rate of GDP, at least since the early 1980s,[11] so that the intertemporal budget constraint is fulfilled according to (ii) in Proposition 10.2. Thus, the hypothesis of an overall sustainable fiscal policy cannot be rejected for France. Next, we look at Germany.

---

[11] This also holds for Germany, Italy and Portugal.

**10.3.2. Germany**

As Figure 10.3 shows at the beginning of the mid-1970s the German government was confronted with high debt ratios accompanied with permanent primary deficits. Furthermore, in Figure 10.4 two episodes of a sharp rise in the growth rate of public debt can be observed followed by periods with budgetary discipline and lower increasing debt ratios. In the mid-1970s the debt ratio increases very rapidly, due to the oil shock, which also caused a recession with the rise of the unemployment rate. This fact is highlighted in Figure 10.3 by the solid line for debt to GDP ratio and the dotted lines for the primary surplus. The second sharp increase of the debt ratio was caused by the German unification and began in the early 1990s as the GDP growth rates slowed down.

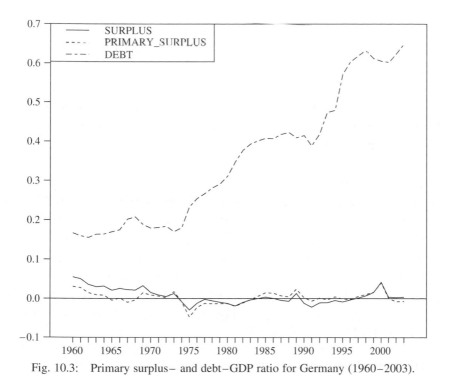

Fig. 10.3:   Primary surplus– and debt–GDP ratio for Germany (1960–2003).

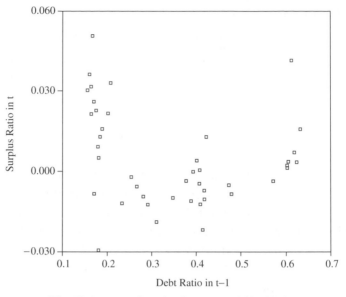

Fig. 10.4:    $s_t$ vs. $b_{t-1}$ for Germany (1960–2003).

If debt ratios smaller than 0.2 are disregarded a weak positive slope for the regression line can be realized. Yet, the entire data set clearly show the phases of fiscal consolidation in the 1990s and the consolidation efforts to join the EMU (see Figure 10.3).

Next, we explore if the test procedure agrees with our presumptions. For Equation 10.14 we get the estimates in Table 10.3.

The $\bar{\beta}$ coefficient of 0.148 is significant at all ratios and indicates a strong positive response of the primary surplus to a higher debt in the previous period. The same effect is observed for the variables' net interest payment and business cycle and the coefficients are both highly significant. But a significantly positive effect of the social surplus on the primary surplus cannot be observed. The good fit of the data is reflected in the relatively high $R^2$ of 0.642 and a DW-statistic of 1.181, although there still must be other variables involved to explain the remaining structure of the residuals. Finally, let us look at the other three regressions which are summarized in Table 10.4.

Table 10.3: Estimates for Equation 10.14 (dependent variable: $s_t$).

| | Coefficient | Standard error (*T*-statistic) |
|---|---|---|
| Constant | −0.002 | 0.005 (−0.415) |
| $b_{t-1}$ | 0.148 | 0.043 (3.467) |
| Social$_t$ | −0.068 | 0.255 (−0.266) |
| Int$_t$ | −2.552 | 0.670 (−3.810) |
| YVAR$_t$ | 0.240 | 0.060 (3.967) |
| $R^2$/DW | 0.642/1.181 | |

In the first test, with $s_t$ as the dependent variable, all parameters, except the constant, are highly significant and the sustainability coefficient $\bar{\beta}$ has a positive sign. The second test, with the $s_t^{soc}$ as the dependent variable, shows a slightly different scenario. The $\bar{\beta}$ coefficient of 0.078 is only significant at the 10% level and the net interest payments and the constant term are insignificant. Looking at $R^2$ and the DW-statistic we draw the conclusion that the first model fits better than the other two. As for France, the estimation of Equation 10.17 does not produce statistically significant results. Nevertheless, the coefficients have the same signs as in the other estimations.

Calculating $\beta = \bar{\beta} + \alpha_2 r$, with $r = 0.04$ the average long-term real interest rate in Germany over the period considered, demonstrates that $\beta$ is strictly positive. Thus, as for the case

Table 10.4: Estimates for Equations 10.15–10.17, Germany.

| | Dependent variable, $s_t$ | | Dependent variable, $s_t^{soc}$ | | Dependent variable, $s_t^{soc}$ | |
|---|---|---|---|---|---|---|
| | Coefficient | *T*-statistic | Coefficient | *T*-statistic | Coefficient | *T*-statistic |
| Constant | −0.001 | −0.270 | −0.011 | −1.720 | −0.005 | −0.806 |
| $b_{t-1}$ | 0.153 | 4.411 | 0.078 | 1.840 | 0.018 | 1.192 |
| Int$_t$ | −2.676 | −5.995 | −0.851 | −1.609 | | |
| YVAR$_t$ | 0.241 | 4.103 | 0.219 | 3.114 | | |
| $R^2$ | 0.641 | | 0.241 | | 0.038 | |
| DW | 1.177 | | 1.045 | | 0.883 | |

of France our estimations suggest that Germany has followed a sustainable fiscal policy. In all estimations the primary surplus ratio increases with a rising debt ratio suggesting that the intertemporal budget constraint is met.

The Chow breakpoint test and the $F$-test on equal variances suggest that German unification in 1990 generated a structural break at that period.[12] Therefore, we have split the sample into two parts and estimated Equation 10.14 for the two sub-samples. One period is from 1960 to 1989 and the other one from 1990 to 2003. For the first sub-sample the results of our model remain basically unchanged ($R^2 = 0.820$ and DW $= 0.979$) and the $\bar{\beta}$-value increases to 0.378 ($T$-statistic $= 5.448$). The other parameters, except for the social surplus, show strong significance and the expected sign. In the second sub-sample almost all estimates are insignificant which is possibly due to the small data set. Nevertheless, the coefficient $\bar{\beta}$ with a value of 0.162 is significantly different from zero at the 10% level ($T$-statistic $= 1.833$). Our presumption that the unification significantly influenced the fiscal policy of Germany seems to be supported by the test.

### 10.3.3. Italy

Since the mid-1980s, Italy has shown a fast growing debt ratio accompanied by a permanent primary deficit. Faced with the criteria for joining the EMU in 1999, fiscal policy changed its course and the Italian government has lowered the deficits and at the beginning of the 1990s, surplus stopped the growth of public debt ratio. Although, the debt criteria could not be fulfilled at the start of the EMU, Italy joined the EMU in 1999. The trends of Italian fiscal policy are shown in Figure 10.5.

An overall consolidation effort of the fiscal policy in response to higher debt ratios is suggested by Figure 10.6 in which the primary

---

[12] Details are again available on request.

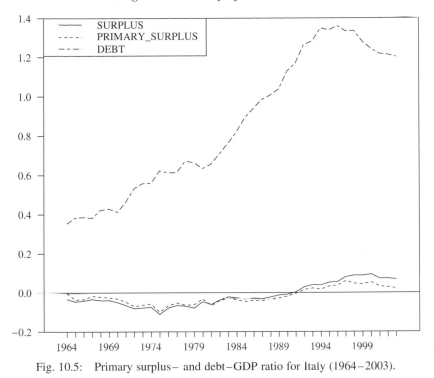

Fig. 10.5:   Primary surplus– and debt–GDP ratio for Italy (1964–2003).

surplus ratio is plotted against the debt ratio. Apparently the Italian government tried to increase the surplus ratio in order to stabilize the growing indebtedness.

This conclusion is also reached by the results of our test. The estimation of the Equation 10.14 yields the results in Table 10.5.

The response parameter $\bar{\beta}$ is 0.163 and significant at all levels ($T$-statistic $= 6.956$), meaning that the aforementioned conjecture of a sustainable fiscal policy holds in spite of the extraordinarily high initial debt ratio. The other estimates are all significantly different from zero although the social surplus effect is only small with a coefficient of 0.053. Finally, the $R^2$ reaches 0.911 and the DW-statistic is 1.071. The latter suggests that there might still be some structure in the residual which is not covered by our framework.

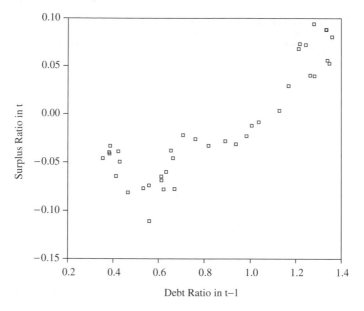

Fig. 10.6:    $s_t$ vs. $b_{t-1}$ for Italy (1964–2003).

Next, we have estimated Equations 10.15–10.17. The results are shown in Table 10.6.

Those estimates confirm our results above. The Italian fiscal policy points to sustainability in the long run in spite of the initial high debt–income ratio. Both $\bar{\beta}$-coefficients of 0.199 and 0.131 in Equations 10.15 and 10.16, respectively, are positive and significant

Table 10.5:    Estimates for Equation 10.14.

|  | Coefficient | Standard error ($T$-statistic) |
|---|---|---|
| Constant | −0.122 | 0.013 (−9.461) |
| $b_{t-1}$ | 0.163 | 0.023 (6.956) |
| Social$_t$ | −0.531 | 0.274 (−1.933) |
| Int$_t$ | −0.525 | 0.131 (−4.000) |
| YVAR$_t$ | 0.128 | 0.024 (5.339) |
| $R^2$/DW | | 0.911/1.071 |

Table 10.6:    Estimates for Equations 10.15–10.17, Italy.

| | Dependent variable, $s_t$ | | Dependent variable, $s_t^{soc}$ | | Dependent variable, $s_t^{soc}$ | |
|---|---|---|---|---|---|---|
| | Coefficient | T-statistic | Coefficient | T-statistic | Coefficient | T-statistic |
| Constant | −0.143 | −19.393 | −0.103 | −14.045 | −0.019 | −2.963 |
| $b_{t-1}$ | 0.199 | 18.525 | 0.131 | 13.246 | $2 \times 10^{-6}$ | 2.438 |
| $Int_t$ | −0.628 | −5.714 | −0.434 | −4.290 | | |
| $YVAR_t$ | 0.138 | 5.938 | 0.118 | 5.195 | | |
| $R^2$ | 0.906 | | 0.812 | | 0.004 | |
| DW | 0.997 | | 1.109 | | 0.163 | |

suggesting that corrective measures in balancing the budget, or running a surplus, have been taken. This holds although the estimation of Equation 10.17 yields a $\bar{\beta}$-coefficient which is virtually zero. But again, this equation is characterized by an extremely small $R^2$ and DW-statistic.

Calculating $\beta = \bar{\beta} + \alpha_2 r$ demonstrates that this coefficient is strictly positive, as for France and Germany. For Italy the average long-term real interest rate is $r = 0.023$ over the period we consider. This relatively small values is due to very high inflation rates in Italy in the mid-1970s and in the early 1980s.

## 10.3.4. Portugal

Another candidate for testing sustainability of fiscal policy is Portugal which has also been in the news for violating the Maastricht criteria. The situation in Portugal differs from Italy in the fact that Portugal's indebtedness is relatively small, but it primarily suffered from persistent deficits in the last years as shown in Figure 10.7. The main difference to the other countries is that Portugal's net interest payments affects its budget in an extreme way, i.e. the primary surplus is nearly zero over most of the sample period but paying the debt service generates a public deficit.

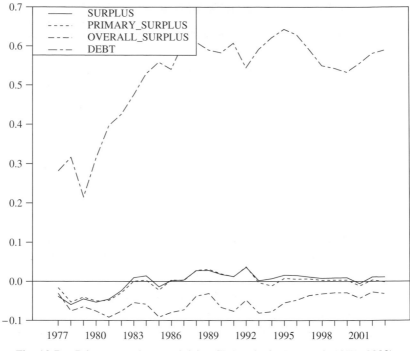

Fig. 10.7:   Primary surplus– and debt–GDP ratio for Portugal (1977–2003).

Despite the problem of the high net interest payments Portugal shows a positive relationship between primary surplus and debt ratios as can be observed from Figure 10.8.

The estimation of Equation 10.14 for Portugal gives the results in Table 10.7.

The main parameter $\bar{\beta}$ with a value of 0.164 is positive and significant at all usual levels ($T$-statistic $= 6.547$). The same holds for the constant and the business cycle variable. Yet, the latter shows a negative sign, which means if the economy is growing the surplus will be reduced. As in the case of France the business cycle upswing has also a negative effect on the surplus but in the case of France, it was not significantly different from zero. The remaining variables' social

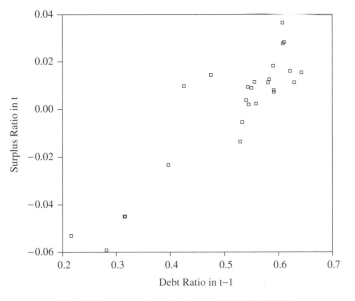

Fig. 10.8:   $s_t$ vs. $b_{t-1}$ for Portugal (1977–2003).

surplus and interest payments do not have a significant effect on the primary surplus.

In contrast to the other countries the primary surplus ratio rises with higher interest payments although the coefficient $\alpha_2$ is not statistically significant. The $R^2$ value of 0.861 and the DW-statistic of 1.812 indicate that the data are very well represented by Equation 10.14. Estimating Equations 10.15–10.17 gives results as shown in Table 10.8.

Table 10.7:   Estimates for Equation 10.14.

|  | **Coefficient** | **Standard error (*T*-statistic)** |
|---|---|---|
| Constant | −0.083 | 0.012 (−7.112) |
| $b_{t-1}$ | 0.164 | 0.025 (6.547) |
| Social$_t$ | 0.314 | 0.364 (0.863) |
| Int$_t$ | 0.014 | 0.093 (0.154) |
| YVAR$_t$ | −0.051 | 0.014 (−3.691) |
| $R^2$/DW | 0.861/1.811 | |

Table 10.8:   Estimates for Equations 10.15–10.17, Portugal.

| | Dependent variable, $s_t$ | | Dependent variable, $s_t^{soc}$ | | Dependent variable, $s_t^{soc}$ | |
|---|---|---|---|---|---|---|
| | Coefficient | $T$-statistic | Coefficient | $T$-statistic | Coefficient | $T$-statistic |
| Constant | −0.085 | −6.789 | −0.090 | −6.829 | −0.095 | −11.588 |
| $b_{t-1}$ | 0.161 | 7.073 | 0.150 | 6.663 | 0.176 | 10.576 |
| Int$_t$ | 0.054 | 0.466 | 0.181 | 1.848 | | |
| YVAR$_t$ | −0.043 | −1.938 | −0.015 | −0.880 | | |
| $R^2$ | 0.858 | | 0.780 | | 0.749 | |
| DW | 1.833 | | 1.697 | | 1.466 | |

The results in Table 10.8 are not very surprising if one looks at Figure 10.8. It can be explained by the small distance between the primary surplus series excluding the social surplus ($s_t$) and including the social surplus ($s_t^{soc}$), that is by the almost balanced social budget. The parameters of interest in Equations 10.15 and 10.16 are both positive and significant and take the value 0.161 and 0.150, respectively ($T$-statistics = 7.393 and 6.663). Even Equation 10.17 produces statistically significant results and acceptable values for $R^2$ and for the DW-statistic.

### 10.3.5.  US

Finally we will look at the fiscal policy trend of the US. Many authors have focused their attention on the sustainability of fiscal policy in the US. This issue is back in the news due to the actual deficit caused by the Iraq war and the tax cuts to stimulate the US economy. We first consider the graph giving the time series of US debt- and primary surplus ratios and the scatter plot of these two variables (Figure 10.9).

The primary surplus ratio excluding the social surplus is almost always positive. Until the Reagan Administration took over in 1980

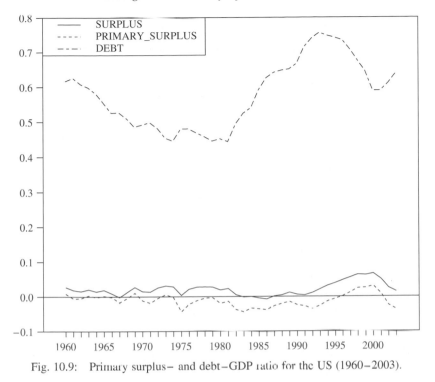

Fig. 10.9: Primary surplus– and debt–GDP ratio for the US (1960–2003).

the debt ratio fell and began to grow until the Democrats won the White House back in 1992. Then, in the 1990s the debt ratio started significantly declining (Figure 10.10).

Concerning the scatter plot a weak positive relationship can be observed even if the volatility around the imaginary regression line increases. This suggests that those outliers may cause problems with the residuals and are likely to show up in a poor DW-statistic and possibly a low $R^2$. For the first regression we get the result in Table 10.9.

All coefficients are highly significant and $\bar{\beta}$ is positive so that sustainability cannot be rejected. As our regression shows the US government tried to compensate the additional debt by running a higher surplus a year later. Interestingly, a negative value of the business cycle is estimated. As in the case of Portugal, a growing

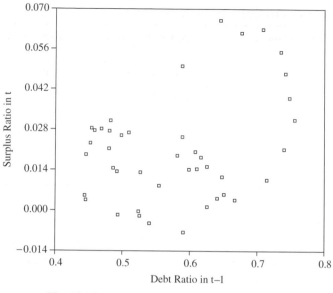

Fig. 10.10:   $s_t$ vs. $b_{t-1}$ for the US (1960–2003).

economy will reduce the surplus. Also, if a social surplus is produced the surplus will be reduced, meaning that the government will take advantage of the good social position and lowers its efforts to run a surplus. Our conjecture of a low $R^2$ and a poor DW-statistic is verified, they take values of 0.375 and 0.656, respectively. Table 10.10 summarizes the results for the next estimations.

Table 10.9:   Estimates for Equation 10.14.

|  | Coefficient | Standard error (*T*-statistic) |
|---|---|---|
| Constant | −0.056 | 0.017 (−3.309) |
| $b_{t-1}$ | 0.165 | 0.035 (4.683) |
| $Social_t$ | −0.600 | 0.266 (2.259) |
| $Int_t$ | −1.617 | 0.381 (−4.242) |
| $YVAR_t$ | −0.138 | 0.036 (−3.778) |
| $R^2$/DW | 0.376/0.656 | |

Table 10.10: Estimates for Equations 10.15–10.17, US.

| | Dependent variable, $s_t$ | | Dependent variable, $s_t^{soc}$ | | Dependent variable, $s_t^{soc}$ | |
|---|---|---|---|---|---|---|
| | Coefficient | T-statistic | Coefficient | T-statistic | Coefficient | T-statistic |
| Constant | − 0.044 | − 2.853 | − 0.063 | − 4.114 | − 0.036 | − 2.299 |
| $b_{t-1}$ | 0.167 | 4.515 | 0.164 | 4.453 | 0.041 | 1.497 |
| $Int_t$ | − 1.310 | − 3.607 | − 1.821 | − 5.613 | | |
| $YVAR_t$ | − 0.178 | − 4.071 | − 0.111 | − 2.768 | | |
| $R^2$ | 0.289 | | 0.342 | | 0.048 | |
| DW | 0.409 | | 0.794 | | 0.548 | |

The poor quality of our estimation remains and suggests to include other variables to properly model the outliers in these time series. Yet, all parameters are significant and the $\bar{\beta}$s have the expected sign. For the US the average long-term real interest rate was $r = 0.026$ for the period of 1960–2003 implying that $\beta = \bar{\beta} + \alpha_2 r > 0$ holds. Thus, our findings seem to verify Bohn's results when he characterized the US fiscal policy to be sustainable even if we do not use the same data and include additional components in the framework.

It should also be mentioned that for the US interest rates have been lower than the growth of GDP which would indicate dynamic inefficiency. However, in a stochastic framework it is the relation between the growth rate and the rate of return on risky capital which determines whether an economy is dynamically efficient and Abel et al. (1989) provide strong evidence that the US economy is dynamically efficient.

## 10.4. CONCLUSION

This chapter has analyzed the question of whether fiscal policy is sustainable in selected Euro-area countries. We have focused on those countries which are characterized by a high debt ratio or which recently have violated the 3% Maastricht deficit criteria. We have undertaken this study by following up an approach that Bohn (1998) has developed to study sustainability of fiscal policy in the US. Theoretically, we could show that if the primary surplus to GDP ratio of the government increases linearly with a rising ratio of public debt to GDP the fiscal policy is sustainable for dynamically efficient economies.

Our empirical results suggest that fiscal policies in the countries under consideration are sustainable. The reason for this is that governments take corrective actions as a result of rising debt ratios by increasing the primary surplus ratio. This, however, implies that the intertemporal budget constraint of the government, which should be fulfilled in the far future when time approaches infinity, has immediate implications for the period budget constraint.

So, the compliance with the intertemporal budget constraint implies that either public spending must decrease with a rising public debt ratio or the tax revenue must increase. Looking at actual fiscal policy one realizes that it is not a rise in the tax revenue but a decline in public spending, which generates primary surpluses. As to the component of public spending which has been reduced mostly, it can be seen that in many countries public investment has been decreased. Public investment is likely to be the variable that can be reduced most easily. Thus, the decline of public investment as a result of a rising public debt may be explained, a fact which can also be observed empirically (see, e.g. Gong et al., 2001; Heinemann, 2002). Thus, although the fiscal policy we studied for the Euro-area economies can be considered sustainable, in the long-run, high debt ratios may have negative repercussion for the growth rates of economies.

## APPENDIX A10. PROPOSITION 10.2 WITH A TIME-VARYING INTEREST RATE AND GDP GROWTH RATE

If Equation 10.7 holds and the interest rate and the GDP growth rate are not constant the discounted level of government debt,

$\exp(-\int_0^t r(\tau)\mathrm{d}\tau)B(t)$, is given by

$$\exp\left(-\int_0^t r(\tau)\mathrm{d}\tau\right)B(t)$$

$$= e^{-\beta t}\left[B(0) - \alpha Y(0)\int_0^t \exp\left(\beta\tau - \int_0^\tau (r(\mu) - \gamma(\mu))\mathrm{d}\mu\right)\mathrm{d}\tau\right],$$

with $r(\cdot)$ and $\gamma(\cdot)$ the time-varying interest rate and GDP growth rate, respectively, and $\alpha$ and $\beta$ as in Equation 10.7. For $\beta > 0$ and $\alpha \geq 0$ it is immediately seen that the intertemporal budget constraint holds. For $\beta > 0$ and $\alpha < 0$ the intertemporal budget constraint holds for $\lim_{\tau \to \infty} \int_0^\tau (r(\mu) - \gamma(\mu))\mathrm{d}\mu = \infty$.

## APPENDIX B10. DATA

*Source*: OECD Economic Outlook Statistics and Projections.

We use the data set corresponding to those published in the June 2003 issue of the OECD Economic Outlook. Especially, we take the entire data set for the Government Account and the series for Gross Domestic Product at Market prices (GDP).

The data for the four Euro-area countries are expressed in euro (EUR). For each country, pre-1999 data were converted from national currency using the irrevocable conversion euro rates. The data are expressed in millions of EUR or USD, respectively.

# CHAPTER 11

# Stabilization of Public Debt and Macroeconomic Performance

## 11.1. INTRODUCTION

The above stated trends toward excessive deficits of some of the Euro-area member states in the 1980s has called for fiscal consolidation and debt stabilization already before the introduction of the Euro in January 1999. In fact the Maastricht Treaty of 1992 laid the groundwork for such stabilization efforts.

In the 1990s empirical studies had already emerged which called into question the expansionary effects of Keynesian deficit spending. The researchers studied the question of whether a rise in public spending shows positive or negative effects on the growth rate of an economy. Perotti (1999), for example demonstrates that low levels of debt or deficit are likely to generate positive effects of public expenditure shocks, while high levels of public debt lead to negative effects. Giavazzi and Pagano (1990) studied the fiscal consolidations in Denmark and Ireland in the 1980s and showed that in these countries a drastic cut in public deficits led to a sharp increase in private consumption. Alesina and Perotti (1995) reach a similar result. In addition to the two countries mentioned above, those authors consider Belgium, Canada, Italy, Portugal and Sweden over the time period form the mid-1980s to the beginning of the 1990s. In each of these countries the primary deficit was strongly reduced while the growth rate of private consumption was positive and larger than in the years prior to the adjustment.

The question of whether fiscal consolidation and debt stabilization show, in the short run, positive or negative effects on macroeconomic performance was of great relevance for European countries which joined the Economic and Monetary Union (EMU). Since the transition to EMU has been characterized by considerable need for monetary and fiscal consolidation efforts it is important to analyze the effects of that fiscal policy on the economic performance. Moreover, one may want to know the growth effects of the strict fiscal rules that were introduced at the start of the Euro. van Aarle et al. (1999), for example study the economic impact of fiscal retrenchment on economic activity during the transition towards EMU. They analyze whether countries under fiscal stress show different reactions to public policy measures compared to other countries. In their paper, an economy is supposed to be under fiscal stress if its primary budget gap is larger than $-0.05$ (in absolute terms). They find strong effects of adjustments in government spending on private consumption and investment for countries under fiscal stress. For countries which are not under fiscal stress fiscal consolidation shows negative effects as to private consumption and investment.

In this chapter we will pursue a similar line of research. Our goal is to study the impact of public deficit and public debt on real variables, such as investment and GDP, for some countries of the EU. Further, we intend to clarify whether countries which seem to have large deficits and debt experience different effects of fiscal policies compared to countries with low deficits and debt.

The rest of this chapter is organized as follows. In the next section we conduct Granger causality tests in order to test empirically what effects the reduction of fiscal deficit and debt has. Here, we will not consider the connection between economic growth and fiscal variables but focus on detrended GDP and public debt. Then, we construct sustainability indicators for a finite time horizon and study whether countries, which seem to have less sustainable policies experience different effects of public debt and deficits compared to countries with sustainable policies. Finally, we test whether the effect of public deficit on GDP depends on whether the debt ratio is high or low.

## 11.2. GRANGER-CAUSALITY TESTS

First, we consider the impact of debt and deficits on real GDP. To do so we have to detrend real GDP. We do this by following the standard macroeconometric approach as suggested, e.g. in King et al. (1988) or Campbell (1994). That is we assume that the log of real GDP follows a linear time trend, i.e. $\ln(\text{GDP}) = a + bt$, with $t$ the time, and estimate that equation with OLS. The detrended variable then is given by

$$\tilde{y}_t \equiv \frac{\ln(\text{GDP}) - (\hat{a} + \hat{b}t)}{\hat{a} + \hat{b}t}, \qquad (11.1)$$

with $\hat{a}$ and $\hat{b}$ the OLS estimates for $a$ and $b$.

To perform this test the following equation is estimated

$$y_t = c + \alpha_1 y_{t-1} + \cdots + \alpha_p y_{t-p} + \beta_1 x_{t-1} + \cdots + \beta_p x_{t-p} + u_t,$$

with $c$ a constant and $u_t$ a stochastic error term. If the hypothesis

$$H_0 : \beta_1 = \cdots = \beta_p = 0$$

can be rejected the variable $x$ has a statistically significant effect on $y$. We tested whether public debt and public deficits have a negative impact on detrended real GDP($\tilde{y}_t$). In all tests we have set $p = 3$ and $p = 5$. We have set $p = 3$ and $p = 5$ because we think that 3 and 5 years are a reasonable and large enough time lag over which public deficit and public debt can help to predict detrended GDP.

Table 11.1 gives the results for $p = 3$ and $p = 5$ with the results for $p = 5$ in parenthesis if they differ from the ones obtained for $p = 3$. We consider the following core countries of the EU: Belgium, France,

Table 11.1:    Granger causality test of $b$ and $d$ on GDP.

|        | $\tilde{y}_t$ caused by $b$ | $\tilde{y}_t$ caused by $d$ |
|--------|-----------------------------|-----------------------------|
| B      | insig.                      | insig.                      |
| F      | insig.                      | insig.                      |
| G      | insig.                      | insig.                      |
| I      | $-$* (insig.)               | insig. $(+$**$)$            |
| Nl     | $-$** $(-$*$)$              | $-$* (insig.)               |
| Sp     | $+$**                       | insig. $(+$**$)$            |
| Swe    | insig.                      | insig.                      |
| All    | $-$**                       | $-$**                       |

*, significant at the 5% significance level;
**, significant at the 1% significance level;
insig, not significant at the 1 and 5% level.

Germany, Italy, Netherlands, Spain and Sweden.[1] "All" in the table means that the countries in the sample have been pooled, i.e. put together in one sample. In order to get an idea of whether the effect of public debt and deficit is positive or negative we ran correlations between detrended GDP and current and lagged debt and deficit, respectively which, however, we do not report here. The data we use are annual and from OECD (1999a,b) and from European Commission (1998) and cover the time period from 1970 to 2000.[2]

Table 11.1 shows that the debt–GDP ratio has a negative impact on detrended real GDP in Italy (for $p = 3$) and the Netherlands, while this effect is significantly positive in Spain. In all other countries no significant effect of the debt–GDP ratio on detrended GDP could be found. For Spain there is a positive effect of the debt–GDP ratio on detrended GDP. This could be due to cumulated past government expenditure exerting a positive effect on GDP. However, since this only holds for Spain this conclusion must be considered with care. As concerns the deficit–GDP ratio, a significant negative effect on detrended GDP could be detected

---

[1] In all tables we use the following abbreviations: B, Belgium; F, France; G, Germany; I, Italy; Nl, Netherlands; Sp, Spain; Swe, Sweden.
[2] The data for 1998–2000 are projections.

only for the Netherlands and this also becomes insignificant setting $p = 5$. In all other countries, this effect is not significant except Italy and Spain (for $p = 5$), where this effect is positive. So our conjecture that public deficits may have a stimulating effect on GDP must be considered with care since only for Italy and Spain and only with $p = 5$ a significantly positive result could be found.

Pooling all countries one gets an unambiguous result. In this case, Table 11.1 shows that there is a statistically significant negative effect of both the debt–GDP ratio and the deficit–GDP ratio on detrended GDP. In our view this result is the most reliable due to the large data basis. Further, we think that the countries under consideration are relatively homogeneous so that pooling these countries does not pose too great a problem.

Other implications of our theoretical model were that private investment is crowded out by public debt and public deficits. Further, our model also implies a crowding-out effect of public investment by public debt. The results of the empirical studies analyzing these questions are shown in Table 11.2. There, we test whether the public debt–GDP ratio, $b$, and the public deficit–GDP ratio, $d$, have a statistically significant effect on detrended private investment, $i$, where private investment was detrended by applying

Table 11.2: Granger causality test of $b$ and $d$ on $i$ and of $b$ on $i_p$.

| | $i_t$ **caused by** $b$ | $i_t$ **caused by** $d$ | $i_{pt}$ **caused by** $b$ |
|---|---|---|---|
| B | $-$ ** | $-$ ** | insig. $(-\ast)$ |
| F | insig. | $-\ast$ | insig. |
| G | insig. | insig. | $-\ast$ |
| I | insig. | insig. | insig. |
| Nl | $+$ ** $(+\ast)$ | $-\ast$ (insig.) | $-\ast$ $(-\ast\ast)$ |
| Sp | insig. $(+\ast\ast)$ | insig. | insig. |
| Swe | insig. $(-\ast)$ | insig. | insig. |
| All | $-$ ** | $-$ ** | insig. |

$\ast$, significant at the 5% significance level;
$\ast\ast$, significant at the 1% significance level;
insig, not significant at the 1 and 5% level.

Equation 11.1. Further, we also tested whether detrended public investment, $i_\mathrm{p}$, is significantly affected by $b$. Again, Table 11.2 gives the results for $p = 3$ and $p = 5$ with the results for $p = 5$ in parenthesis if they differ from the ones obtained for $p = 3$.[3]

This table shows that only in Belgium and in Sweden (with $p = 5$) there is a significantly negative effect of public debt on detrended private investment. In all other countries this relation is insignificant, in the Netherlands, and in Spain for $p = 5$, it is even positive. As to the effect of public deficit on private investment, this effect is statistically significant and negative for Belgium, France and the Netherlands (for $p = 3$), while in all other countries it is not statistically significant. If we pool all data in one sample we again get a clear result. In this case, both the debt–GDP and the deficit–GDP ratio have a negative effect on private investment.

Further, from Table 11.2 it can be seen that the hypothesis of a high public debt–GDP ratio crowding out public investment must be rejected for almost all countries. Only for Germany, for the Netherlands and for Belgium (with $p = 5$) we found a statistically significant negative effect of the public debt–GDP ratio on public investment. In all other countries this effect is not statistically significant. This also holds if we pool the data. In this case, public debt does not have a significant effect on public investment either.

A similar outcome is obtained when testing whether the ratio of public debt to GDP and the ratio of public deficit to GDP affect detrended real private consumption. As concerns the public debt–GDP ratio we could find a significant effect of that ratio on consumption in Belgium (significantly negative) for $p = 3$ and $p = 5$, in France (significantly negative for $p = 5$) and in Spain (significantly positive) for $p = 3$ and $p = 5$. In all other countries as well as in our pooled data set this effect was not significant at the 5 or 1% level. The deficit–GDP ratio has a significantly negative effect on

---

[3] Again, we ran correlations between the variables and current and lagged public debt and deficit to get an idea about the sign.

private consumption only in Spain (for $p = 3$ and $p = 5$) and in France (for $p = 5$). In all other countries as well as in the pooled data set there was no significant effect at the 5 or 1% significance level.

An interesting question is whether countries with unsustainable policies experience different effects of public debt and deficits compared to sustainable countries. To answer this question we next look at the sustainability of fiscal policy in EU countries.

## 11.3. SUSTAINABILITY INDICATORS OF FISCAL POLICY IN FINITE TIME

For studying the sustainability of fiscal policy of EU countries from a practical perspective we can use the budget constraint of the government and employ the following differential equation

$$\dot{B}(t) = G(t) - T(t) + r(t)B(t), \qquad B(0) = B_0, \qquad (11.2)$$

with $B(t)$ government debt at time $t$, $G(t)$ total public spending and $r(t)$ the interest rate, all in real terms. For a constant real interest rate a given fiscal policy is sustainable if Equation 11.3 holds.

$$\lim_{t \to \infty} B(t) \exp[-rt] = 0 \qquad (11.3)$$

This condition is equivalent to requiring that the discounted sum of future primary surpluses equals initial debt, i.e.

$$B_0 = -\int_0^t D(s) \exp[-rt] \mathrm{d}s \qquad (11.4)$$

must hold, with $D$ the primary deficit.

Equations 11.3 and 11.4 have often been used in practice to test whether a given fiscal policy is sustainable.[4] Another and slightly different approach to measure whether fiscal policies are sustainable is proposed by Blanchard et al. (1990), which can gives some information in the medium run. An advantage of the Blanchard

---

[4] See also Chapter 11 for more theoretical foundations of sustainability tests.

approach is that it gives a quantitative measure indicating the gap between the actual fiscal policy and a sustainable fiscal policy. Therefore, we adopt in this chapter the approach worked out by Blanchard et al. (1990). In that contribution it is argued that it is more useful to rewrite the budget constraint in terms of ratios to GDP, since economies grow over time. This gives[5]

$$\dot{b} = g - \tau + (r - w)b, \qquad b(0) = b_0, \qquad (11.5)$$

with $w$ the growth rate of real GDP and $b = B/\text{GDP}$, $g = G/\text{GDP}$, $\tau = T/\text{GDP}$. A given fiscal policy is sustainable if

$$b_0 = -\int_0^t (g(s) - \tau(s))\exp[-(r - w)s]ds \qquad (11.6)$$

holds for $t \to \infty$. Solving for $\tau$ gives the (constant) sustainable tax ratio $\tau_s$. The deviation of the actual tax ratio $\tau$ from the sustainable tax ratio $\tau_s$ then is an indicator for sustainability. If $\tau_s - \tau$ is positive the sustainable tax ratio is larger than the actual, and the government has to raise taxes or reduce spending to achieve sustainability. If the reverse holds, i.e. if $\tau_s - \tau$ is negative the actual tax ratio is larger than the one which guarantees sustainability and the fiscal policy is sustainable.

To get implementable indicators within finite time Blanchard et al. (1990) impose the requirement that the debt–GDP ratio returns to its initial value. This yields the sustainable tax rate in finite time, $\tau_{sf}$, as (for details as to the derivation see Blanchard et al., 1990, p.15–17)

$$\tau_{sf} = (r - w)\left(b_0 + (1 - \exp[-(r - w)t])^{-1}\right.$$
$$\left. \times \int_0^t (g + h)\exp[(r - w)s]ds\right). \qquad (11.7)$$

---

[5] In the following we again omit the time argument $t$.

Since we are interested in the question of whether the effects of fiscal policy on the private economy depend on the fiscal discipline in a country we are interested in a medium term indicator of sustainability. We believe that the decisions of private individuals are affected by the fiscal position of a country in the medium term, rather than by its fiscal position in the short term or long term. An approximation to (Equation 11.7 $- \tau$) in the medium term is

$$((5 \text{ years average of } g) + (r - w)b_0) - \tau. \qquad (11.8)$$

Next we compute Equation 11.8 for the countries we also considered in the last section. Figures 11.1 and 11.2 show the results for the time period from 1982 to 2000.

With the exception of Spain and Sweden none of the countries under consideration have sustainable fiscal policies in the mid-nineties. This outcome is similar to the result obtained by Grilli (1988).

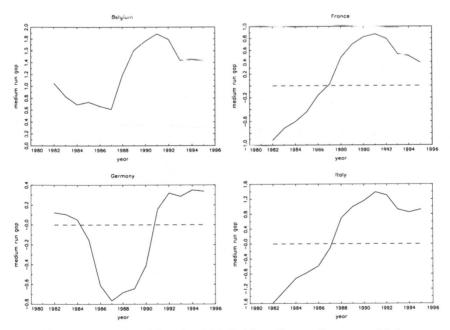

Fig. 11.1:  Results of Equation 11.8, Belgium, France, Germany and Italy.

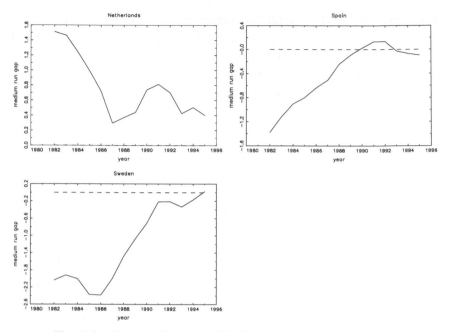

Fig. 11.2:    Results of Equation 11.8, Netherlands, Spain and Sweden.

He conducts unit root tests for 10 EU countries and concludes that up to 1987 all EU countries with the exception of Germany and Denmark have unsustainable policies.[6]

However, it can also be realized that in the 1990s the fiscal positions have become better, i.e. convergence towards sustainable policies can be observed in all countries. This holds especially for France and the Netherlands. The reason for that outcome are the Maastricht criteria which required the deficit–GDP and the debt–GDP ratio not to exceed 3 and 60%, respectively. Nevertheless, Belgium and Italy are characterized by highly unsustainable fiscal policies with a medium run gap of about 1.4 and 0.9, respectively. It should also be mentioned that the Netherlands were also characterized by highly unsustainable

---

[6] Other studies which address the question of sustainability of public debt in EU countries are, e.g. Wickens (1993) and Feve and Henin (1996).

fiscal policies at the beginning of the eighties with a medium run gap which is almost as high as for Belgium and Italy. However, in the beginning of the nineties the Netherlands drastically changed their fiscal policy and succeeded to get an almost sustainable fiscal policy until the mid of the nineties. For Germany one realizes a sharp increase in the medium term gap at the beginning of the nineties due to the large increase in public deficits and public debt caused by German unification.[7] There is again an increase in the medium term gap in 1993 which is due to the recession in this year.

We should also like to point out that all of those countries had a negative medium term gap until the end of the seventies. This means that fiscal policies had been sustainable in the medium run in the countries we consider up to the seventies.

Next we try to clarify whether countries which differ with respect to the sustainability of their fiscal policies also experience different effects of fiscal policies.

Looking at Tables 11.1 and 11.2 we can try to establish a relation between the results of the Granger causality tests of the last section and the sustainability tests of this section. However, it is difficult to come to a clear answer. On the one hand, in Table 11.1 we found a statistically significant Granger causality of public debt in Italy (with $p = 3$) and in the Netherlands, two countries which are or were unsustainable in the 1980s and 1990s, respectively. But, on the other hand, there is an insignificant effect of public debt in Belgium, which is also to be considered as unsustainable. A similar observation holds as concerns the effects of public deficits.

The same holds when one looks at the effects of public debt and deficit on private and public investment. As one can see from Table 11.2 there is no unambiguous relationship between these effects and the sustainability of countries. For example, on the one hand, public deficits exert a negative effect on private investment in Belgium and the Netherlands (for $p = 3$), which can be considered

---

[7] For a more detailed test, see Greiner and Semmler (1999a).

as unsustainable. However, on the other hand, there is also a negative relation in France which must be considered as sustainable while in all other countries this effect is not significant including Italy which is likely to have had an unsustainable policy. Similar conclusions hold when one looks at the other results of the Granger causality tests in this table.

So, the overall conclusion is that there is no clear relation between the effects of public debt and of public deficits and the sustainability of fiscal policies. There are some hints that countries which appear to have unsustainable policies for some time period are more likely to have negative effects of public debt and deficits. However, there are also counter-examples so that this cannot be accepted as a fact.

## 11.4. TESTING A NON-LINEAR RELATIONSHIP

In section 11.2 we have seen that public deficit has a negative impact on detrended GDP when the countries are pooled. In this section we want to study whether this relationship depends on the debt–GDP ratio or whether it is independent of this variable. That is we want to test whether the effects of public deficit on detrended real GDP differ according to whether the debt ratio in an economy is low or high.

To get insight into the relation between public debt, public deficit and GDP we estimate a non-linear equation which assumes that the effect of public deficit on detrended GDP depends on the debt–GDP ratio. This is done by assuming that the coefficient giving the impact of public deficit on detrended GDP is a function of the debt–GDP ratio. As to the latter function we assume a polynomial of degree 3. More concretely, we estimate the following equation,

$$\tilde{y}_t = \alpha + \beta \tilde{y}_{t-1} + \theta(b_t)d_t, \tag{11.9}$$

with

$$\theta(b_t) = \theta_0 + \theta_1 b_t + \theta_2 b_t^2 + \theta_3 b_t^3. \tag{11.10}$$

Equations 11.9 and 11.10 state that detrended GDP depends on its own lagged value and on the deficit ratio $d_t$, where the effect of the deficit ratio is assumed to be affected by the debt ratio $b_t$. If $\theta(b_t)$ is positive the deficit ratio has a positive impact on detrended GDP if it is negative the reverse holds. Further, since $\theta(\cdot)$ depends on the debt ratio the effect of the deficit ratio on detrended GDP also depends on the debt ratio.

Estimating Equation (11.9) for the pooled data set with non-linear least squares gives the following result:

| Estimated parameter | Value | Standard deviation |
|---|---|---|
| $\alpha$ | 0.00012 | 0.00012 |
| $\beta$ | 0.775 | 0.044 |
| $\theta_0$ | 0.015 | 0.026 |
| $\theta_1$ | $-0.112$ | 0.129 |
| $\theta_2$ | 0.169 | 0.189 |
| $\theta_3$ | $-0.075$ | 0.084 |

Figure 11.3 gives the curve of $\theta_t$ and of $b_t$, showing a negative relation for a wide range of $b_t$ after $b_t$ passes a threshold. This implies that the public deficit–GDP ratio has a negative impact on the detrended GDP if the ratio of the debt to GDP passes a certain threshold. In fact, in our estimation, if the debt–GDP ratio is smaller than roughly 15% a marginal increase in the public deficit–GDP

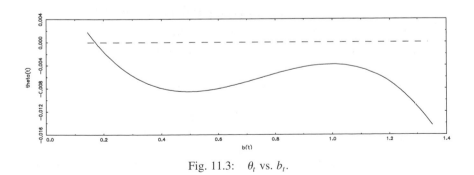

Fig. 11.3:   $\theta_t$ vs. $b_t$.

ratio has a positive impact on detrended GDP. We also estimated an equation assuming a linear relationship between the public deficit–GDP ratio and detrended output, i.e. we assumed $\theta$ to be a constant parameter to be determined by OLS. We have obtained a statistically significant estimated value for $\theta$ of $\theta = -0.008$. This shows that a linear regression might overlook the region where deficit spending has a positive macroeconomic effect.

## 11.5. CONCLUSION

In this chapter we have studied the effects of public deficit and debt on the macroeconomic performance of some EU countries. We could obtain the following main results.

The Granger causality tests showed no unambiguous results concerning the effects of public deficit and public debt on detrended GDP when studying single countries. Further, there are some hints that countries which seem to have large deficits and debt are more likely to experience negative effects of an increase of public debt on GDP. However, this result is too vague to be accepted as a fact. Looking at the crowding-out effect of public debt and public deficit, again no unambiguous result could be obtained. The same holds if one looks at the effect of public debt on public investment.

When pooling the data in one sample we get mostly unambiguous results. In this case public debt and public deficit both exert a negative influence on detrended GDP. The same holds as concerns the crowding-out effect. When all countries are pooled there is a statistically significant negative effect of public debt and deficit on detrended private investment.

Estimating a non-linear equation for the pooled data set with detrended GDP as the dependent variable which is explained by its own lagged values and by the public deficit–GDP ratio multiplied by the public debt–GDP ratio showed that for smaller values of the debt–GDP ratio public deficits have a stimulating effect on detrended GDP. For higher debt–GDP levels an increase in public deficits goes along with a decrease in detrended GDP as predicted by our model.

Evaluating our estimations we think that the results obtained for the pooled data are the most reliable ones because the data basis is the largest in this case. Therefore, we might conclude that public debt and deficits have negative effects as to GDP and lead to crowding out only once a certain threshold of debt is reached.

We also want to note that levels for which public deficits may have stimulating effects on GDP appear to be small in our non-linear regression. But this may be due to the quality of data and time period we considered. Since our data started in the seventies where public policies have been characterized by chronic deficits, it is probably that the positive effects of public deficits on macroeconomic performance are not very distinct. Yet, we have also found evidence that a linear regression may be quite misleading.

PART III

# Monetary and Fiscal Policy Interactions

As mentioned in Chapter 1, fiscal policy is not to be seen independent of monetary policy. The interaction of monetary and fiscal policies is a recurring theme in macroeconomics and has also been a crucial issue in a highly integrated economic area as the European Union. Monetary policy can be accommodative to fiscal policy or counteractive. On the basis of the previous two parts, this part is devoted to the analysis of monetary and fiscal policy interactions of the Euro-area. In Chapter 12 we will explore fiscal regimes for several Euro-area countries and, taking Italy as an example, study interactions between the common monetary policy and fiscal policy of member states. In Chapter 13, however, we will explore time-varying monetary and fiscal policy interactions as well as the role of expectation in interactions between the two policies.

CHAPTER 12

# Monetary and Fiscal Policy Interactions in the Euro-Area

## 12.1. INTRODUCTION

Recently, the monetary and fiscal policy interaction has been an important topic in macroeconomics and a crucial issue in the highly integrated economic area such as the European Union (EU). Economists have stated that the efficiency of monetary policy might be affected by fiscal policy through its impact on demand and by modifying the long-term conditions for economic growth. On the other hand, the monetary policy may be accommodative to the fiscal policy or counteractive. The monetary and fiscal policy interaction seems to be more important for the Euro-area than for other economies, since the member states of the EMU have individual fiscal authorities, but the monetary policy is pursued by a single monetary authority, the ECB. Therefore, this chapter is devoted to the analysis of monetary and fiscal policy interactions in the Euro-area. Although there are some papers on monetary and fiscal policy interactions at the theoretical level, not much empirical evidence has been presented so far. We will, therefore, focus on the empirical evidence of monetary and fiscal policy interactions in the Euro-area, exploring not only monetary and fiscal policy interactions inside the core countries of the Euro-area, namely in Germany, France and Italy, but also study the interactions between the fiscal policy of an individual country and the common monetary policy.

The remainder of this chapter is organized as follows. In section 12.2 we present briefly the recent literature of monetary and fiscal policy interactions. In section 12.3 we undertake some VAR estimations of the fiscal regime and Granger-Causality tests on monetary and fiscal policy instruments. In this section we also undertake a VAR estimation of the Italian fiscal policy and the common monetary policy. Section 12.4 concludes this chapter.

## 12.2. RECENT LITERATURE ON MONETARY AND FISCAL POLICY INTERACTIONS

Although there are numerous studies on the interactions of monetary and fiscal policies, we may divide up the literature into four main trends.

### 12.2.1. The fiscal theory of the price level determination

The "fiscal theory of the price level" (FTPL) was mainly developed by Leeper (1991), Sims (1994, 1997, 2001a) and Woodford (1994, 1995, 2001a) and has recently attracted much attention. This kind of research studies the impact of the so-called "non-Ricardian" fiscal policy. The non-Ricardian fiscal policy, disregarding the inter-temporal solvency constraint of the government, explores the paths of the government taxes, debt and expenditure. In this version the price level in equilibrium has to adjust in order to ensure government solvency. It has been shown that the non-Ricardian fiscal policy may change the stability conditions of the monetary policy. Benhabib et al. (2001), for example, explore conditions under which monetary policy rules that set the interest rate as an increasing function of the inflation rate, incur aggregate instability and claim that these conditions may be affected by the monetary-fiscal regime. We will present the FTPL briefly below.

Woodford (1995, p. 3) describes how the fiscal policy may affect the equilibrium price level as follows: the real value of the net assets of the private sector (the net government liabilities) can be reduced by an increase in the price level. The reduction of private-sector wealth may reduce the demand for goods and services because of the wealth effect. Since there is only one price level that results in equilibrium with aggregate demand being equal to aggregate supply, the price level may be changed because of the changes in expectations regarding future government budgets that may have similar wealth effects such that the equilibrium can be maintained. Therefore, according to the FTPL, the fiscal policy may play an important role in the price level determination for two reasons: the size of the outstanding nominal government debt may influence the effects of price-level changes on aggregate demand, and moreover, the expected future government debt may have some wealth effects.

Let $p_t$ denote the price level at date $t$, $W_t$ the nominal value of beginning-of-period wealth, $g_t$ government purchases in period $t$, $T_t$ the nominal value of net taxes paid in period $t$, $R_t^b$ the gross nominal return on bonds held from period $t$ to $t + 1$ and $R_t^m$ the gross nominal return on the monetary base and define further the following variables:

$$\tau_t = T_t/p_t, \qquad \text{(real tax)},$$

$$\Delta_t = (R_t^b - R_t^m)/R_t^b \qquad \text{("price" of holding money)},$$

$$r_t^b = R_t^b(p_t/p_{t+1}) - 1, \qquad \text{(real rate of return on bonds)},$$

$$m_t = M_t/p_t \qquad \text{(real balances)}.$$

Given the predetermined nominal value of net government liabilities $W_t$ and the expectations at date $t$ regarding the current and future values of the real quantities and relative prices, the equilibrium condition in Woodford (1995) that determines the price level $p_t$ at date $t$ can be expressed as

$$\frac{W_t}{p_t} = \sum_{s=t}^{\infty} \frac{(\tau_s - g_s) + \Delta_s m_s}{\prod_{j=t}^{s-1}(1 + r_j^b)}. \tag{12.1}$$

Assuming long-run price flexibility, although prices may be sticky in the short run, Woodford (1995) gives a simple interpretation to the mechanism by which the price level adjusts to satisfy Equation 12.1. In short, changes in the nominal value of outstanding government liabilities or the size of the real government budget deficits expected at some future dates may be inconsistent with an equilibrium at the existing price level. These changes may make households believe that their budget set has been expanded and, as a result, increase their demand. Woodford (1995) further points out that an excess demand will appear and that the price level will be raised so that the households will adjust their estimates of wealth to the quantity that allows them to buy the quantity of goods supplied by the economy. Woodford (1995, p. 15) further explores this problem with a specific example. Assume that $T_t$ can be set as

$$T_t = p_t x_t - \Delta_t M_t,$$

with $x_t$ being an exogenous sequence, then it can be shown that Equation 12.1 becomes

$$\frac{W_t}{p_t} = \sum_{s=t}^{\infty} \rho^{s-t} \frac{u'(y_s - g_s)}{u'(y_t - g_t)} [x_s - g_s]$$

with $u(\cdot)$ being the household's utility function and $y_t$ the income. $\rho$ is a discount factor between 0 and 1. The equation above shows that $p_t$ can be determined without being affected by money and interest rate.

Woodford (1995) emphasizes that in one special case, the so-called "Ricardian" policy regime, fiscal policy fails to play any role in price-level determination. The FTPL has attracted much attention and extensive research has been undertaken to discuss monetary and fiscal policy interactions in this framework. Woodford's work has been very important for the Euro-area in particular, where the Masstricht criteria have restricted the member states' deficit by 3% and the debt by 60% of the GDP. These criteria would make sense if one expects, as the FTLP suggests, that fiscal policy has price effects. Further elaborations on the FTLP can be found, for example, in Ljungvist and Sargent (2000, Chapter 17) and Linnemann and Schabert (2002).

Although the FTPL has attracted much attention, it has been criticized for empirical as well as logical reasons. Buiter (2002), for example, claims that the FTPL "confuses budget constraints and equilibrium conditions", two crucial factors in a market-economy model. Canzonerie et al. (2000) undertake some empirical research to test whether the "Ricardian" or "non-Ricardian" regime could be obtained in time series data for a particular country. With US data from 1951 to 1995, they conclude that the US fiscal regime seemed to have been "Ricardian" rather than "non-Ricardian" and find that the conclusion is robust to different subperiods of data.

### 12.2.2. Strategic interactions between monetary and fiscal policies

Some researchers have tried to explore monetary and fiscal policy interactions from a strategic perspective. Examples include Catenaro (2000), van Aarle et al. (1995), Buti et al. (2001), Wyplosz (1999), and van Aarle et al. (2002). van Aarle et al. (1995), for example, extend the analysis of Tabellini (1986) and reconsider the interaction between fiscal and monetary authorities in a differential game framework. They derive explicit solutions of the dynamics of the fiscal deficit, inflation and government debt in the cooperative and Nash open-loop equilibria. van Aarle et al. (2002) discuss three alternative policy regimes in a stylized dynamic model of the EMU in both symmetric and asymmetric settings: non-cooperative monetary and fiscal policies, partial cooperation and full cooperation.

### 12.2.3. Empirical research on monetary and fiscal policy interactions

Though most researchers explore monetary and fiscal policy interactions at a theoretical level, there is some empirical work although admittedly not much. Besides the empirical research by Canzonerie et al. (2001) studying the fiscal regime of the US with VAR models, some other researchers have also explored how monetary and fiscal policies may have interacted in some countries. Examples include Mélitz (1997, 2000), van Aarle and Gobbin (2003), Muscatelli et al. (2002) and Smaghi and Casini (2000). Mélitz (1997), for example, uses pooled data for all 15 member states of the EU except Luxembourg, and five other OECD countries to undertake some estimation and finds that coordinated macroeconomic policy existed, claiming that an easy fiscal policy leads to a tight monetary policy and vice versa. Muscatelli et al. (2002) estimate VAR models with both constant and time-varying parameters for the G7 countries while Smaghi and Casini (2000) undertake an investigation into the cooperation between the monetary and fiscal institutions. They compare the situations prior to EMU and in its first year and argue that something was lost when the Euro-area countries moved into the EMU. In particular, the dialogue and cooperation between budgetary and monetary authorities within the EMU can be improved.

### 12.2.4. Monetary and fiscal policy interactions in open economies

The analysis of monetary and fiscal policy interactions has also been extended to open economies and examples include Leith and Wren-Lewis (2000), Mélitz (2000), van Aarle et al. (2002), Sims (1997), Chamberlin et al. (2002), Clausen and Wohltmann (2001) and Beetsma and Jensen (2002). The monetary and fiscal policy interactions between two or more countries, especially between member states of the EMU, are usually the focus of such research. This is quite a crucial problem for the Euro-area, since the member states have their own fiscal authorities but monetary policy is pursued by a single monetary authority, the ECB.

## 12.3. MONETARY AND FISCAL POLICY INTERACTIONS IN THE EURO-AREA

In this section we will explore some empirical evidence on monetary and fiscal policy interactions in the Euro-area employing a VAR model. Two problems are to be tackled. First following Canzonerie, Cumby and Diba (hereafter referred to as CCD), we will test whether the fiscal regime of the Euro-area has been "Ricardian" or "non-Ricardian" so that we can infer whether the assumption of the FTPL holds in Euro-area countries. We will use a different method from that of Chapter 10. Second, taking Italy as an example, we will study how the fiscal policy in member states of the EU has interacted with the common monetary policy. Moreover, we will also refer to some empirical evidence of van Aarle and Gobbin (2003) and Muscatelli et al. (2002) to see how monetary and fiscal policies may have interacted in the Euro-area.

### 12.3.1. Tests of the fiscal regime

In Chapter 10 we have already undertaken some tests on the fiscal policy sustainability in the Euro-area and find that most of the countries in the Euro-area seem to have implemented sustainable fiscal policies since the 1970s. In this section we will test fiscal regimes with VAR models following CCD, who test the interactions between two variables, surplus and government liabilities. This is an approach different from that employed in Chapter 10. From the impulse functions of the VAR model we can explore whether the fiscal regimes have been Ricardian or non-Ricardian.

We will undertake similar estimations for France and Germany. Both the primary surplus (total surplus minus net interest payments) and debt are scaled by dividing them by GDP. The surplus $S_t$ and the debt $B_t$ stand for the (primary) surplus/GDP ratio and (government) debt/GDP ratio. A preliminary impression on the surplus and debt of Germany (1967.1–1998.4) and France

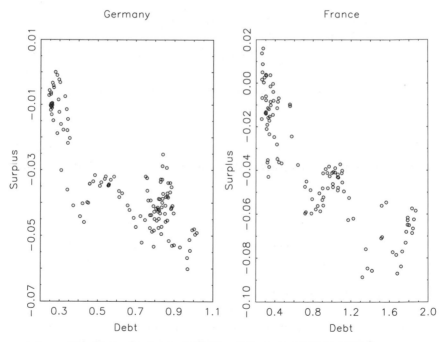

Fig. 12.1:   Surplus and liability of Germany (1967.1–1998.4)
and France (1971.1–1998.4).

(1970.1 – 1998.4) can be obtained from Figure 12.1. We observe a negative relationship between the surplus and debt in both countries. The correlation coefficient of $S_t$ and $B_t$ is as significant as $-0.840$ in Germany and $-0.852$ in France.[1]

In order to explore how the surplus and debt respond to each other dynamically, we follow CCD and undertake a VAR estimation for both. The estimation results for Germany with $T$-statistics in parentheses are shown below:

$$S_t = \underset{(1.007)}{-0.001} + \underset{(10.045)}{1.088\,S_{t-1}} - \underset{(1.061)}{0.162\,S_{t-2}} + \underset{(0.310)}{0.046\,S_{t-3}}$$

$$\underset{(1.027)}{-0.100\,S_{t-4}} - \underset{(2.594)}{0.056\,B_{t-1}} + \underset{(1.594)}{0.044\,B_{t-2}}$$

$$+ \underset{(0.218)}{0.006\,B_{t-3}} + \underset{(0.052)}{0.001\,B_{t-4}}, \quad R^2 = 0.960,$$

$$B_t = \underset{(1.136)}{0.004} - \underset{(2.140)}{1.162\,S_{t-1}} + \underset{(0.425)}{0.326\,S_{t-2}} + \underset{(0.012)}{0.009\,S_{t-3}}$$

$$\underset{(0.267)}{-0.130\,S_{t-4}} + \underset{(8.122)}{0.885\,B_{t-1}} + \underset{(0.565)}{0.078\,B_{t-2}}$$

$$\underset{(0.622)}{-0.087\,B_{t-3}} + \underset{(0.718)}{0.077\,B_{t-4}}, \quad R^2 = 0.996.$$

In order to evaluate the effects of debt on surplus and the reverse, we present the impulse responses of $S_t$ and $B_t$ to one SD innovations

---

[1] Quarterly data are used. The data source of the net interest payments is the OECD Statistical Compendium. The sources of other data are OECD and IMF. For the net interest payments we have only semi-annual data. In order to obtain the missing quarterly data of the net interest payments, we have proceeded as follows: first we compute the average value of the semi-annual interest payments from year to year. Second we compute the average interest rate from year to year with quarterly data. We then compute the missing data of the net interest payments by multiplying the average net interest payments per year with one plus the percent deviation of the interest rate from its average value.

with different ordering in Figures 12.2 and 12.3 (- - - denotes confidence interval, ± 2SE).

Both Figures 12.2 and 12.3 indicate that one SD innovation in $S_t$ induces a negative response of $B_t$ and similarly, one SD innovation of $B_t$ induces a negative response of $S_t$. This is just what the non-Ricardian fiscal regime implies. If we use fewer lags (two lags, for example) of $S_t$ and $B_t$ for the estimation, similar results are obtained. The evidence above seems to confirm a non-Ricardian fiscal regime in Germany in the period covered.

Now we come to the case of France. The quarterly data cover 1970.1 – 1998.4 with the same data source as for Germany. The result

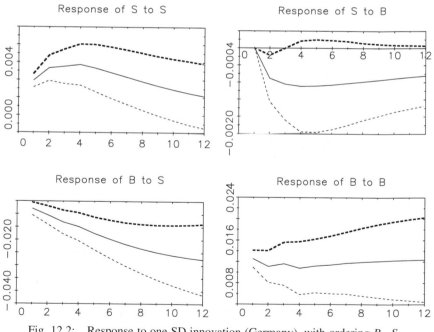

Fig. 12.2:   Response to one SD innovation (Germany), with ordering $B_t$, $S_t$.

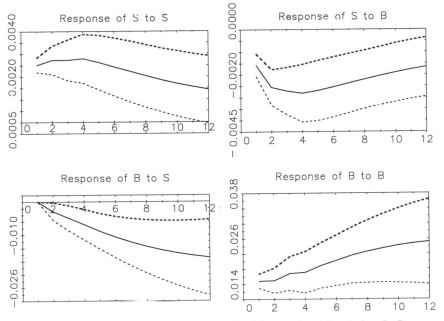

Fig. 12.3:   Response to one SD innovation (Germany), with ordering $S_t$, $B_t$.

of the VAR estimation reads as (*T*-statistics in parentheses)

$$S_t = \underset{(1.097)}{-0.001} + \underset{(10.083)}{0.999\,S_{t-1}} + \underset{(0.819)}{0.114\,S_{t-2}} - \underset{(1.880)}{0.259\,S_{t-3}}$$

$$- \underset{(0.318)}{0.032\,S_{t-4}} - \underset{(0.244)}{0.003\,B_{t-1}} - \underset{(1.720)}{0.021\,B_{t-2}}$$

$$- \underset{(0.527)}{0.006\,B_{t-3}} + \underset{(2.164)}{0.024\,B_{t-4}}, \quad R^2 = 0.945,$$

$$B_t = \underset{(0.082)}{-0.001} - \underset{(3.020)}{2.242\,S_{t-1}} - \underset{(0.135)}{0.141\,S_{t-2}} + \underset{(1.079)}{1.116\,S_{t-3}}$$

$$- \underset{(0.829)}{0.635\,S_{t-4}} + \underset{(4.524)}{0.383\,B_{t-1}} + \underset{(2.105)}{0.194\,B_{t-2}}$$

$$- \underset{(1.704)}{0.157\,B_{t-3}} + \underset{(6.385)}{0.534\,B_{t-4}}, \quad R^2 = 0.992.$$

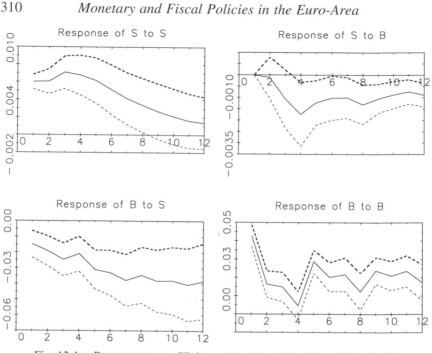

Fig. 12.4:　Response to one SD innovation (France), with ordering $B_t$, $S_t$.

We show the impulse responses of $S_t$ and $B_t$ to one SD innovations with different ordering in Figures 12.4 and 12.5 (- - - denotes confidence interval, $\pm$ 2SE).

From Figures 12.4 and 12.5 we find that one SD innovation of $S_t$ always induces a negative response of $B_t$ and one SD innovation of $B_t$ also induces a negative response of $S_t$. This is similar to the case of Germany. Therefore, the estimation also seems to indicate that the fiscal regime was a non-Ricardian rather than a Ricardian one in France. Similar results are obtained from the estimation of $S_t$ and $B_t$ with two lags.

The VAR estimation following CCD seems to favor the conclusion that, unlike the case of the US tested by CCD, Germany and France appear to have pursued a non-Ricardian rather than Ricardian fiscal policy in the past decades. In the FTPL Woodford (1995) maintains that the non-Ricardian fiscal regime rather than

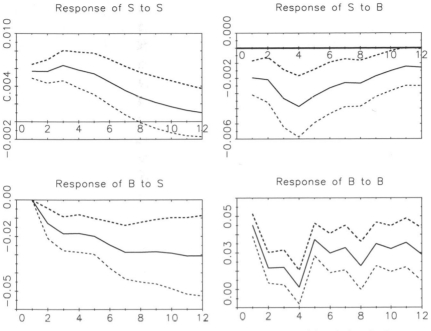

Fig. 12.5:   Response to one SD innovation (France), with ordering $S_t$, $B_t$.

the Ricardian one may be the common case. He considers the Ricardian fiscal regime only as a special case, in which the fiscal policy plays but a small role in the price level determination. The evidence of Germany and France appears to confirm, to some extent, the claim of Woodford (1995).[2]

Above we have explored fiscal regimes in France and Germany by way of VAR estimation. The estimation results seem to favor the conclusion that both countries have implemented unsustainable fiscal policy. This is, however, different from the conclusion in Chapter 10, where we tested fiscal regimes of both countries, following the estimation of Bohn (1995, 1998) and concluded that

---

[2] Of course, given the low inflation rate of France and Germany, in particular in the 1990s, the FTPL seems to miss some other important variables to realistically explain price dynamics.

fiscal policies of the two countries are sustainable. Our conclusion from the current chapter is more in line with those from some earlier studies, see Greiner and Semmler (1999b) for example. This difference results from how sustainability of fiscal policy is defined. As mentioned in Chapter 10, Bohn (1995, 1998) argues that sustainability of fiscal policy is too easily rejected in traditional studies because of problems in the so-called no-Ponzi game condition. The difference of these results indicates that it may be advisable to pursue new tests for sustainability of fiscal policy. Recently, Greiner, Koeller and Semmler (2005), for example, study time-varying reactions to fiscal policy imbalances.

### 12.3.2. Granger-Causality tests of monetary and fiscal policy interactions

Next, we come to another important question: how have monetary and fiscal policies interacted in the Euro-area? Can we obtain some information on fiscal policy from the monetary policy and the other way round? We will first undertake a Granger-Causality test for monetary and fiscal policy instruments. Subsequently, we will discuss some evidence of monetary and fiscal policy interactions in the Euro-area provided by Muscatelli et al. (2002).

In the research below we take the surplus and the short-term interest rate as the instruments of fiscal and monetary policies, respectively. The countries to be studied include France, Germany and Italy. Because the short-term interest rate of Italy is not available, we take the official discount rate instead. The Italian surplus data are not available for 1991.4–1993.4. In order to approximate the surplus of Italy during this period, we assume that the government revenue has the same growth rate of the surplus and then compute the surplus using the growth rate of the government revenue from 1991.4 to 1993.4. The short-term interest rates of France and Germany are measured by the 3-month treasury bill rate and the German call money rate, respectively.

The goal of the Granger-Causality test is to explore whether there is Granger-Causality between the short-term interest rate and the surplus in the three countries. According to the FTPL, the fiscal regime plays a certain role in the price level determination. Therefore, we will also undertake a Granger-Causality test for the surplus and inflation to see whether there exists any Granger-Causality between these two variables. The results of the Granger-Causality tests are presented in Table 12.1, where $S$, $R$ and $\pi$ denote the surplus, interest rate and inflation rate, respectively, and $\rightarrow$ stands for "Granger-causes". "Y" (yes) indicates that one variable Granger-causes the other and "N" (no) indicates that one variable does not Granger-cause the other. The inflation rate is measured by the changes in the consumer price index (CPI).

From Table 12.1 we find that in the cases of Germany and Italy, the surplus does not Granger-cause the short-term interest rate, no matter whether 4 or 8 lags are used in the tests. The case of France is, however, somewhat different: $S$ Granger-causes $R$ with both 4 and 8 lags. $R$ does not Granger-cause $S$ in the case of Germany with either 4 or 8 lags, but it Granger-causes $S$ in France and Italy with 8 lags. The Granger-Causality between $S$ and $\pi$ also differs across countries. $S$ does not Granger-cause $\pi$ in Italy with either 4 or 8 lags. It does not Granger-cause $\pi$ with 8 lags in Germany and France but does Granger-cause $\pi$ with 4 lags in these two countries.

The Granger-Causality tests tell us whether the fiscal and monetary instruments contain some information about each other.

Table 12.1: Granger-Causality tests at 5% significance level of significance (1970.1 – 1998.4).

| Country | $S \rightarrow R$ | $R \rightarrow S$ | $S \rightarrow \pi$ | $\pi \rightarrow S$ |
|---|---|---|---|---|
| Germany | N* N** | N* N** | Y* N** | N* N** |
| France | Y* Y** | N* Y** | Y* N** | Y* N** |
| Italy | N* N** | Y* Y** | N* N** | N* Y** |

* denotes test with 4 lags and ** with 8 lags. *Data sources*: OECD an IMF

The next problem is to explore how these variables may have interacted in the Euro-area. Muscatelli et al. (2002) undertake some structural (time-varying and Bayesian) VAR tests of monetary and fiscal policy interactions for the G7 countries. The endogenous variables used include the output gap, inflation rate, fiscal stance and the call money rate. A similar VAR estimation has been undertaken by van Aarle and Gobbin (2001). The endogenous variables they use include the inflation rate, output growth, change in the short-term interest rate, real government revenue growth and real government spending growth. van Aarle and Gobbin (2003) explore the cases of Japan, the US and the member states of the EU and the aggregate economy of the Euro-area. Muscatelli et al. (2002) find that the monetary and fiscal policy interactions are asymmetric and different for different countries. That is, in the cases of the US and UK, an easy fiscal policy might imply an easy monetary policy, but no changes in the monetary policy are implied by the changes in fiscal policy in the cases of Italy, Germany and France.

Note that the evidence from Muscatelli et al. (2002) and van Aarle and Gobbin (2003) refers to monetary and fiscal policy interactions within the individual countries studied. As mentioned before, the problem of monetary and fiscal policy interactions may be more important for the Euro-area than for other countries because the member states have individual fiscal authorities, but the monetary policy is pursued by a single monetary authority, the ECB. Therefore, it is necessary to explore the interaction between the fiscal policies in the member states and the common monetary policy. Next, we take the German call money rate $R_t$ as the common monetary policy instrument and, taking Italy as an example, explore the interaction between Italian fiscal policy and the common monetary policy. Peersman and Smets (1999) justify taking the German rate as the common monetary policy instrument and use it to explore the monetary policy in the Euro-area.

To be more precise, we undertake a VAR estimation of the Italian $S_t$ and German $R_t$ to explore how the common monetary policy may have affected the Italian fiscal policy from 1979 to 1998. The estimation with data from 1979.1 to 1998.4 gives us the following results (*T*-statistics in parentheses):

$$S_t = \underset{(0.893)}{0.018} + \underset{(1.992)}{0.195\,S_{t-1}} + \underset{(0.944)}{0.094\,S_{t-2}} + \underset{(0.264)}{0.026\,S_{t-3}}$$

$$+ \underset{(5.761)}{0.553\,S_{t-4}} + \underset{(0.026)}{0.016\,R_{t-1}} - \underset{(0.570)}{0.532\,R_{t-2}}$$

$$+ \underset{(0.266)}{0.249\,R_{t-3}} - \underset{(2.164)}{0.392\,R_{t-4}}, \quad R^2 = 0.661,$$

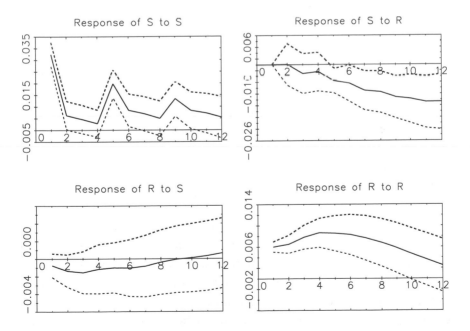

Fig. 12.6:   The response to one SD innovation with ordering Italian $S_t$, German $R_t$.

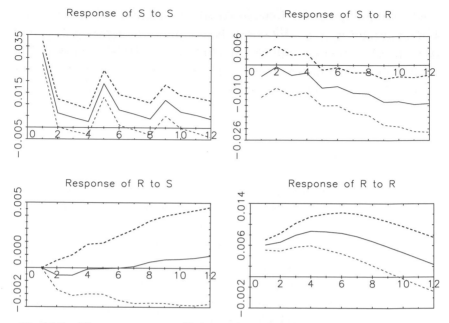

Fig. 12.7:   The response to one SD innovation with ordering German $R_t$, Italian $S_t$.

$$R_t = \underset{(1.893)}{0.007} - \underset{(0.949)}{0.017}\, S_{t-1} + \underset{(0.243)}{0.005}\, S_{t-2} + \underset{(1.098)}{0.020}\, S_{t-3}$$

$$+ \underset{(0.093)}{0.002}\, S_{t-4} + \underset{(9.168)}{1.079}\, R_{t-1} + \underset{(0.793)}{0.138}\, R_{t-2}$$

$$- \underset{(0.722)}{0.126}\, R_{t-3} - \underset{(1.493)}{0.180}\, R_{t-4}, \quad R^2 = 0.938.$$

The result indicates that the common monetary policy does not affect the Italian fiscal policy much since the $T$-statistics of the coefficients of $R_{t-i}$ ($i = 1,...,4$) in the first equation are insignificant. Moreover, the coefficients of $S_{t-i}$ ($i = 1,...,4$) in the second equation also have insignificant $T$-statistics. Similar results are obtained from the estimation with two lags. The impulse responses of the Italian $S_t$ and German $R_t$ with different ordering are shown in Figures 12.6 and 12.7. Although the estimation above shows that $R_t$ does not affect $S_t$ much, both Figures 12.6 and 12.7 indicate that the one SD innovation of $R_t$ induces a negative response of $S_t$. This implies that the Italian fiscal policy might have been weakly counteractive to the common monetary policy before 1998. The one SD innovation of $S_t$, however, induces only a weak response of $R_t$ around zero.

## 12.4. CONCLUSION

This chapter has, in a preliminary way, explored the monetary and fiscal policy interactions in the Euro-area. We first have presented the recent literature on this problem. We have then undertaken some estimation with VAR models for France and Germany to test the fiscal regimes and find that the two countries were endangered to have implemented a non-Ricardian fiscal policy in some time periods. This has implications for the so-called fiscal theory of price level, which proposes that the price level has to adjust to ensure the government solvency under a non-Ricardian fiscal regime and that the Ricardian fiscal regime is only a special case. We have also undertaken some Granger-Causality tests for the fiscal policy and find the results differ across countries. Yet, overall one needs to remark that the fiscal policy may only be one of numerous factors, as discussed in part I of this book, impacting the price level. Fiscal policy, if associated with productive government spending, as studied in Part II of the book, can also counteract inflation pressures.

# CHAPTER 13

# Time-Varying Monetary and Fiscal Policy Interactions

### Abstract

In the previous chapter we have undertaken some preliminary study on the monetary and fiscal policy interactions in the Euro-area. This chapter is to explore time-varying interactions between monetary and fiscal policies with a State-Space model. Note that in the previous chapter only backward-looking behavior is considered. A question is whether the forward-looking behavior should also be taken into account. Therefore, in this chapter we will also undertake some estimation to explore the role of expectations in the interdependence of the two policies.

## 13.1. MONETARY AND FISCAL POLICY INTERACTIONS IN A STATE-SPACE MODEL WITH MARKOV-SWITCHING

Muscatelli et al. (2002) employ a VAR model to explore the monetary and fiscal policy interactions in the Euro-area. Another interesting study is undertaken by von Hagen et al. (2001). They set up a macroeconomic model and estimate it with the three-stage least squares. The goal of that model is to explore the interactions between the fiscal policy and real output, and between the fiscal policy and monetary conditions. The three endogenous variables used are the fiscal policy, monetary policy and real GDP growth. Because there might be regime changes in economies, in this section we will undertake some estimation of time-varying monetary and fiscal policy interactions.

In order to explore whether there are regime changes in monetary and fiscal policy interactions (and if so, how they have changed), we employ a State-Space model with Markov-switching. To some extent this is similar to Muscatelli et al. (2002), who apply a State-Space VAR model to explore the regimes of monetary and fiscal policy interactions. Our method differs from theirs in that we assume Markov-switching in the variance of the shocks and the drifts of time-varying parameters in the State-Space model. The problem of a traditional State-Space model without Markov-switching is that the changes of the time-varying parameters may be exaggerated. This problem was recognized by Sims (2001b) in a comment on Cogley and Sargent (2001). A reasonable choice seems to be setting up a VAR model with the fiscal policy, monetary policy, output gap and inflation rate as endogenous variables and then estimating time-varying parameters in a State-Space model with Markov-switching. In so doing we have to estimate a large number of parameters and the efficiency of the results will be reduced. Therefore, we will only estimate a single equation below. This should not affect the conclusion significantly since we are mainly interested in the interactions between monetary and fiscal policy variables.

As in the previous chapter we measure the monetary policy with the short-term interest $R$ and the fiscal policy with the primary surplus $S$. Since we have found some Granger-Causality of the short-term interest rate affecting the surplus, we will just estimate the following equation:

$$S_t = \alpha_{1t} + \alpha_{2t}S_{t-1} + \alpha_{3t}R_{t-1} + \varepsilon_t, \qquad (13.1)$$

where $\varepsilon_t$ is a shock with normal distribution and zero mean. In fact, the surplus may also be affected by the inflation rate and output gap, but as mentioned above, we ignore these effects just to reduce the number of parameters to be estimated. Note that we assume $\alpha_i$ $(i = 1...3)$ are time-varying and moreover, we assume the variance of the shock $\varepsilon_t$ is not constant but has Markov-switching property. Defining $X_t$ and $\phi_t$ as

$$X_t = (1 \ S_{t-1} \ R_{t-1}),$$

$$\phi_t = (\alpha_{1t} \ \alpha_{2t} \ \alpha_{3t})',$$

Equation (13.1) can be rearranged as

$$S_t = X_t \phi_t + \varepsilon_t.$$

Recall that we assume that the shock $\varepsilon_t$ has a Markov-switching variance. Following Kim and Nelson (1999), we simply assume that $\varepsilon_t$ has two states of variance with Markov property, namely

$$\varepsilon_t \sim N(0, \sigma^2_{\varepsilon,SS_t}),$$

with

$$\sigma^2_{\varepsilon,SS_t} = \sigma^2_{\varepsilon,0} + (\sigma^2_{\varepsilon,1} - \sigma^2_{\varepsilon,0})SS_t, \qquad \sigma^2_{\varepsilon,1} > \sigma^2_{\varepsilon,0},$$

and

$$\Pr[SS_t = 1 | SS_{t-1} = 1] = p,$$

$$\Pr[SS_t = 0 | SS_{t-1} = 0] = q,$$

where $SS_t = 0$ or $1$ indicates the states of the variance of $\varepsilon_t$ and Pr stands for probability. The time-varying vector $\phi_t$ is assumed to follow the following path

$$\phi_t = \bar{\Phi}_{SS_t} + F\phi_{t-1} + \eta_t, \qquad \eta_t \sim N(0, \sigma^2_\eta), \qquad (13.2)$$

where $\bar{\Phi}_{SS_t}(SS_t = 0 \text{ or } 1)$ denotes the drift of $\phi_t$ under different states, and $\bar{\Phi} = (\bar{\alpha}_1 \bar{\alpha}_2 \bar{\alpha}_3)$. $F$ is a diagonal matrix with constant elements, $\eta_t$ is a vector of shocks of normal distribution with zero mean and constant variance. $\sigma_\eta^2$ is assumed to be a diagonal matrix.[1] Moreover, we assume $E(\varepsilon_t \eta_t) = 0$. The State-Space model of Markov-switching can now be presented as

$$S_t = X_t \phi_t + \varepsilon_t, \qquad \varepsilon_t \sim N(0, \sigma_{\varepsilon,SS_t}^2), \qquad (13.3)$$

$$\phi_t = \bar{\Phi}_{SS_t} + F\phi_{t-1} + \eta_t, \qquad \eta_t \sim N(0, \sigma_\eta^2). \qquad (13.4)$$

Let $Y_{t-1}$ denote the vector of observations available as of time $t-1$. In the usual derivation of the Kalman filter in a State-Space model without Markov-Switching, the forecast of $\phi_t$ based on $Y_{t-1}$ can be denoted by $\phi_{t|t-1}$. Similarly, the matrix denoting the mean squared error of the forecast can be written as

$$P_{t|t-1} = E[(\phi_t - \phi_{t|t-1})(\phi_t - \phi_{t|t-1})'|Y_{t-1}],$$

where $E$ is the expectation operator.

In the State-Space model with Markov-switching, however, the forecast of $\phi_t$ is based on $Y_{t-1}$ as well as on the random variable $SS_t$ taking on the value $j$ and on $SS_{t-1}$ taking on the value $i$ ($i$ and $j$ equal 0 or 1):

$$\phi_{t|t-1}^{(i,j)} = E[\phi_t|Y_{t-1}, SS_t = j, SS_{t-1} = i],$$

and correspondingly the mean squared error of the forecast is

$$P_{t|t-1}^{(i,j)} = E[(\phi_t - \phi_{t|t-1})(\phi_t - \phi_{t|t-1})'|Y_{t-1}, SS_t = j, SS_{t-1} = i].$$

---

[1] Theoretically, the elements of $F$ and the variance of $\eta_t$ may also have Markov-switching property, but since there are already many parameters to estimate, we just ignore this possibility to improve the efficiency of estimation. Note that if the elements of $F$ are larger than 1 in absolute value, that is, if the time-varying parameters are non-stationary, we should abandon the assumption of Equation (13.2) and assume a random walk path for the time-varying vector $\phi_t$.

Conditional on $SS_{t-1} = i$ and $SS_t = j$ $(i, j = 0, 1)$, the Kalman filter algorithm for our model reads as follows:

$$\phi_{t|t-1}^{(i,j)} = \bar{\Phi}_j + F\phi_{t-1|t-1}^i, \tag{13.5}$$

$$P_{t|t-1}^{(i,j)} = FP_{t-1|t-1}^i F' + \sigma_\eta^2, \tag{13.6}$$

$$\xi_{t|t-1}^{(i,j)} = S_t - X_t \phi_{t|t-1}^{(i,j)}, \tag{13.7}$$

$$\nu_{t|t-1}^{(i,j)} = X_t P_{t|t-1}^{(i,j)} X_t' + \sigma_{\varepsilon,j}^2, \tag{13.8}$$

$$\phi_{t|t}^{(i,j)} = \phi_{t|t-1}^{(i,j)} + P_{t|t-1}^{(i,j)} X_t' [\nu_{t|t-1}^{(i,j)}]^{-1} \xi_{t|t-1}^{(i,j)}, \tag{13.9}$$

$$P_{t|t}^{(i,j)} = (I - P_{t|t-1}^{(i,j)} X_t' [\nu_{t|t-1}^{(i,j)}]^{-1} X_t) P_{t|t-1}^{(i,j)}, \tag{13.10}$$

where $\xi_{t|t-1}^{(i,j)}$ is the conditional forecast error of $S_t$ based on information up to time $t - 1$ and $\nu_{t|t-1}^{(i,j)}$ is the conditional variance of the forecast error $\xi_{t|t-1}^{(i,j)}$. It is clear that $\nu_{t|t-1}^{(i,j)}$ consists of two parts $X_t P_{t|t-1}^{(i,j)} X_t'$ and $\sigma_{\varepsilon,j}^2$. When there is no Markov-Switching property in the shock variance, $\sigma_{\varepsilon,j}^2$ is constant. In order to make the Kalman filter algorithm above operable, Kim and Nelson (1999) developed some approximations and managed to collapse $\phi_{t|t}^{(i,j)}$ and $P_{t|t}^{(i,j)}$ into $\phi_{t|t}^j$ and $P_{t|t}^j$ respectively.[2]

On the basis of the theoretical background of the State-Space model with Markov-switching, we undertake the estimation for France and Germany below. Using the French data from 1971.1 to 1998.4,

---

[2] As for the details of the State-Space model with Markov-Switching, the reader is referred to Kim and Nelson (1999, Chapter 5). The program applied below is based on the Gauss Programs developed by Kim and Nelson (1999).

we obtain the following results (SD in parentheses):

$$\sigma_\eta = \begin{pmatrix} 0.001 \\ {\scriptstyle(0.001)} & 0 & 0 \\ 0 & 0.000 \\ {\scriptstyle(0.006)} & 0 \\ 0 & 0 & 0.040 \\ {\scriptstyle(0.006)} \end{pmatrix},$$

$$F = \begin{pmatrix} -0.591 \\ {\scriptstyle(0.198)} & 0 & 0 \\ 0 & 0.763 \\ {\scriptstyle(0.279)} & 0 \\ 0 & 0 & -0.190 \\ {\scriptstyle(0.195)} \end{pmatrix},$$

$$\bar{\Phi}_0 = \begin{pmatrix} 0.007 \\ {\scriptstyle(0.002)} \\ 0.232 \\ {\scriptstyle(0.274)} \\ -0.064 \\ {\scriptstyle(0.024)} \end{pmatrix}, \qquad \bar{\Phi}_1 = \begin{pmatrix} 0.137 \\ {\scriptstyle(0.005)} \\ 0.242 \\ {\scriptstyle(0.289)} \\ -0.132 \\ {\scriptstyle(0.057)} \end{pmatrix},$$

$$p = \underset{(0.021)}{0.971}, \quad q = \underset{(0.046)}{0.928}, \quad \sigma_{\varepsilon,0} = \underset{(0.001)}{0.000}, \quad \sigma_{\varepsilon,1} = \underset{(0.001)}{0.009},$$

with the maximum likelihood function being $-415.770$. The fact that the elements of $F$ are all smaller than 1 in absolute terms indicates that the time-varying parameters are stationary. This justifies our adoption of Equation (13.2). The difference of $\sigma_\varepsilon$ in states 0 and 1 is relatively obvious: 0.009 with the SD being 0.001 in state 1 and 0.000 with the SD being 0.001 in state 0. The difference between $\bar{\alpha}_2$ in state 1 and state 0 is not obvious, but the difference of $\bar{\alpha}_3$ between state 1 and state 0 is relatively obvious: $-0.132$ with the SD being 0.057 in state 1 and $-0.064$ with the SD being 0.024 in state 0.

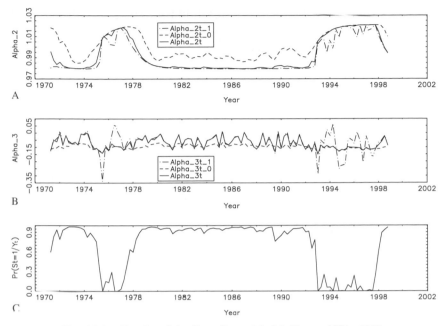

Fig. 13.1:   Results of the State-Space Model: France 1971–1998.

Next, we present the time-varying paths of the coefficients in Figure 13.1.

Figure 13.1A presents the time-varying path of $\alpha_2$ under different states. $\alpha_{2,0}$ is the path of $\alpha_2$ under state 0 and $\alpha_{2,1}$ the path of $\alpha_2$ under state 1. We also present the expected path of $\alpha_i(i = 2, 3)$ in Figure 13.1, which is computed as the weighted sum of $\alpha_{i,0}$ and $\alpha_{i,1}$ with the probability as weights, namely,

$$\alpha_i = \Pr[SS_t = 0|Y_t]\alpha_{i,0} + \Pr[SS_t = 1|Y_t]\alpha_{i,1}.$$

The paths of $\alpha_3$ in different states are shown in Figure 13.1B while Figure 13.1C presents the probability of being in state 1 given the observation $Y_t$. From Figure 13.1C we find that the economy is probably in state 1 most of the time except in the mid-1970s and the 1990s. There seem to be some significant changes in the time-varying parameters around 1975, 1979 and 1993. The switching of $\alpha_3$

indicates the changes of the monetary and fiscal policy interactions in France. The monetary and fiscal policy interactions are somewhat different in states 1 and 0 in the 1970s and 1990s. $\alpha_3$ evolves between 0 and $-0.10$ in both states most of the time except that it experienced some relatively obvious changes around 1972 and in the 1990s in state 1. Moreover, it is relatively smooth in state 0, remaining close to $-0.10$. The evidence seems to imply that there is no strong interaction between the monetary and fiscal policies in France and they might have been counteractive to each other if anything.

The German data from 1967.1 to 1998.4 generate the following results with SD in parentheses

$$
\sigma_\eta = \begin{pmatrix} 0.000 \\ (0.002) & 0 & 0 \\ 0 & 0.034 \\ (0.016) & 0 \\ 0 & 0 & 0.000 \\ (0.010) \end{pmatrix}, \quad F = \begin{pmatrix} -0.201 \\ (0.182) & 0 & 0 \\ 0 & 0.653 \\ (0.097) & 0 \\ 0 & 0 & -0.384 \\ (0.706) \end{pmatrix},
$$

$$
\bar{\Phi}_0 = \begin{pmatrix} -0.006 \\ (0.002) \\ 0.274 \\ (0.076) \\ -0.057 \\ (0.033) \end{pmatrix}, \quad \bar{\Phi}_1 = \begin{pmatrix} 0.002 \\ (0.001) \\ 0.369 \\ (0.092) \\ -0.037 \\ (0.026) \end{pmatrix},
$$

$$
p = 0.898, \quad q = 0.929, \quad \sigma_{\varepsilon,0} = 0.0015, \quad \sigma_{\varepsilon,1} = 0.0017,
$$
$$
(0.051) \qquad (0.055) \qquad (0.0007) \qquad (0.0003)
$$

with the maximum likelihood function being $-565.456$.

From the estimate of $F$ we know that all time-varying parameters are stationary. Unlike the case of France, the differences between and $\bar{\phi}$ and $\sigma_\varepsilon$ in state 0 and state 1 are not really obvious. We present the paths of the time-varying coefficients of Germany in Figure 13.2.

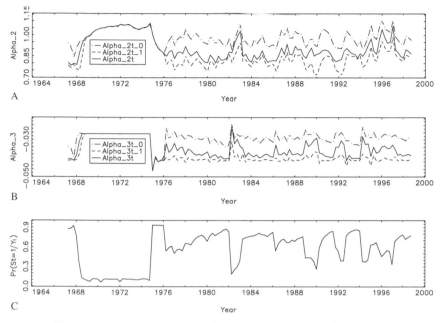

Fig. 13.2:    Results of the State-Space Model: Germany 1967–1998.

The fact that $\alpha_3$ in Figure 13.2B lies between $-0.03$ and $-0.05$ in both states indicates some weak interaction between the fiscal and monetary policies in Germany, that is, the two policies have been counteractive to each other if anything. This is similar to the case of France. The economy is probably in state 1 most of the time except between 1968 and 1975 and moreover, the time-varying parameters in state 0 and state 1 were close to each other from 1968 to 1975.

Above we have estimated the time-varying monetary and fiscal policy interactions in France and Germany in the past decades with a State-Space model with Markov-switching. The results indicate that there have not been strong interactions between the two policies in the two countries and, if anything, they have been counteractive to each other. This seems to be consistent with the view of many historical observers of the monetary and fiscal policies in those two countries in the 1980s and 1990s. This is also the conclusion of Mélitz (1997) who finds that fiscal and monetary policies tend to move in opposite directions using the pooled data for some OECD countries.

## 13.2. MONETARY AND FISCAL POLICY INTERACTIONS WITH FORWARD-LOOKING BEHAVIOR

Above we explored the interactions between monetary and fiscal policies with little attention paid to forward-looking behavior. The question concerned is, therefore, whether the fiscal or monetary policy takes the future behavior of the other into account. In order to consider forward-looking behavior, we assume that the surplus can be modelled as

$$S_t = \alpha_0 + \sum_{i=1}^{m} \alpha_i S_{t-i} + \alpha_{m+1} y_{t-1} + \alpha_{m+2} E[R_{t+n} | \Omega_t] + \varepsilon_t, \quad (13.11)$$

where $y_t$ denotes output gap, $E$ the expectation operator and $\Omega_t$ the information available to form the expectation of the future short-term interest rate $R_{t+n}$. $\varepsilon_t$ is iid with zero mean and constant variance. After eliminating the unobserved forecast variables from the equation above, we have the following equation

$$S_t = \alpha_0 + \sum_{i=1}^{m} \alpha_i S_{t-i} + \alpha_{m+1} y_{t-1} + \alpha_{m+2} R_{t+n} + \eta_t, \quad (13.12)$$

where $\eta_t = \alpha_{m+2}\{E[R_{t+n} | \Omega_t] - R_{t+n}\} + \varepsilon_t$. Let $u_t$ be a vector of variables within the information set $\Omega_t$ for the expectation of the future short-term interest rate. Since $E[\eta_t | u_t] = 0$, Equation (13.12) implies the following set of orthogonality conditions that will be employed for the estimation:

$$E\left[ S_t - \alpha_0 - \sum_{i=1}^{m} \alpha_i S_{t-i} - \alpha_{m+1} y_{t-1} - \alpha_{m+2} R_{t+n} | u_t \right] = 0. \quad (13.13)$$

We will apply GMM to estimate the unknown parameters for Germany with quarterly data from 1970.1 to 1998.4.

The instruments include the 1–4 lags of the short-term interest rate, output gap, the first difference of the inflation rate and the surplus and a constant. An MA(4) autocorrelation correction is undertaken. The output gap of Germany is measured by the percent deviation of log industrial production index from its HP filtered trend. In the estimation below we take $m = 4$. The results with different $n$ are shown in Table 13.1 with T-Statistics in parentheses. We also present the J-statistics to illustrate the validity of the over-identifying restrictions.

From Table 13.1 we find that $\alpha_6$ has always a positive sign and that its T-Statistics are not significant enough with $n = 0$ and $n = 1$, but in case $n = 2$ and $n = 3$ it has significant T-Statistics. This seems to indicate that the future short-term interest rate may have affected the current fiscal policy, but not greatly. Similar results are obtained from the estimation with two lags of the surplus. Note that the coefficient on the output gap has insignificant T-Statistics.

Table 13.1:    GMM Estimation of Equation (13.11) for Germany.

| Parameter | $n$ | | | |
|---|---|---|---|---|
| | **0** | **1** | **2** | **3** |
| $\alpha_0$ | − 0.002 | − 0.004 | − 0.006 | − 0.008 |
| | (1.678) | (2.294) | (3.380) | (3.689) |
| $\alpha_1$ | 1.166 | 1.128 | 1.111 | 1.077 |
| | (14.282) | (13.746) | (13.991) | (13.567) |
| $\alpha_2$ | − 0.341 | − 0.320 | − 0.315 | − 0.298 |
| | (3.340) | (3.140) | (3.094) | (3.002) |
| $\alpha_3$ | 0.231 | 0.201 | 0.160 | 0.145 |
| | (2.176) | (1.920) | (1.539) | (1.393) |
| $\alpha_4$ | − 0.101 | − 0.074 | − 0.044 | − 0.030 |
| | (1.202) | (0.898) | (0.547) | (0.369) |
| $\alpha_5$ | − 0.008 | − 0.003 | 0.003 | 0.014 |
| | (0.708) | (0.244) | (0.215) | (1.049) |
| $\alpha_6$ | 0.017 | 0.034 | 0.051 | 0.071 |
| | (1.066) | (1.700) | (2.558) | (2.781) |
| $R^2$ | 0.947 | 0.946 | 0.944 | 0.936 |
| J-St. | 0.109 | 0.101 | 0.096 | 0.095 |

## 13.3. CONCLUSION

In this chapter we have explored the problem of how monetary and fiscal policies have interacted over time. Employing a State-Space model with Markov-switching, we have estimated the time-varying parameters of a simple model and find that for both France and Germany there seem to have been no strong interactions between the monetary and fiscal policies. They have been, in contrast to the US (at least in the 1990s), counteractive to each other if anything.

The last problem we have tackled is whether fiscal policy took the expectations of the future monetary policy into account and vice versa. That is, we have explored monetary and fiscal policy interactions with forward-looking behavior and found that the German fiscal policy has not been affected greatly by expectations of monetary policy.

# REFERENCES

Abel, A. B., Mankiw, N. G, Summers, L. H. and Zeckhauser, R. J. (1989). Assessing dynamic efficiency: theory and evidence. *Review of Economic Studies*, *56*, 1–19.

Aguiar, A. and Martins, M. M. F. (2002). Trend, cycle, and nonlinear trade-off in the Euro-area 1970–2001. *CEMPRE*, Universidade do Porto, FEP Working Paper 122.

Alesina, A. and Perotti, R. (1995). Fiscal expansions and fiscal adjustments in OECD countries. *Economic Policy*, *21*, 205–248.

Altug, S. (1989). Time to build and aggregate fluctuations: some new evidence. *International Economic Review*, *30*, 889–920.

Arby, M. F. (2001). Long-run trend, business cycles and short-run shocks in real GDP. State Bank of Pakistan Working Paper No. 01 (URL: http://www.sbp.org.pk/publications/wpapers/wp01.pdf).

Arrow, K. J. (1962). The economic implications of learning by doing. *Review of Economic Studies*, *29*, 155–173.

Aschauer, D. A. (1989). Is public expenditure productive? *Journal of Monetary Economics*, *23*, 177–200.

Ball, L. (1997). Efficient rules for monetary policy. NBER Working Paper No. 5952.

Ball, L. (1999). "Policy rules for open economies," in *Monetary Policy Rules*, J. B. Taylor, (ed.), Chicago: University of Chicago Press, pp. 127–144.

Barro, R. J. (1979). On the determination of public debt. *Journal of Political Economy*, *87*, 940–971.

Barro, R. J. (1990). Government spending in a simple model of endogenous growth. *Journal of Political Economy*, *98*, 103–125.

Barro, R. J. and Sala-i-Martin, X. (1992). Public finance in models of economic growth. *Review of Economic Studies*, *59*, 645–661.

Baxter, M. and King, R. (1995). Measuring business cycles: approximate Band-Pass filters for economic time series. NBER Working Paper No. 5022.

Beck, G. W. and Wieland, V. (2002). Learning and control in a changing economic environment. *Journal of Economics Dynamics and Control*, *26*, 1359–1377.

Beetsma, R. M. W. J. and Jensen, H. (2002). Monetary and fiscal policy interactions in a micro-founded model of a monetary union. ECB Working Paper No. 166.

Bellman, R. (1957). *Dynamic Programming*, Princeton: Princeton University Press.

Benhabib, J. and Schmitt-Grohé, S. (2001). The perils of Taylor rule. *Journal of Economic Theory*, *96*, 40–69.

Benhabib, J., Schmitt-Grohé, S. and Uribe, M. (1998). The perils of the Taylor rules. Star Center for Applied Economics, NYU, Working Paper.

Benhabib, J., Schmitt-Grohé, S. and Uribe, M. (2001). Monetary policy and multiple equilibria. *American Economic Review, 91*, 166–186.

Bernanke, B. and Gertler, M. (1999). Monetary policy and asset price volatility. Federal Reserve Bank of Kansas City, Economic Review, fourth quarter, pp. 17–51.

Beyn, W. J., Pampel, T. and Semmler, W. (2001). Dynamic optimization and skiba sets in economic examples. *Optimal Control Applications and Methods, 22*(5/6), 251–280.

Blanchard, O. J. (1981). Output, the stock market and interest rates. *American Economic Review, 71*, 410–425.

Blanchard, O. J. (1998). *Unemployment and Real Wages: A Basic Model*, MIT Press, Manuscript.

Blanchard, O. J. (2003). *Macroeconomics*, Upper Saddle River: Prentice Hall.

Blanchard, O. J. (2005). "Monetary policy and unemployment," in *Monetary Policy and Unemployment—US, Euro-Area and Japan*, W. Semmler (ed.), London: Routledge.

Blanchard, O. J., Chouraqui, J.-C., Hagemann, R. P. and Sartor, N. (1990). The sustainability of fiscal policy: New answers to an old question. *OECD Economic Studies, 15*, 7–36.

Blanchard, O. J. and Fischer, S. (1989). *Lectures on Macroeconomics*, Cambridge, MA: MIT Press.

Blanchard, O. J. and Katz, L. (1997). What we know and do not know about the natural rate of unemployment. *Journal of Economic Perspectives, 11*(1), 51–72.

Blanchard, O. J. and Summers, L. (1986). "Hysteresis and the European unemployment problem," in *NBER Macroeconomics Annual 1*, S. Fischer (ed.), pp. 15–78.

Blanchard, O. J. and Summers, L. (1988). Beyond the natural rate hypothesis. *American Economic Review, 78*, 182–187.

Blanchard, O. J. and Watson, M. (1982). "Bubbles, rational expectations, and financial markets," in *Crisis in the Economic and Financial Structure*, P. Wachtel (ed.), Lexington: Lexington Books, pp. 410–425.

Blanchard, O. J. and Wolfers, J. (2000). The role of shocks and institutions in the rise of European unemployment: the aggregate evidence. *Economic Journal, 110*, C1–C33.

Blinder, A. S. and Solow, R. M. (1973). Does fiscal policy matter? *Journal of Public Economics, 2*, 291–337.

Bohn, H. (1995). The sustainability of budget deficits in a stochastic economy. *Journal of Money, Credit and Banking, 7*, 257–271.

Bohn, H. (1998). The behavior of US public debt and deficits. *Quarterly Journal of Economics, 113*, 949–963.

Boivin, J. (2001). *The Fed's Conduct of Monetary Policy: Has it Changed and Does it Matter?* Columbia Business School, Manuscript.

Brock, W. A. and Malliaris, A. G. (1989). *Differential Equations, Stability and Chaos in Dynamic Economics*, Amsterdam: North-Holland.

Buiter, W. H. (2002). The fiscal theory of the price level: a critique. *Economic Journal*, *112*(481), 459–480.

Buti, M., Roeger, W. and In't Veld, J. (2001). *Monetary and Fiscal Policy Interactions Under the Stability Pact*, European University Institute.

Cagetti, M., Hansen, L. P., Sargent, T. J. and Williams, N. (2002). Robustness and pricing with uncertain growth. *The Review of Financial Studies*, *15*(2), 363–404.

Calvo, G. (1983). Staggered prices in a utility-maximizing framework. *Journal of Monetary Economics*, *12*, 383–398.

Campbell, J. (1994). Inspecting the mechanism: an analytical approach to the stochastic growth model. *Journal of Monetary Economics*, *33*, 463–506.

Canzoneri, M. B., Cumby, R. E. and Diba, B. T. (2001). Is the price level determined by the needs of fiscal solvency? *American Economic Review*, *91*(5), 1221–1238.

Canzonerie, M. B., Cumby, R. E. and Diba, B. T. (2001). Is the price level determined by the needs of fiscal solvency? *American Economic Review*, *91*, 1221–1238.

Carlstrom, C. T. and Fuerst, T. S. (2000). Money growth rules and price level determinacy. Manuscript, Federal Reserve Bank of Cleveland, and Department of Economics, Bowling Green State University.

Catenaro, M. (2000). *Macroeconomic Policy Interactions in the EMU: A Case for Fiscal Policy Coordination*, Universita' di Milano Bicocca and UniS, Manuscript.

Cecchetti, S. (1988). The case of the negative nominal interest rates: new estimates of the term structure of interest rates during the Great Depression. *Journal of Political Economy*, *96*, 1111–1141.

Chadha, J. S. and Nolan, C. (2004). Output, inflation and the New Keynesian Phillips curve, *International Review of Applied Economics*, *18*(T.3), 271–288.

Chadha, J. and Schellekens, P. (1998). Utility functions for central bankers: the not so drastic quadratic. LSE Financial Market Group, Discussion Paper 308.

Chamberlin, G., Hall, S., Henry, B. and Vines, D. (2002). Coordinating monetary and fiscal policies in an open economy. Manuscript, Management School, Imperial College London, Centre for International Macroeconomics, Oxford University.

Chari, V., Christiano, L. and Kehoe, P. (1994). Optimal policy in a business cycle model. *Journal of Political Economy*, *102*, 617–652.

Chen, Z. and Epstein, L. G. (2000). Ambiguity, risk and asset returns in continuous time. RCER Working Paper 474.

Chen, P. and Flaschel, P. (2004). *Testing the Dynamics of Wages and Prices for the US Economy*, CEM Working Paper 67, Bielefeld: University of Bielefeld.

Chiarella, C., Franke, R., Flaschel, P. and Semmler, W. (2001). Output, interest and the stock market: An alternative to the jump variable technique. *Bulletin of the Czech Econometric Society*, *13*, 1–30.

Choi, K. and Jung, C. (2003). *Structural Changes and the US Money Demand Function*, Department of Economics, Ohio University, Manuscript.

Chow, G. (1993). Statistical estimation and testing of a real business cycle model. Econometric Research Program, Research Memorandum No. 365, Princeton University.

Christiano, L. and Eichenbaum, M. (1992). Current real business cycle theories and aggregate labor market fluctuation. *American Economic Review*, 82, 430–472.

Christiano, L. and Gust, L. (1999). "Comment," in *Monetary Policy Rules*, J. B. Taylor (ed.), Chicago: The University of Chicago Press.

Citibase (1992). Database.

Clarida, R., Gali, J. and Gertler, M. (1998). Monetary policy rules in practice: some international evidence. *European Economic Review*, 42, 1033–1067.

Clarida, R., Gali, J. and Gertler, M. (1999). The science of monetary policy: a New Keynesian perspective. *Journal of Economic Literature*, XXXVII, 1661–1701.

Clarida, R., Gali, J. and Gertler, M. (2000). Monetary policy rules and macroeconomic stability: evidence and some theory. *Quarterly Journal of Economics*, CXV(1), 147–180.

Clausen, V. and Wohltmann, H.-W. (2001). *Monetary and Fiscal Policy Dynamics in an Asymmetric Monetary Union*, University of Essen and University of Kiel, Manuscript.

Clouse, J. H., Orphanides, A., Small, D. and Tinsley, P. (2003). Monetary policy when the nominal short-term interest rate is zero. *Topics in Macroeconomics*, 3(1) (article 12).

Coenen, G. and Wieland, V. (2003). The zero-interest-rate bound and the role of the exchange rate for monetary policy in Japan. ECB Working Paper No. 218.

Cogley, T. and Sargent, T. J. (2001). Evolving post-world war II US inflation dynamics. *NBER Macroeconomics Annual*, 16(1), 331–373.

Cogley, T. and Sargent, T. J. (2002). Drifts and volatilities: monetary policies and outcomes in the post WWII US. Federal Reserve of Atlanta, Working Paper No. 2003-25.

Corsetti, G. and Pesenti, P. (1999). Stability, asymmetry and discontinuity: the launch of European Monetary Union. Brookings Papers on Economic Activity 2, December, pp. 295–372.

Dechert, W. D. (1984). Has the Averch–Johnson effect been theoretically justified? *Journal of Economic Dynamics and Control*, 8, 1–17.

Deutsche Bundesbank (1983). Revidierte Ergebnisse der gesamtwirtschaftlichen Finanzierungsrechnung fuer die Jahre 1950 bis 1959. Frankfurt am Main.

Deutsche Bundesbank (1994). Ergebnisse der gesamtwirtschaftlichen Finanzierungsrechnung fuer West-Deutschland 1960 bis 1992. Frankfurt am Main.

Deutsche Bundesbank (1996). Ergebnisse der gesamtwirtschaftlichen Finanzierungsrechnung fuer Deutschland 1990 bis 1995. Statistische Sonderveroeffentlichung 4. Frankfurt am Main.

Deutsche Bundesbank Monthly Report (1999). April, pp. 47–63.

Deutsche Bundesbank (2000). Kerninflation als Hilfsmittel der Preisanalyse. *Monatsberichte*, Jg. 52(4).

Diamond, P. A. (1965). National debt in a neo-classical growth model. *American Economic Review*, 55, 1126–1150.

Dolado, J. J., María-Dolores, R. and Naveira, M. (2001). *Are Central Bank's Reaction Functions Asymmetric? Evidence for Some Central Banks*, Department of Economics, Universidad Carlos III de Madrid.

Dolado, J. J., María-Dolores, R. and Ruge-Murcia, F. J. (2002). *Nonlinear Monetary Policy Rules: Some New Evidence for the US*, Departmento de Economía, Universidad Carlos III de Madrid, Working Paper 02-29.

Domar, E. D. (1957). *Essays in the Theory of Economic Growth*, Oxford: Oxford University Press.

Dupasquier, C. and Ricketts, N. (1998). *Nonlinearities in the Output–Inflation Relationship: Some Empirical Results for Canada*, Bank of Canada, Working Paper 98-14.

Dupor, W. (2001). *Nominal Prices Versus Asset Price Stabilization*, Wharton School, University of Pennsylvania, Working Paper.

Easterly, W. and Rebelo, S. (1993). Fiscal policy and economic growth. *Journal of Monetary Economic Growth, 32*, 417–458.

Economic Report of the President (1994). United States Government Printing Office, Washington.

Eggertsson, G. and Woodford, M. (2003). *The Zero Bound on Interest Rates and Optimal Monetary Policy*, Princeton University, Manuscript.

Eller, J. W. and Gordon, R. J. (2003). Nesting the New Keynesian Phillips Curve within the Mainstream model of US inflation dynamics. *CEPR Conference*, the Phillips curve revisited.

Epstein, L. and Schneider, M. (2001). Recursive multiple priors. Rochester Center for Economic Research, Working Paper No. 485.

European Commission, (1998). *Statistical Annex. European Economy 65*, Brussels: Directorate for Economic and Financial Affairs.

Evans, G. W. and Honkapohja, S. (2001). *Learning and Expectations in Macroeconomics*, Princeton: Princeton University Press.

Fair, R. C. (2000). Testing the NAIRU model for the United States. *The Review of Economics and Statistics, 82*, 64–71.

Feve, P. and Henin, P. Y. (1996). Assessing Maastricht sustainability of public deficits in a stochastic environment. Manuscript, CEPREMAP, Paris, Paper presented at the CEEA-Symposium on Problems of European Monetary Union, Frankfurt, November 1996.

Filardo, A. J. (1998). New evidence on the output cost of fighting inflation. *Economic Review*, pp. 33–61 (third quarter).

Filardo, A. J. (2000). Monetary policy and asset prices. Federal Reserve Bank of Kansas City.

Fischer, S. (1993). The role of macroeconomic factors on growth. *Journal of Monetary Economics, 32*, 485–512.

Flaschel, P., Semmler, W. and Gong, G. (2001). A Keynesian macroeconometric framework for the analysis of monetary policy rules. *Journal of Economic Behavior and Organization, 46*, 101–136.

Flaschel, P., Kauermann, G. and Semmler, W. (2004). *Testing Wage and Price Phillips Curves for the United States*, CEM Working Paper 68, Bielefeld: University of Bielefeld.

Flaschel, P. and Krolzig, H.-M. (2002). *Wage and Price Phillips Curve*, CEM Working Paper 66, Bielefeld: University of Bielefeld.

Fuhrer, J. and Moore, G. (1995). Inflation persistence. *Quarterly Journal of Economics*, *110*, 127–159.

Galí, J. and Gertler, M. (1999). Inflation dynamics: a structural econometric analysis. *Journal of Monetary Economics*, *44*, 195–222.

Galí, J., Gertler, M. and López-Salido, J. D. (2001a). European inflation dynamics. *European Economics Review*, *45*, 1237–1270.

Galí, J., Gertler, M. and López-Salido, J. D. (2001b). Notes on estimating the closed form of the hybrid new Phillips curve. Manuscript.

Galí, J., Gertler, M. and López-Salido, J. D. (2005). Robustness of the Estimates of the hybrid New Keynesian Phillips curve. forthcoming, Journal of Monetary Economics.

Gerlach, S. and Smets, F. (2000). MCIs and monetary policy. *European Economic Review*, *44*, 1677–1700.

Gerlach, S. and Svensson, L. E. O. (2002). Money and inflation in the Euro-area: a case for monetary indicators? CEPR, Discussion Paper Series 2002, No. 3392.

Giannoni, M. P. (2002). Does model uncertainty justify caution? Robust optimal monetary policy in a forward-looking model. *Macroeconomic Dynamics*, *6*, 111–144.

Giavazzi, F. and Pagano, M. (1990). "Can severe fiscal adjustments be expansionary?," in *NBER Macroeconomics Annual*, O. Blanchard and S. Fischer (eds.), Cambridge, MA: MIT Press.

Giordani, P. and Söderlind, P. (2002). Solutions of macromodels with Hansen–Sargent robust policies: summary and some extensions. SSE/EFI Working Paper Series in Economics and Finance No. 499.

Gong, G., Greiner, A. and Semmler, W. (2001). Growth effects of fiscal policy and debt sustainability in the EU. *Empirica, Journal of Applied Economics and Economic Policy*, *28*(1), 3–19.

Gonzalez, F. and Rodriguez, A. (2003). Robust control: a note on the response of the control to changes in the "free" parameter. Manuscript, Department of Economics, University of Texas at Austin.

Gordon, R. J. (1997). The time-varying NAIRU and its implications for economic policy. *Journal of Economic Perspectives*, *11*, 11–32.

Graham, L. and Snower, D. J. (2002). The return of the long-run Phillips curve. Institute for the Study of Labor (IZA), Discussion paper No. 646.

Greiner, A., Koeller, U. and Semmler, W. (2005). Testing Sustainability of German Fiscal Policy: Evidence for the Period 1960-2003, CESIFO working paper No. 1386, Center for Economic Studies & Ifo Institute for Economic Research, Munich.

Greiner, A. and Semmler, W. (1996). Multiple steady states, indeterminacy and cycles in a basic model of endogenous growth. *Journal of Economics*, *63*, 79–99.

Greiner, A. and Semmler, W. (1999a). An endogenous growth model with public capital and government debt. *Annals of Operations Research*, *88*, 65–79.

Greiner, A. and Semmler, W. (1999b). An inquiry into the sustainability of German fiscal policy: some time series tests. *Public Finance Review*, *27*, 221–237.

Greiner, A. and Semmler, W. (2003). "Monetary Policy, Non-Uniqueness of Steady States and Hysteresis Effects," in *Modelling and Control of Economic Systems 2002*, R. Neck (ed.), Oxford: Elsevier Science Ltd., pp. 323–328.

Greiner, A., Semmler, W. and Gong, G. (2005). *The Forces of Economic Growth: A Time Series Perspective*, Princeton: Princeton University Press.

Grilli, V. (1988). "Seignorage in Europe," in *A European Central Bank? Perspectives on Monetary Unification after Ten Years of the EMS*, M. De Cecco and A. Giovannini (eds.), Cambridge: Cambridge University Press.

Grüne, L. (1997). An adaptive grid scheme for the discrete Hamilton–Jakobi–Bellman equation. *Numerische Mathematik, 75*, 319–337.

Grüne, L. (2001). Numerik Optimaler Steuerung. Lecture notes, Department of Mathematics, University of Bayreuth.

Grüne, L. and Semmler, W. (2004a). Using dynamic programming with adaptive grid scheme for optimal control problems in economics. *Journal of Economics Dynamics and Control, 28*, 2427–2456.

Grüne, L. and Semmler, W. (2004b). Asset-pricing constrained by past consumption decisions. CEM Working Paper, University of Bielefeld.

Grüne, L., Semmler, W. and Sieveking, M. (2004). Creditworthiness and thresholds in a credit market model with multiple equilibria. *Economic Theory, 25*(2), 287–315.

Hall, R. (1988). Intertemporal substitution in consumption. *Journal of Political Economy, 96*, 339–357.

Hamilton, J. D. (1994). *Time Series Analysis*, Princeton: Princeton University Press.

Hamilton, J. D. and Flavin, M. (1986). On the limitations of government borrowing: a framework for empirical testing. *American Economic Review, 76*, 808–819.

Hansen, L. P. (1982). Large sample properties of generalized method of moments estimators. *Econometrica, 50*, 1029–1054.

Hansen, L. P. and Sargent, T. J. (1999). Robustness and commitment: a monetary policy example. Manuscript, March 1999.

Hansen, L. P. and Sargent, T. J. (2001a). Time inconsistency of robust control? Manuscript.

Hansen, L. P. and Sargent, T. J. (2001b). Robust control and model uncertainty. The American Economic Review: Papers and Proceedings, 2, 2001.

Hansen, L. P. and Sargent, T. J. (2003). Robust Control and Economic Uncertainty. Book manuscript.

Harvey, A. C. (1989). *Time Series Models*, Oxford: Phillip Allan Publishers Ltd.

Harvey, A. C. (1990). *Forecasting, Structural Time Series Models and the Kalman Filter*, Cambridge: Cambridge University Press.

Heinemann, F. (2002). Factor mobility, government debt and the decline in public investment. ZEW Discussion Paper No. 02-19 (URL: ftp://ftp.zew.de/pub/zew-docs/dp/dp0219.pdf).

Hornstein, A. and Uhlig, H. (2000). What is the real story for interest rate volatility? *German Economic Review, 1*(1), 43–67.

Howitt, P. and McAffee, R. P. (1992). Animal spirits. *American Economic Review, 82*(3), 493–507.

Jones, L. E., Manuelli, R. E. and Rossi, P. E. (1993). Optimal taxation in models of endogenous growth. *Journal of Political Economy*, *101*(3), 485–517.

Judd, K. L. (1998). *Numerical Methods in Economics*, Cambridge, MA: MIT Press.

Judge, G. G., Hill, R. C., Griffiths, W. E., Luetkepohl, H. and Lee, T.-C. (1985). *Introduction to the Theory of Econometrics*, New York: Wiley.

Kalaba, R. and Tesfatsion, L. (1989). Time-varying linear regression via flexible least squares. *Computers and Mathematics Applications*, *17*, pp. 1215–1245.

Karanassou, M., Sala, H. and Snower, D. J. (2005). A reappraisal of the inflation–unemployment tradeoff. *European Journal of Political Economy*.

Kato, R. and Nishiyama, S. (2005). Optimal monetary policy when the interest rates are bounded at zero. *Journal of Economic Dynamics and Control*, *29*(1–2), 97–133.

Kent, C. and Lowe, P. (1997). Asset price bubbles and monetary policy. Research Bank of Australia, Manuscript.

Kierman, C. U. and Lippi, F. (1999). Central bank independence, centralization of wage bargaining, inflation and unemployment: theory and some evidence. *European Economic Review*, *43*, 1395–1434.

Kim, C.-J. and Nelson, C. R. (1999). *State-Space Models with Regime Switching*, Cambridge, MA: MIT Press.

Kim, D., Osborn, D. R. and Sensier, M. (2002). *Nonlinearity in the Fed's Monetary Policy rule*, University of Manchester, Manuscript.

King, R. G., Plosser, C. I. and Rebelo, S. T. (1988). Production, growth and business cycles I: the basic neo-classical model. *Journal of Monetary Economics*, *21*, 195–232.

Kremers, J. M. (1988). US federal indebtedness and the conduct of fiscal policy. *Journal of Monetary Economics*, *23*, 219–238.

Laxton, D., Rose, G. and Tambakis, D. (1999). The US Phillips curve: the case for asymmetry. *Journal of Economic Dynamics and Control*, *23*, 1459–1485.

Leeper, E. M. (1991). Equilibria under 'active' and 'passive' monetary and fiscal policies. *Journal of Monetary Economics*, *27*, 129–147.

Leith, C. and Wren-Lewis, S. (2000). Interactions between monetary and fiscal policies. *Economic Journal*, *110*(March), 93–108.

Levin, A., Wieland, V. and Williams, J. C. (1999). "Robustness of simple monetary policy rules under model uncertainty," in *Monetary Policy Rules*, J. B. Taylor (ed.), Chicago: The Chicago University Press.

Linnemann, L. and Schabert, A. (2002). *Monetary and Fiscal Policy Interactions when the Budget Deficit Matters*, Department of Economics, University of Cologne, Manuscript.

Ljungvist, L. and Sargent, T. J. (2000). *Recursive Macroeconomic Theory*, Cambridge, MA: MIT Press.

Lucas, R. (1988). On the mechanics of economic development. *Journal of Monetary Economics*, *22*, 3–42.

Lucas, R. (1990). Supply-side economics: an analytical review. *Oxford Economic Papers*, *42*, 293–316.

Ludvigson, S. and Steindel, C. (1999). How important is the stock market effect on consumption? *Federal Reserve Bank of New York, Economic Policy Review*, (July), pp. 29–52.

Luetkepohl, H. and Herwartz, H. (1996). Specification of varying coefficient time series models via generalized flexible least squares. *Journal of Econometrics*, *70*, 261–290.

Mankiw, N. G. (2001). The inexorable and mysterious tradeoff between inflation and unemployment, *Economic Journal, 111,* May 2001, C45–C61.

Marimon, R. and Scott, A. (1999). *Computational Methods for the Study of Dynamic Economies*, New York: Oxford University Press.

McCallum, B. T. (1984). Are bond-financed deficits inflationary? A Ricardian analysis. *Journal of Political Economy*, *92*(1), 123–135.

Mehra, R. (1998). On the volatility of stock prices: an exercise in quantitive theory. *International Journal of System Sciences*, *29*, 1203–1211.

Mélitz, J. (1997). Some cross-country evidence about debt, deficits and the behavior of monetary and fiscal authorities. CEPR Discussion Paper No. 1653.

Mélitz, J. (2000). Some cross-country evidence about fiscal policy behavior and consequences for EMU. European Economy Reports and Studies, Public debt and fiscal policy in EMU, *2*(1).

Mendizábal, H. R. (2005). The behavior of money velocity in low and high inflation countries. *Forthcoming in Journal of Money, Credit and Banking.*

Meyer, L. H. (2000). Structural change and monetary policy. FRB speech.

Meyer, L. H., Swanson, E. T. and Wieland, V. (2001). NAIRU uncertainty and nonlinear policy rules. Board of Governors of the Federal Reserve System, Finance and Economics Discussion Series No. 2001-01.

Milesi-Ferretti, G. M. and Roubini, N. (1994). Optimal taxation of human capital and physical capital in endogenous growth models. NBER Working Paper No. 4882.

Mishkin, F. S. (2003). *The Economics of Money, Banking, and Financial Markets*, Reading, MA: Addison Wesley.

Mortensen, D. T. (1989). The persistence and indeterminancy of unemployment in search equilibrium. *Scandinavian Journal of Economics*, *91*, 347–370.

Muscatelli, V. A., Tirelli, P. and Trecroci, C. (2002). *Monetary and Fiscal Policy Interactions Over the Cycle: some empirical evidence*, Manuscript, University of Glasgow.

Musgrave, J. C. (1992). Fixed reproducible wealth in the United States, revised estimates. *Survey of Current Business*, *72*, 106–137.

Newey, W. K. and West, K. D. (1987). A simple, positive-definite, heteroskedasticity and autocorrelation consistent covariance matrix. *Econometrica*, *55*, 703–708.

Nobay, A. R. and Peel, D. A. (2003). Optimal monetary policy in a model of asymmetric central bank preferences. *Economic Journal*, *113*(489), 657–665.

OECD (1998). Statistical Compendium. CD-ROM 1998, OECD, Paris.

OECD (1999a). Statistical Compendium. CD-ROM 1999, OECD, Paris.

OECD, (1999b). *Fiscal Positions and Business Cycle Statistics*, Paris: Organisation for Economic Development and Cooperation.

Orphanides, A. and van Norden, S. (2002). The unreliability of output gap estimation in real time. *The Review of Economics and Statistics*, *84*(4), 569–583.

Orphanides, A. and Wieland, V. (2000). Inflation zone targeting. *European Economic Review, 44*, 1351–1387.

Orphanides, A. and Wilcox, D. (1996). The opportunistic approach to disinflation. Finance Economic Discussion Paper Series 96-24, Federal Reserve Board.

Orphanides, A. and Williams, C. (2002). Imperfect knowledge, inflation expectations and monetary policy. FRBSF Working Paper 2002-04.

Pedroni, P. (1992). *Human Capital, Endogenous Growth and Co-integration for Multi-Country Panels*, Department of Economics, Colombia University, mimeo.

Peersman, G. and Smets, F. (1999). *Uncertainty and the Taylor Rule in a Simple Model of the Euro-area Economy*, Proceedings of the Federal Reserve Bank of San Francisco.

Perotti, R. (1999). Fiscal policy in good times and bad. *Quarterly Journal of Economics, 114*, 1399–1436.

Petruzzello, S. (1995). *Political Control of 'Explosive' Budget Deficits*, Department of Economics, Columbia University, mimeo.

Pfähler, W., Hofmann, U. and Bönte, W. (1996). Does extra public infrastructure capital matter? An appraisal of empirical literature. *Finanzarchiv NF, 53*, 68–112.

Phelps, E. S. and Zoeg, G. (1998). Natural-rate theory and OECD unemployment. *Economic Journal, 108*, 782–801.

Phillips, A. W. (1958). The relation between unemployment and the rate of change of money wages in the United Kingdom, 1861–1957. *Economica, 25*, 283–299.

Rigobon, R. and Sack, B. (2001). Measuring the reaction of monetary policy to the stock market. NBER Working Paper 8350.

Romer, P. M. (1986). Increasing returns and long-run growth. *Journal of Political Economy, 94*, 1002–1037.

Romer, P. M. (1990). Endogenous technical change. *Journal of Political Economy, 98*, 71–102.

Rotemberg, J. and Woodford, M. (1996). Oligopolistic pricing and the effects of aggregate demand on economic activity. *Journal of Political Economy*, 1153–1207.

Rotemberg, J. and Woodford, M. (1999). "Interest rate rules in an estimated sticky price model," in *Monetary Policy Rules*, J. B. Taylor, (ed.), Chicago: The University of Chicago Press.

Roubini, N. and Sachs, J. (1989a). Government spending and budget deficits in the industrial countries. *Economic Policy, 4*, 99–132.

Roubini, N. and Sachs, J. (1989b). Political and economic determinants of the budget deficits in the industrial democracies. *European Economic Review, 33*, 903–938.

Rudebusch, G. D. and Svensson, L. E. O. (1999). "Policy rules for inflation targeting," in *Monetary Policy Rules*, J. B. Taylor (ed.), London: The University of Chicago Press.

Sachverständigenrat zur Begutachtung der gesamtwirtschaftlichen Lage (1993). Zeit zum Handeln-Antriebskräfte Starken, Jahresgutachten 1993/94, Metzler-Poeschel, Stuttgart.

Sachverständigenrat zur Begutachtung der gesamtwirtschaftlichen Lage (1995). Im Standortwettbewerb, Jahresgutachten 1995/96, Metzler-Poeschel, Stuttgart.

Sack, B. and Wieland, V. (2000). Interest-rate smoothing and optimal monetary policy: a review of recent empirical evidence. *Journal of Economics and Business*, *52*(1/2), 205–228.

Sargent, T. T. (1986). *Rational Expectations and Inflations*, New York: Harper & Row.

Sargent, T. J. (1987). *Dynamic Macroeconomic Theory*, Cambridge, MA: Harvard University Press.

Sargent, T. J. (1999). *The Conquest of American Inflation*, Princeton: Princeton University Press.

Sargent, T. J. and Wallace, N. (1975). "Rational" expectations, the optimal monetary instrument, and the optimal money supply rule. *Journal of Political Economy*, *83*(2), 241–254.

Schaling, E. (2004). The nonlinear Phillips curve and inflation forecast targeting: Symmetric Versus Asymmetric Monetary Policy Rules. *Journal of money, credit and banking 36*(3), 361–386.

Scharnagl, M. (1998). The stability of German money demand: not just a myth. *Empirical Economics*, *23*, 355–370.

Semmler, W. and Gong, G. (1996). Estimating parameters of real business cycle models. *Journal of Economic Behavior and Organisation*, *30*, 301–325.

Semmler, W. and Sieveking, M. (1999). *Optimal and Non-optimal Equilibria in Dynamic Economic Models*, Bielefeld: Department of Economics, University of Bielefeld.

Semmler, W. and Sieveking, M. (2000). Critical debt and debt dynamics. *Journal of Economic Dynamics and Control*, *24*, 1124–1144.

Semmler, W. and Wöhrmann, P. (2004). Credit risk and sustainable debt: a model and estimations of why the Euro is stable in the long-run. *Economic Modelling*, *21*(6), 1145–1160.

Semmler, W. and Zhang, W. (2004). Monetary policy with nonlinear Phillips curve and endogenous Nairu. GEM Working Paper, www.wiwi uni-bielefeld.de/cem.

Shiller, R. (1984). *Market Volatility*, Cambridge, MA: MIT Press.

Sidrauski, M. (1967). Rational choice and patterns of growth in a monetary economy. *American Economic Review*, *57*, 534–544.

Sims, C. A. (1994). A simple model for study of the determinacy of the price level and the interaction of monetary and fiscal policy. *Economic Theory*, *4*, 381–399.

Sims, C. A. (1997). Fiscal foundations of price stability in open economies. Manuscript, Princeton University.

Sims, C. A. (2001a). Comment on Sargent and Cogley's "evolving US postwar inflation dynamics". Manuscript, Princeton University.

Sims, C. A. (2001b). Fiscal aspects of central bank independence. Manuscript, Princeton University.

Smaghi, L. B. and Casini, C. (2000). Monetary and fiscal policy co-operation: institutions and procedures in EMU. *The Journal of Common Market Studies*, *38*(3), 375–555.

Smets, F. (1997). Financial asset prices and monetary policy: theory and evidence. Bank for International Settlements, Working Paper No. 47.

Söderström, U. (2002). Monetary policy with uncertain parameters. *Scandinavian Journal of Economics*, *104*(1), 125–145.

Staiger, D., Stock, J. H. and Watson, M. W. (1996). How precise are estimates of the natural rate of unemployment? NBER Working Paper 5477.

Statistisches Bundesamt Wiesbaden (1974). *Lange Reihen zur Wirtschaftsentwicklung*, Stuttgart, Mainz: W. Kohlhammer.

Statistisches Bundesamt Wiesbaden (1984). *Volkswirtschaftliche Gesamtrechnungen*, Fachserie 18, Reihe S.7, Stuttgart: Metzler-Poeschel.

Statistisches Bundesamt Wiesbaden (1991). *Volkswirtschaftliche Gesamtrechnungen*, Fachserie 18, Reihe S.17, Stuttgart: Metzler-Poeschel.

Statistisches Bundesamt Wiesbaden (1994). *Volkswirtschaftliche Gesamtrechnungen*, Fachserie 18, Reihe 1.3, Stuttgart: Metzler-Poeschel.

Statistisches Bundesamt Wiesbaden (1995a). *Volkswirtschaftliche Gesamtrechnungen*, Fachserie 18, Reihe 1.2, Stuttgart: Metzler-Poeschel.

Statistisches Bundesamt Wiesbaden (1995b). *Statistisches Jahrbuch für die Bundesrepublik Deutschland*, Stuttgart: Metzler-Poeschel.

Stiglitz, J. (1997). Reflections on the natural rate hypothesis. *Journal of Economic Perspectives*, *11*, 3–10.

Stokey, N. L., Lucas, R. E. Jr. and Prescott, E. C. (1996). *Recursive Methods in Economic Dynamics*, Cambridge, MA: Harvard University Press.

Sturm, J.-E., Kuper, G. H. and de Haan, J. (1998). "Modelling government investment and economic growth on a macro level," in *Market Behaviour and Macroeconomic Modelling*, S. Brakman, H. van Ees and S. K. Kuipers (eds.), London: Mac Millan/St Martin's Press, pp. 359–406.

Svensson, L. E. O. (1997). Inflation forecast targeting: implementation and monitoring inflation targets. *European Economic Review*, *41*, 1111–1146.

Svensson, L. E. O. (1999a). Inflation targeting as a monetary policy rule. *Journal of Monetary Economics*, *43*, 607–654.

Svensson, L. E. O. (1999b). Inflation targeting: some extensions. *Scandinavian Journal of Economics*, *101*(3), 337–361.

Svensson, L. E. O. (2000). Robust control made simple. Manuscript, Department of Economics, Princeton University.

Svensson, L. E. O. (2002). The inflation forecast and the loss function. Discussion Papers Series. Center for Economic Policy Research London, No. 3365.

Svensson, L. E. O. (2003). What is wrong with Taylor rule? Using judgement in monetary policy through targeting rules. *Journal of Economic Literature*, *41*, 426–477.

Tabellini, G. (1986). Money, debt and deficits in a dynamic game. *Journal of Economic Dynamics and Control*, *10*, 427–442.

Tambakis, D. N. (1998). Monetary policy with a convex Phillips curve and asymmetric loss. IMF Working Paper 98/21.

Taylor, J. B. (1993). Discretion versus policy rules in practice. *Carnegie–Rochester Conference Series on Public Policy*, *39*, 195–214.

Taylor, J. B. (1999a). *Monetary Policy Rules*, Cambridge/Chicago: NBER Publication/ University of Chicago Press.

Taylor, J. B. (1999b). The Robustness and efficiency of monetary policy rules as guidelines for interest rate setting by the European Central Bank. *Journal of Monetary Economics*, *43*(3), 655–679.

Taylor, J. B. (1999c). "A historical analysis of monetary policy rules," in *Monetary Policy Rules*, J. B. Taylor (ed.), Chicago: University of Chicago Press.

Taylor, J. B. and Uhlig, H. (1990). Solving nonlinear stochastic growth models: a comparison of alternative solution methods. *Journal of Business and Economic Statistics*, *8*, 1–17.

Tetlow, R. J. and von zur Muehlen, P. (2003). Avoiding Nash inflation: Bayesian and robust responses to model uncertainty, Finance and Economics Discussion Series, Federal Reserve Board.

Trehan, B. and Walsh, C. E. (1991). Testing intertemporal budget constraints: theory and applications to US Federal budget and current account deficits. *Journal of Money, Credit and Banking*, *23*, 206–223.

Tucci, M. P. (1990). A note on flexible least squares. *Journal of Economic Dynamics and Control*, *14*, 175–182.

Tucci, M. P. (1997). Adaptive control in the presence of time-varying parameters. *Journal of Economic Dynamics and Control*, *22*, 39–47.

Tullio, G., de Souza, E. and Giucca, P. (1996). "The demand for money functions in Europe and in Germany before and after the Berlin Wall," in *Inflation and Wage Behaviour in Europe*, P. de Grauwe, S. Micossi and G. Tullio (eds.), Oxford: Clarendon.

Turnovsky, S. J. (1995). *Methods of Macroeconomic Dynamics*, Cambridge, MA: MIT Press.

Turnovsky, S. J. and Fisher, W. H. (1995). The composition of government expenditure and its consequences for macroeconomic performance. *Journal of Economic Dynamics and Control*, *19*, 747–787.

Ullersma, C. A. (2003). The zero lower bound on nominal interest rates and monetary policy effectiveness: a survey. OCFEB, RM0203.

van Aarle, H. G. and Gobbin, N. (2003). Monetary and fiscal policy transmission in the Euro-area: evidence from a structural VAR analysis. *Journal of Economics and Business*, *55*(5–6), 609–638.

van Aarle, B., Bovenberg, L. and Reith, M. (1995). Monetary and fiscal policy inter-action and government debt stabilization. Discussion Paper from Tilburg University No. 1, Center for Economic Research.

van Aarle, B., Engwerda, J., Plasmans, J. and Weeren, A. (1999). Monetary and fiscal policy design under EMU: a dynamic game approach. CESIFO Working Paper 262, Tilburg University.

van Aarle, B., Engwerda, J. and Plasmans, J. (2002). Monetary and fiscal policy interaction in the EMU: a dynamic game approach. *Annals of Operations Research*, *109*, 229–264.

van Ewijk, C. (1991). *On the Dynamics of Growth and Debt*, Oxford: Oxford University Press.

van Ewijk, C. and van de Klundert, T. (1993). "Endogenous technology, budgetary regimes and public policy," in *The Political Economy of Government Debt*, H. A. A. Verbon and A. A. M. Van Winden Frans (eds.), Amsterdam: North-Holland, pp. 113–136.

Varian, H. R. (1975). "A Bayesian approach to real estate assessment," in *Bayesian Econometrics and Statistics in Honour of Leonard J. Savage*, S. E. Fienberg and A. Zellner (eds.), Amsterdam: North-Holland, pp. 195–208.

Vega, J. (1998). Money demand stability: evidence from Spain. *Empirical Economics, 23*, 387–400.

Vickers, J. (1999). *Monetary Policy and Asset Prices*, Bank of England, mimeo.

von Hagen, J., Hallett, A. H. and Strauch, R. (2001). Budgetary consolidation in EMU. CEPR Working Paper No. 148.

White, H. (1980). A heteroskedasticity-consistent covariance estimator and direct test for heteroskedasticity. *Econometrica, 48*, 817–838.

Wickens, M. (1993). The sustainability of fiscal policy and the Maastricht conditions. Centre for Economic Forecasting, London Business School, Discussion Paper No. 10-93.

Wicksell, K. (1898). *Interest and Prices*, London: Macmillan, English translation by R.f. Kahn 1936.

Wieland, V. (2000). Monetary policy, parameter uncertainty and optimal learning. *Journal of Monetary Economics, 46*, 199–228.

Wilcox, D. W. (1989). The sustainability of government deficits: implications of the present-value borrowing constraint. *Journal of Money, Credit and Banking, 21*, 291–306.

Wolters, J., Teräsvirta, T. and Lütkepohl, H. (1998). Modeling the demand for M3 in the united Germany. *The Review of Economics and Statistics, 80*(3), 399–409.

Woodford, M. (1994). Monetary policy and price level determinacy in a cash-in-advance economy. *Economic Theory, 4*, 345–380.

Woodford, M. (1995). Price-level determinacy without control of a monetary aggregate. *Carnegie–Rochester Conference Series on Public Policy, 43*, 1–46.

Woodford, M. (1996). Control of the public debt: a requirement for price stability. NBER Working Paper 5684.

Woodford, M. (2001a). Fiscal requirements for price stability. *Journal of Money, Credit and Banking, 33*, pp. 669–728.

Woodford, M. (2001b). The Taylor rule and optimal monetary policy. *American Economic Review, 91*(2), 232–237.

Woodford, M. (2003a). *Interest and Prices: Foundations of a Theory of Monetary Policy*, Princeton: Princeton University Press.

Woodford, M. (2003b). Optimal interest-rate smoothing. *Review of Economic Studies, 70*(4), 861–886.

Wyplosz, C. (1999). Economic policy coordination in EMU: strategies and institutions. CEPR.

Zhang, W. and Semmler, W. (2005). Monetary policy rules under uncertainty: empirical evidence, adaptive learning and robust control. *Forthcoming in Macroeconomic Dynamics*.

# *Author Index*

# Subject Index